Baxter
9·55

S. WEIR MITCHELL

As a Psychiatric Novelist

S. WEIR MITCHELL

As a Psychiatric Novelist

---

by DAVID M. REIN

Preface by C. P. Oberndorf

INTERNATIONAL UNIVERSITIES PRESS, INC.

New York   New York

MANUFACTURED IN THE UNITED STATES OF AMERICA

CONTENTS

		PAGE
Preface by C. P. Oberndorf		vii
Foreword		xiii
I.	MITCHELL'S PHILADELPHIA BACK-GROUND	1
II.	MITCHELL'S EARLY STUDIES OF SNAKE VENOM AND OF NERVE INJURIES	13
III.	"THE CASE OF GEORGE DEDLO": A STORY BASED ON MITCHELL'S STUDY OF NERVE INJURIES	23
IV.	MITCHELL'S CASE STUDIES OF NERVOUS AILMENTS: MATERIAL FOR FICTION	34
V.	MITCHELL'S SCIENTIFIC ATTITUDE TOWARD HIS CHARACTERS	51
VI.	DETERIORATION OF CHARACTER	61
	Dr. Wendell	61
	Richard Darnell	79
VII.	THE COUCH-LOVING INVALIDS	85
	Octopia Darnell	85
	Constance Trescot	101
	Ann Penhallow	118
VIII.	DUAL PERSONALITY	126
	Mary Reynolds	126
	Mr. J. C.	129
	Sibyl Maywood	131

IX. DIPSOMANIA 145
    Roger Grace 145
    Peter Lamb 152
X. INSANITY 155
    Philetus Richmond 155
    Mr. Hapworth 163
    John Greyhurst 171
XI. MITCHELL AS A NOVELIST 178
BIBLIOGRAPHY 203

INTRODUCTION

By C. P. OBERNDORF, M.D.

A proverbial commonplace has it that truth is stranger than fiction, and both intentionally and unconsciously, writers of fiction are continuously drawing upon their own experiences for detail and reaction. To physicians, more than other professional groups, is granted the opportunity and privilege of observing closely and listening in silent sympathy to the intimate life stories of other people, and literature numbers among its writers several physicians who have turned their progressive information and knowledge into fiction. Doctors Anton Chekov and Conan Doyle may well continue to attract readers for centuries. Today, Somerset Maugham and A. J. Cronin, formerly physicians, have attained the highest distinction in the world of letters.

Psychiatrists and psychoanalysts, even more than general practitioners, acquire deep insight into the origin and motivation of human behavior from the revelations of patients, which are relatively uninfluenced by him. Freud himself received the Goethe Prize in literature, perhaps the highest award for German authors, for the forcible, yet vivid quality of his profuse scientific productions and of his case presentations, which were often as fascinating as the best imaginative creations. Yet very few members of the specialty of psychiatry have ventured into fiction writing, where the dramatic incidents unfolded in the office might be presented for the entertainment and instruction of the average reader.

An exception to this, and a very notable one, is S. Weir Mitchell, an eminent neurologist in the days when psychiatry as we know it today had not developed and the various forms of emotional disturbances were treated by the neuropsychiatrist, to use a more modern hybrid term. One of Mitchell's novels, *Hugh Wynn, Quaker,* in its day was a best seller, another expression which might have puzzled Mitchell. The wide range and popularity of Mitchell's fiction would make Rein's scholarly re-examination of these works distinctly valuable as a literary study alone.

On the other hand, novelists and poets from the earliest times have understood the dynamics of thought and the unconscious which Freud embodied into the system of psychology, which he called psychoanalysis, and which has profoundly influenced all contemporary psychiatry, at least in America. He selected from the Greek tragedy *Oedipus Rex* by Sophocles, the name of the complex for that family drama which is the core of many an individual's neurotic conflict.

So, too, Herman Melville had struggled with the torture of psychic conflict some fifty years before Freud in *Moby Dick,* and reported it with such vividness and force that the centennial of its publication was cause for wide celebration in 1951. And he dedicated the book with "my admiration for his genius" to Nathaniel Hawthorne, a similarly tortured soul, who in *The Scarlet Letter* has given us possibly the most understanding account of the ravages of the sense of guilt on the mind and body of its unhappy clerical victim.

Let us return to Melville's *Moby Dick.* Here, Ahab is described as "gnawed within and scorched without with the infixed, unrelenting fangs of some incurable idea," an obsession in psychiatric terminology. Immediately following this observation, an inquiry is posed regarding the crew of the whaler *Pequod,* "by what evil malice their souls were possessed that at times his hate seemed almost theirs; the White Whale as much their insufferable foe as his; how all this came to be—what the White Whale was to them, or how to their *unconscious* [italics mine] understandings, also in some dim unexpected way, he might have seemed the gliding great demon of the seas of life—all this to explain deeper than Ishmael can go." The significance of productions such as *Moby Dick, Gulliver's Travels* and *Hamlet* have been subjected to outstanding psychoanalytic interpretation since Freud first applied his method in 1907 to Wilhelm Jensen's little book *Gradiva,* and to a Dream of Leonardo da Vinci.

To speculate about the meaning of the White Whale in *Moby Dick,* of the Albatross in Coleridge's *Ancient Mariner,* by correlating a part or the whole of the context of the book or poems with the author's personal life history and reactions has become an avocation for many analysts. To me, some of these speculative investigations appear to be of little comparable value, and a synthesis of the selective association of the analyst to the context, which may not be those of the author.

Perhaps for this reason it is just as well that the author of this book on S. Weir Mitchell is not a psychiatric psychoanalyst and therefore does not feel obligated to hunt for hidden or symbolic implications in Mitchell's numerous novels, but evaluates them on the level at which they were written. As Rein implies, the abnormal characters which Mitchell presents consistently behaved in real life much as he described them in his stories. Here Mitchell has followed the descriptive psychiatry of his French and German contemporaries, and like them, he prided himself on the scientific accuracy of his observations.

That Mitchell was more progressive in his grasp of the general psychiatric problems than the vast majority of American psychiatrists in the latter years of the nineteenth century is amply evidenced by his address in 1890 before the American Medico-psychological Association (now the American Psychiatric Association). Here, he criticized scathingly the almost universal indifference of its members to research in the vast field of mental disorder. That his blast had little effect is apparent from the fact that so little had been undertaken in this direction that a group, headed by the Swiss-trained Adolf Meyer, in 1910 organized the American Psychopathological Association, composed of men whose interests in psychiatry extended beyond custodial care.

True to this scientific training, Mitchell focused his attention intensively upon the physiological aspects of life and upon the world outside, possibly because he primarily hesitated to examine closely the powerful drives which men are inclined to repress and conceal. Thus, for example, he misses completely in his discussion of the sleepwalking scene in Lady Macbeth the phenomenon and emergencies of repressed impulses during the sleep so beautifully illustrated by his more sensitive and yet medically untrained literary brother, Thomas Hardy, in *Tess of the D'Urbervilles*. Here, the strict moral code of the grave clergyman, Angel Clare, also under the impulses of profound emotional upheaval, walks in his sleep, and during it lavishes upon Tess all the love and tenderness he felt for her, but felt obligated to suppress during his waking hours. A similar position is apparent in the case of the alcoholism of Philetus Richmond in Mitchell's *Far in the Forest*, to take at random an example from the wide range of psychopathological manifestations Mitchell included in his novels. He carefully evades consideration of the possibility of secret marital incompatibility between the aging husband of sixty-five and his far younger wife as a basis for the husband's flight into alcoholism late in life as the solution of his psychological problems.

Mitchell's cultural conservatism reinforced his factual and scientific tendencies. These, in turn, prevented a search in his disturbed characters for repressed crude forces, especially the sexual ones, a study of which had previously been published by Dr. Ingersoll, a rural New York physician; an unequivocal emphasis on the emotional interplay of mind and body, so ably noted by Dr. Amariah Brigham, founder of the American Psychological Association, and an appreciation of concepts, so distinctly precursory to Freud, brilliantly formulated by Dr. Oliver Wendell Holmes in 1870 in his Phi Beta Kappa address in Harvard "Mechanics in Thought and Morals."

This latter essay must have been known to Mitchell, who at one time courted the favor of Holmes as a physician who had made an envied place for himself in literature, such as young Mitchell hoped to achieve, and of course, eventually did. So, too, he must have been acquainted with the three psychiatric novels of Holmes, written a generation previously. Certainly, no one will quarrel with Rein's opinion that Mitchell was "a more skilled story teller than Holmes," even though today his style appears antiquated and formal and some of his plots, like those of Cambridge autocrat, also are tedious and labored.

I think, too, that no psychiatrist would question Rein's statement that Mitchell did not make "the fullest use of his psychiatric experiences and his understanding," although the depth of the latter is definitely problematical.

In contrast to Mitchell, Holmes' specialty, after a brief time spent in general medical practice, was anatomy, which Chair he occupied at Harvard. This makes the flashes of modern psychiatric insights which illuminated so brightly his pedestrian tales all the more noteworthy. Two differences are apparent in these two eminent medical men of letters, who dealt fictionally with the abnormal. Holmes limited each novel to the delineation of a single abnormal character, with vagaries which can be considered as more or less typical and consistent. Mitchell's main characters would be considered normal, but into the scene he introduced several abnormal personages, with a limited and at times inadequate portrayal.

The second difference lies in the essential intellectual characteristics of the two men. The Bostonian Brahman spoke freely, heatedly and fearlessly about any topic he chose, and the range was enormous, from a relentless campaign against those physicians who refused to accept the contagiousness of puerperal fever to almost atheistic attacks against Calvinist ideas of predestination which lingered stubbornly in some of the Bostonian churches.

The Philadelphia Mainliner, probably fearful of revealing the weaknesses of the entrenched favored class into which he was born and inferentially also of himself, remained prudish, dispassionate, and failed to express, if he remotely discerned them, the emotionally determined motivations of society and his fictional characters, whom he observed so meticulously but prejudicially.

Such a comparison of these two psychiatrically oriented novelists is not irrelevant though it may be unimportant and academic. In any case the reader will have the opportunity to make his own appraisal from the ably written pages of Rein's careful, thorough and critical review of the life and work of a man of many accomplishments who had few professional peers when at the zenith of his career.

FOREWORD

In recent years novelists have made increasing use of the findings of psychiatry. One of the first novelists in America to utilize such information was Dr. S. Weir Mitchell. By his experience as a specialist in nervous disorders, he had become an outstanding pioneer psychiatrist before he wrote his first novel. In this study I have tried to show how Mitchell, throughout his literary career, utilized in his fiction the attitudes, principles, and experience he acquired in his medical research and practice.

I was first introduced to the work of S. Weir Mitchell by Professor Lyon N. Richardson. His enthusiastic interest in the novels of Mitchell and Holmes, particularly in their psychiatric content, led me to the present study. Throughout the progress of this work his readiness at all times to be helpful and his many constructive suggestions have been invaluable.

In Philadelphia I was given important assistance by John Alden and by Miss Mabel Zahn. I am grateful, too, for the co-operation I received from the Historical Society of Pennsylvania and from the Library of the College of Physicians of Philadelphia, where I found a large number of my sources.

My chief source of unpublished material was in the home of Mitchell's granddaughter, Sarah Worthington Macdonough. She offered me access to a wealth of unpublished letters, diaries, and other manuscripts. Her graciousness made this part of my work particularly pleasant.

For encouragement and helpfulness I am indebted to Professor Finley M. K. Foster, and for valuable suggestions to

Miss Lottie M. Maury and to Professors Hazen C. Carpenter, Frederick L. Taft and William E. Umbach. I feel particularly grateful to Professor Robert L. Shurter, whose interest has been a constant stimulus, and to my wife, who has assisted at all stages of this work.

D.M.R.

"I have just finished a novel which I have been fooling over now for three years and find, always a little to my surprise, sometimes to my regret, that I get a clinical picture into my books of some form of mental disorder. When somebody, if ever, comes to review my books as a whole, he will probably recognize with astonishment that they include a clinical study of various forms of psychic disorder."

—Dr. Mitchell to Dr. Thayer.[1]

[1] The unpublished letter, dated September 28, 1910, is in the possession of Mitchell's granddaughter, Sarah Worthington Macdonough.

Chapter I

MITCHELL'S PHILADELPHIA
BACKGROUND

IN THE city of Philadelphia, on a building in downtown Walnut Street, there is a tribute engraved in metal for all to see:

On this spot stood
   The House of
S. Weir Mitchell
   Physician. Physiologist.
   Poet. Man of Letters.

He taught the use of rest for the nervous
He created "Hugh Wynne"
He pictured for us "The Red City" in which
He lived & laboured from 1829 until 1914.

   Erected by Franklin Inn of which
he was a founder & first president.

While the novels of Mitchell sold widely in their day—*Hugh Wynne* was a best seller in 1898—they are now hardly noticed, even by scholars. Since Mitchell's death in 1914, however, there have been important changes in our outlook which might predispose us once again to look with favor upon his work. In particular there has been the great influence of Freud and, with it, the invasion of psychiatry into the novel, the drama, the movies, and even the detective story.

1

S. Weir Mitchell, often thought of as the father of American neurology, was a pioneer psychiatrist. He discovered for himself many of the strange tricks disordered mental functions can play upon the body and upon the entire personality. His skill in the treatment of nervous ailments made him famous in both Europe and America. In his fiction he drew, at times extensively, upon his special knowledge and understanding. As a result his novels contain psychiatric elements which the reader of today can appreciate perhaps more fully than Mitchell's less informed contemporaries. Certainly these novels seem worth a second look, in the light of our own day, such as has been given to the psychiatric novels of Oliver Wendell Holmes, the contemporary of Mitchell. When Holmes's novels, long overlooked, were republished in 1943 in condensed form and illuminated by introductions and notes, they were so well received a second edition was soon issued.[1]

Although Holmes and Mitchell were pioneers in the psychiatric novel, although they knew and corresponded with one another, their mutual influence seems to have been less than one might expect. Apparently each wrote quite independently of the other. If their novels were unique in the American literature of the time, it was because each drew upon his own particular medical experience and understanding.

When one looks into the life of Mitchell he is impressed at once with the importance of the man's versatility, for without it those unique novels could not have been written. It took not only a practicing doctor, such as Mitchell was, to write them, but more than that, a doctor who specialized in nervous diseases. Since in Mitchell's day the field of nervous disorders was hardly touched, it took a specialist who became so not by inheriting established knowledge and technique, but by doing the original research and thinking which alone could make him a specialist.

How Mitchell came by his remarkable variety of accomplishments is a story that takes us into his background. It is

[1] Clarence P. Oberndorf, *The Psychiatric Novels of Oliver Wendell Holmes* (New York, 1946).

perhaps no accident that Mitchell, praised as America's most versatile doctor, came from the same city as the versatile Benjamin Franklin. Certainly the Philadelphia that Mitchell grew up in, partly no doubt because of Franklin's influence, was a center of culture and of accomplished personalities. In medicine particularly, Philadelphia was outstanding, offering the first medical school in America, and remaining for over a century the medical center of the nation.[2]

The remarkable characteristic of many Philadelphia doctors was their competence not merely in their chosen profession, but in a variety of other fields. They were, writes Struthers Burt, "encouraged to develop their individual personalities" and to become "generally learned."[3] Mitchell himself, in speaking at the centennial anniversary of the College of Physicians, paid a similar tribute to the early doctors of Philadelphia:

In New England the clergy were for a long time dominant. In New York then, as now, commercial success was the surest road to social position. South of us it was the landholder who ruled with undisputed sway. But in this city—I may say in this state—from the first settlement until today the physician has held an almost unquestioned and somewhat curious pre-eminence. He is and always has been relatively a more broadly important personage here than elsewhere.[4]

Mitchell then went on to explain that doctors had been and still were prominent in the Pennsylvania legislature, as directors of insurance companies, banks, colleges and libraries.[5]

Among the great doctors of early Philadelphia perhaps none was more famous, more remarkable for the breadth of his accomplishments, than Benjamin Rush, one of the signers of

[2] See Nathan G. Goodman, *Benjamin Rush* (Philadelphia, 1934), p. 128.
[3] Struthers Burt, *Philadelphia, Holy Experiment* (New York, 1945), pp. 224-225.
[4] S. W. Mitchell, *Commemorative Address at the Centennial Anniversary of the Institution of the College of Physicians of Philadelphia, January 3, 1887* (Philadelphia, 1887), p. 5.
[5] *Ibid.*, p. 5.

the Declaration of Independence. Rush is particularly important in the study of Mitchell. As a widely educated physician who excelled in fields other than his own, as a most prominent personage, perhaps the most famous American doctor of his time, he played a large part in shaping the Philadelphia tradition of the versatile doctor. Mitchell felt his influence directly, by knowing his life and works, and personally, because Rush was admired intensely by Mitchell's father. The elder Dr. Mitchell was himself, as we shall see, a broadly accomplished man, and he brought up his son to regard as normal the pattern of versatility. Beyond all this, some of Rush's specific ideas about abnormal behavior broke into the territory which Mitchell was to explore so profitably for both his medical work and his fiction.[6]

Mitchell on several occasions paid his respects to Rush. Even in some of his novels Rush appears from time to time, bearing his own illustrious name as he visits professionally one or another fictional character.[7] More importantly, in the centennial address already mentioned, Mitchell praised him as "next to Franklin" the greatest citizen of Pennsylvania:

[6] Present-day scholars assign to Rush an outstanding place among the pioneers of psychiatry. Jay Wharton Fay observes: "He made the first systematic studies in America of abnormal mentality, and used the technique of suggestion a century before the Nancy School. . . . He anticipated the Freudians in the description and even the nomenclature of phobias. He was interested in dual personality, and furnished the writers of psychology textbooks both in Great Britain and America for the next three generations with anecdotal material in abnormal psychology." *American Psychology before William James* (New Brunswick, 1939), p. 72.

Rush's most recent biographer also pays tribute to his contributions: "Rush frequently asked patients to write down an account of their symptoms. They felt better for the writing and often he learned much that was enlightening about them. Was it possible that Rush, in using this procedure, called by Freud mental catharsis, anticipated the theory and practice of the psychoanalyst?" Goodman, *op. cit.*, p. 265.

[7] See S. Weir Mitchell, *The Red City* (New York, 1907), and S. Weir Mitchell, *Hugh Wynne* (New York, 1898). In *Hugh Wynne* Rush attends an older man (Hugh Wynne's father) whose mind is becoming enfeebled. Mitchell undertook to present at some length Rush's analysis of this case—a sure indication of how familiar he felt himself to be with the views of Rush. See *Hugh Wynne*, pp. 391-392, 424.

With reverent doubt of my powers to do justice to the greatest physician this country has produced, I approach the task of briefly recalling to your memories the vivid and emphatic personality of Benjamin Rush. . . .

Let me add, as a thoughtful physician, that no one can read what he wrote—and I have read most of it—without a strong sense of his sagacious and intelligent originality, and admiration of his clear and often fervid style. His work on insanity is a masterpiece.[8]

A study of Rush's accomplishments, their rich variety, helps one appreciate more clearly the broad pattern of Mitchell's achievements. As described by his most recent biographer, Rush was "a great physician, a talented teacher, a competent scientist, an able organizer, a felicitous writer, a vigorous social reformer, an earnest philanthropist, a creative scholar, and a devoted patriot."[9] Not only was he engaged in many activities but his intellectual life was correspondingly diverse:

The whole world of men, things, and ideas was Rush's province. The subjects into which he delved are almost encyclopedic in scope. He was one of the first Americans to plead for the abolition of slavery and for temperance. He recommended the conservation and advantageous utilization of our natural resources. He was one of the early advocates of a thorough-going reform in our penal system and was instrumental in having the death penalty abolished, except in cases of first-degree murder, in Pennsylvania. He offered countless suggestions for making the world a better place in which to live, and he bent every effort to spread his gospel through eloquent speeches and voluminous writings in newspapers, magazines, pamphlets, and books. His style is forceful, enthusiastic, polished, and often dramatic. Indeed, many of his philosophical and biographical essays can still be read with a measure of satisfaction in their high literary quality and enjoyment in their diverse contents.[10]

Rush offered a simple explanation of how he found time to do so much:

8 S. Weir Mitchell, *Commemorative Address,* p. 16.
9 Goodman, *op. cit.,* p. 352.
10 *Ibid.,* p. 296.

I derived rest from fatigue in reading, by writing, and from writing by reading, so as to require no other relaxation of body or mind for many hours. I likewise varied my studies, by which means no one of them ever palled, and I think I preserved my mind in a more pointed state by this practice, to every study. I learned it from Ruisseau's history of his life.[11]

Mitchell followed a quite similar practice, frequently reading at night, particularly novels, to get relaxation from the medical work of the day. He wrote his fiction mostly in the summer time, as part of his recreation.[12] The "best rest for a tired mind," he explained, was "the employment of hitherto unemployed mental faculties."[13]

Mitchell was influenced not only in general by Rush's versatility, but in particular by his work in the field of abnormal psychology. Rush had a special interest in mental disease, for his eldest brother had suffered from it and later, for many years, Rush's own distinguished son.[14] During the thirty years (1783-1813) he was on the staff of the Pennsylvania Hospital Rush devoted much attention to the insane. The mental cases, in those days, were locked up when they became unmanageable, were often tied and sometimes brutally beaten; they were regarded with fear or ridicule, but not with understanding, for even the doctors lacked the knowledge necessary to give systematic treatment, and never suspected, it seems, that such knowledge could ever be obtained. Rush not only studied his patients, but carried on, as Mitchell did after him, a vigorous and effective effort to provide them with better physical and psychological care. He tried to make clear to those who seemed unaware of it that the insane retained their feelings as human beings, that "a sense of corporeal pleasure, of joy, of gratitude,

---

[11] Benjamin Rush, *The Autobiography of Benjamin Rush* (Princeton, 1949), p. 91.

[12] Mitchell's granddaughter, Mrs. S. W. Macdonough, informed me that Mitchell as a rule spent very little time on pure recreation. His relaxation habitually took the form of busy endeavor with only the field of work changed.

[13] S. Weir Mitchell, *John Sherwood* (New York, 1914), p. 88.

[14] Rush, *op. cit.*, pp. 27-28, 288, 369.

of neglect, and of injustice is seldom totally obliterated from their minds."[15] But even more important, he insisted that mental diseases could be brought "under the dominion of medicine by just theories of their seats and proximate causes."[16]

From all this effort Mitchell was to profit much, and particularly from the book which Rush published (1812) as the culmination of his thirty years of study of the insane, *Medical Inquiries and Observations Upon the Diseases of the Mind*. This "masterpiece," as Mitchell called it, was the first such study in America, and was used as a standard reference on the subject for the next half century, all during the formative years of Mitchell's career. No work on such a scale appeared until 1883, when Hammond published his *Treatise on Insanity*. Where Rush's work left off, Mitchell could begin in his own studies of the abnormal mind.

There were, of course, some ideas in the book which Mitchell never could accept,[17] but there were also many important statements similar to passages which were to appear later in Mitchell's writings. From the very first, as we shall see, Mitchell showed, both in his medical work and in his fiction, a clear understanding of the interrelationship between mind and body, an understanding upon which much of his unique contribution was based. This fundamental interrelationship was quite effectively stated by Rush:

15 See Goodman, *op. cit.*, p. 257.

16 *Ibid.*, p. 258.

17 In his attempts to treat the insane, for example, Rush all too often resorted to bloodletting and purges. This practice grew out of his belief that the immediate cause of madness was "seated in the blood-vessels of the brain." *Medical Inquiries and Observations Upon the Diseases of the Mind* (3rd ed.; Philadelphia, 1827), p. 16. Rush's list of indirect causes was very extensive—almost anything that could act upon the blood vessels of the brain: physical causes such as gout, dropsy, consumption, pregnancy, excessive use of ardent spirits, inordinate sexual desires and gratifications, onanism, great pain, unusual labor or exercise, and extremely hot or cold weather; mental causes such as excessive study, inordinate schemes and ambitions, overexertion of the imagination (as in poets), and various emotions such as joy and grief.

Man is said to be a compound of soul and body. However proper this language may be in religion, it is not so in medicine. He is, in the eye of a physician, a single and indivisible being, for so intimately united are his soul and body, that one cannot be moved, without the other. The actions of the former upon the latter are numerous and important. They influence many of the functions of the body in health. They are the cause of many diseases; and if properly directed, they may easily be made to afford many useful remedies.[18]

Mitchell in his treatment of patients suffering from nervous disorders and in his reference to them in fiction revealed a clear understanding of the effect of old associations upon such people, and the value of new surroundings. Here too he was preceded by Rush:

There are several other remedies which act upon the body through the medium of the mind, and that are proper, in this disease, from all its causes. The first of these is, the *Destruction* of all old associations of ideas. Everything a hypochondriac patient sees or hears, becomes tinctured with some sad idea of his disease. Hence the same objects and sounds never fail of renewing the remembrance of it. Change therefore his dress, his room, his habitation, and his company, as often as possible.[19]

Mitchell understood, as his writings indicate, that old associations could get buried beneath the memory, still affecting the victim, who remained unaware of what was happening. This mechanism, too, Rush described in his masterpiece:

Many diseases take place in the body from causes that are forgotten. . . . In like manner, depression of mind may be induced by causes that are forgotten; or by the presence of objects which revive the sensation of distress with which it was at one time associated, but without reviving the cause of it in the memory. The former pupils of the author will recollect several instances of mental pleasure, as well as pain, from association, mentioned by him in his physiological lectures upon the mind, in which the original causes of both had perished in the memory.[20]

[18] Benjamin Rush as quoted in Fay, *op. cit.*, p. 72.
[19] Benjamin Rush, *Medical Inquiries and Observations*, p. 115.
[20] *Ibid.*, p. 44.

It might be pointed out here that one of Mitchell's chief limitations from the point of view of modern psychiatry was also shared by Rush. They both failed, as did most observers until Freud, to give sufficient weight to the factor of sex.[21]

Less illustrious than Rush, but of great influence upon Mitchell, was Weir's father. As an ardent admirer of Rush, he interested his son in the works and ways of that great man; furthermore J. K. Mitchell was himself an outstanding person, a fine example of the pattern of versatility. At the College of Physicians in Philadelphia there is an unpublished manuscript of his, *Vindication of Rush,* a vigorous paper attempting to refute the charge of falsehood that had been brought against the memory of Rush. Brief excerpts are quoted here, not only to indicate the elder Mitchell's great esteem for Rush but also his own literary inclination. The paper begins:

> The unparalleled success of the American Sydenham in the treatment of yellow fever was too much for his persecutors and slanderers to endure, with composure. Hence they ventured, yet generally in a sly way, to denounce him as a liar. It was exceedingly rare, for any one to make a bold, responsible accusation of this sort. And as this affair is occasionally revived by those who know nothing of its merits, a just and true history of yellow fever demands that this thing be fairly and fully analyzed.

There follows a heated defense of Rush, his character, his achievements, and his treatment of yellow fever by bloodletting. The paper closes on a passionate note:

> Do any imagine, why at this late hour, I venture to agitate this question? I reply, that justice and truth are eternal, and alike proper themes of defence and praise, at all times. At the merited castigation of wickedness, I will ever rejoice; and guided by the same spirit, may I never shrink

[21] One of the first physicians in America to discuss sexual repression as a cause of hysteria and other nervous disorders was A. J. Ingersoll in his book *In Health* (Boston, 1877). See Henry Alden Bunker, "American Psychiatric Literature during the Past One Hundred Years," *One Hundred Years of American Psychiatry,* ed. J. K. Hall, Gregory Zilboorg, and Henry Alden Bunker (New York, 1944), pp. 215-216.

from the task imposed on every honest man by the God of truth, to vindicate a good cause, and to hurl back the venomed arrow aimed at the heart of innocence.[22]

As one might surmise from this passage, the elder Mitchell was interested in literature. A volume of poetry he published in 1839 was reviewed by Poe, who called some of the poems "pretty songs" and singled out one as "remarkable for an old-fashioned polish and vigor of versification."[23]

There is extant in the original manuscript, a reply of J. K. Mitchell's to an admirer of his poetry. It may be interesting to note his pride in the American spirit of his verses and in their moral purity as well, for S. Weir, too, was to write much in tribute to the American spirit, particularly in his historical novels, and he too was to take pride in the morality of his writings. The letter, written from Philadelphia, July 25, 1843, is addressed to John Tomlin:

> I am under obligation to you for your politely expressed and very kind notice of my verses, written during the intervals of labour, and without the polish which one of more leisure might have given to them. Still that they please, and find on their light wings a welcome in the far west among those whose country they describe, and whose earliest habits they depict, is to me no slight gratification.
>
> The merit I myself claim, is not for the *poetry*, but the spirit of my lines. Everything nearly, is American, exclusively American, designed to record scenery and manners fast merging themselves in agriculture and civilization. There is also nothing to corrupt morals, or degrade taste in my little book; nor have I lent my muse to the . . . . appetite for the unnatural and corrupting commixture of virtue and vice; by which many modern writers endeavor to render even attractive the latter, by giving to it the gloss of the former.[24]

[22] J. K. Mitchell, *Vindication of Rush,* an unpublished paper in the College of Physicians of Philadelphia. The manuscript, sixteen handwritten pages, is undated.

[23] Anna Robeson Burr, *Weir Mitchell* (New York, 1929), p. 21.

[24] An unpublished letter in the Historical Society of Pennsylvania. His pride in America is revealed perhaps even more clearly in the letter he wrote to General George P. Morris, who dedicated a book to him: "To

J. K. Mitchell was not only himself a versatile person, but he recommended a broad education for people generally. In a *Lecture on Some of the Means of Elevating the Character of the Working Classes* he urged that mechanics, in order to break down class barriers, should engage in "the pursuit of classical and elegant literature,"[25] and he insisted, too, that they did have the time to do it. The Mitchells, it seems, father as well as son, believed as Rush did, in somehow finding time to carry on worthy projects.

Weir's father, aside from all his other interests, was a distinguished doctor who still holds a place in the world of medicine. In *A History of Medicine* Arturo Castiglione describes him as "an excellent practitioner, teacher, and writer," and calls his *Crytogamous Origin of Malarious and Epidemic Fevers* (1849) "an important contribution to the parasitic concept of infectious diseases."[26] Weir himself considered his father the greatest doctor he ever knew, and frequently referred to his specific contributions or to cases from his notebooks.[27] He edited one of his father's books, a collection of five essays, including one on mesmerism which shows clearly the elder Mitchell's interest in abnormal psychology. J. K. Mitchell's approach to this area, so clouded with mysticism, was, like that of his son's after him, scientific. He investigated the evidence concerning animal magnetism, concerning claims of clairvoyance, mind reading and other mystic powers, look-

---

see one's name appended to a dedication by *anyone* of a book so beautiful and so American, could not fail to be highly gratifying to me, who so love my country, that I write almost exclusively about her." The unpublished letter, dated November 28, 1840, is in the Historical Society of Pennsylvania.

25 J. K. Mitchell, *Lecture on Some of the Means of Elevating the Work ing Classes* (Philadelphia, 1834) p. 8. There is a copy of the work in the College of Physicians of Philadelphia.

26 Arturo Castiglione, *A History of Medicine* (New York, 1947), p. 708.

27 See for example *The Annual Oration before the Medical and Chirurgical Faculty of Maryland* (Baltimore, 1877), p. 9. See also S. Weir Mitchell, "Spinal Arthropathies," *American Journal of the Medical Sciences*, LXIX (April, 1875), p. 340.

ing always for the explanation of such phenomena in terms of natural causes. When, for example, a person mystified his audience by naming objects he could not see, J. K. Mitchell pointed out how he could distinguish them by the slight sounds they made when moved or operated.[28] At the end of his study of over 125 pages, he concluded that he had "demonstratively overthrown" the "pretensions" of the believers in mesmerism.[29]

Brought up in the household of such a father, influenced by Rush and the Philadelphia tradition, Mitchell acquired a unique inheritance. He had before him the example of men who approached scientifically areas of human behavior hitherto outside the field of science—versatile men who were actively interested in a wide variety of subjects. It was Mitchell's own versatility,[30] as we shall see, which permitted his particular accomplishment in the novel, the creation of characters based upon his knowledge and experience as a pioneer psychiatrist.

[28] See S. Weir Mitchell's short story "The Mind Reader" where the apparent mystical ability to read minds turns out to be merely an ability to read slight lip movements. "The Mind Reader," *The Guillotine Club and other Stories* (New York, 1910).

[29] J. K. Mitchell, *Five Essays*, ed. S. Weir Mitchell (Philadelphia, 1859), p. 274. It may be interesting here to quote a reference of S. Weir Mitchell's to mysticism. It reveals the same desire for evidence and understanding, the same disdain for mystical explanation: "When I recognize anything as mysterious I want to understand it. The mystic invents mystery, and casts a shroud of perplexing inadequacies, of fanciful explanation, about the simple. There is much that is probably forever unknowable, but let us not add needlessly to the inexplicable." See S. Weir Mitchell, *Dr. North and His Friends* (New York, 1905), p. 218.

[30] In an address to liberal arts students, Mitchell indicated his belief that a scientist who neglects the arts loses scientific ability: "Darwin so narrowed his tastes by absolute devotion to science as to lose the recreative interests of even the best of fiction and to be at last really bored by Shakespeare. I am sure that in the end he was a worse scientific instrument by reason of his acquired indifference to all that lies within the bounds of one vast continent of human product." The unpublished manuscript, undated, is in the possession of Mrs. S. W. Macdonough.

Chapter II

MITCHELL'S EARLY STUDIES OF SNAKE VENOM AND OF NERVE INJURIES

BEFORE MITCHELL engaged very seriously in the writing of fiction he had a well-developed scientific outlook, derived not only from his father and from Benjamin Rush, but from his own early research. Following the advice of Holmes, who felt that patients distrusted physician-writers, Mitchell built his reputation as a doctor and physiologist before he ventured very far in the literary field. From the very first, therefore, his fiction had the benefit of his unique scientific training and experience.

It must be remembered that when Mitchell wrote, there was but little tendency to utilize psychiatry in the novel. There were abnormal characters in fiction, to be sure, based sometimes upon acute observation, but not upon psychiatric principles as they are understood today, not upon that awareness of cause and effect relationships, that knowledge of behavior patterns that distinguishes the best contemporary psychiatrists, permitting them to improve and sometimes cure the mentally ill. Mitchell had to make his own way. He did not deliberately train himself to become a writer of psychiatric fiction, but in his career as a scientist he attained the outlook and the knowledge which made such fiction possible. His preparation as a psychiatric novelist began with his training as a scientist.

Mitchell's interest in science began in his early boyhood. His father's chemical laboratory was a fairyland to him where he could make precipitates of beautiful colors. Once or twice he nearly blew himself up, but remained undiscouraged. He had fun, too, playing with a skeleton kept in a closet. One day, just before his father used it in a lecture, Weir stuck a lump of bread in its mouth.

By comparison with his life at home Weir found school dull. It did little, apparently, to develop the interest and outlook he acquired from his contacts with his father. He submitted to a succession of incompetent teachers, one of whom thrashed his students brutally. As a result he scorned his teachers and loathed his lessons, remembering this period ever after without a pleasant thought. When, at fifteen, he entered the University of Pennsylvania, it took him some time to get adjusted. As a freshman he was at times guilty of disorderly conduct, and of poor scholarship. Even as a sophomore he was reprimanded at least once for his classroom behavior. However, his work improved during the next two years, and at times he stood at the head of his class.[1]

At Jefferson Medical College, which he entered in 1847, he was a determined scholar, studying all day long and often at night drinking strong coffee or taking cold showers to keep awake. Here he was impressed most of all by Dunglison's lectures in physiology. They helped form his lifelong habit of probing apparent mysteries in search of their natural causes. "I think I began to develop then," he recalled, "the desire to leave no riddle unsolved, and this has made the laboratory a delight to me."[2]

[1] See Ernest Earnest, S. *Weir Mitchell: Novelist and Physician* (Philadelphia, 1950), pp. 12-17.

[2] *Ibid.*, p. 45. Years later Mitchell applied for the post of Dr. Dunglison —just how eagerly is indicated in a letter he wrote on May 28, 1863: "After some reflection I concluded myself to write urging your return for the election on Tuesday—I am now able to say to you that I have the voice of every professor now at home as well as the expressed desire of Dr. Dunglison that I should succeed him. Nevertheless I run as I am told the utmost risk owing chiefly to the possible absence of two trustees—

When in March 1850, at the age of twenty-one, he finished his medical course, his zeal for learning was too intense to permit him to settle down into the routine of an ordinary doctor. He decided to go to Paris, an advanced center of medicine, and there continue his studies. On the way he stopped in England and visited a wealthy relative, Alexander Henry. The gentleman, impressed with Weir's enthusiasm, gave him one hundred pounds to buy books and scientific equipment. After some hesitation Weir accepted the gift and, shortly afterwards, when he was studying in Paris, used 140 dollars of it to buy the best microscope he could find. This was a significant purchase, for it indicated his interest in independent research. Microscopes were rare in America, even in hospitals, and at times unobtainable.

Weir spent hours each day not only with his microscope, but with the catheter and other instruments. He studied at first hand cases of tumor and consumption, and did work in gynecology and ophthalmology. He was encouraged in all this experimental study by his teachers, particularly the great physiologist Claude Bernard. "I think so and so must be the case," Mitchell said to him one day. "Why think," replied Bernard, "when you can experiment? Exhaust experiment and then think."[3] Bernard was one of the first to investigate hysterical illness, a field in which Mitchell later made important contributions.

At the end of one year in Europe Weir, deeply impressed with his own ignorance, wanted to continue for another year, but his father's health was failing and he was needed at home.

---

as for myself it is of course no light matter to see the just reward of years of labour slip away for no fault of mine.

"You can understand therefore why I urge you to oblige me by returning for this occasion."

The unpublished letter, which does not contain the name of the addressee, is in the library of the Historical Society of Pennsylvania. Mitchell did not get the post, nor did he ever get any such university appointment. Dr. Edward Schumann of Philadelphia, who knew Mitchell, tells me that Mitchell was deeply disappointed by this failure.

[3] *Ibid.*, p. 64. See also Earnest, *op. cit.*, pp. 22-26.

As a practicing doctor in Philadelphia, however, Weir continued his studies, soon beginning an investigation into the nature of rattlesnake venom. He gave up all his free time to this research, coming to his laboratory at three or four in the afternoon and staying all evening, sometimes till after midnight. Even away from the laboratory his mind reverted to this work. "I took it to sleep with me," he wrote, "and woke to think about it, and found it hard to escape when in church or conversing with people."[4] Other doctors tried in vain to discourage him. "What nonsense to bother yourself about snake poisons!" one of them declared. And another warned that every experiment in the laboratory would lose him a patient.[5]

When Mitchell completed his first extensive study of rattlesnakes, it was published (1860) by the Smithsonian Institution. His remarks in the preface indicate the spirit in which he had carried on his work, undeterred by superstitions, aversions, or the protests of the antivivisectionists. So little study of snake poisons had ever been accomplished, he explained, because of the widespread aversion to snakes, shared even by doctors, an aversion which some people believed was instinctive. This belief, recognized today as fallacious, he brushed aside at once as an unnecessary obstacle to important research. His was the objective approach of the scientist, searching for the facts and drawing whatever conclusions they warranted:

> The conclusions arrived at in the pages of this Essay, rest alone upon experimental evidence. That in so varied and so difficult a research, it may be found that I have sometimes been misled, and at others erred in the interpretation of facts, is no doubt to be anticipated. I began this work, however, without preconceived views, and throughout its prosecution I have endeavored to maintain that condition of mind which is wanted in experimentation, and that love of truth which is the parent of rational inferences.[6]

4 *Ibid.*, pp. 75-76.
5 *Ibid.*, p. 72.
6 S. Weir Mitchell, "Researches Upon the Venom of the Rattlesnake," *Smithsonian Contributions to Knowledge*, XII (1860), pp. iii-iv.

In his introductory chapter, he made additional comments upon his point of view:

> For the researches which form the novel part of the following essay, I claim only exactness of detail and honesty of statement. Where the results have appeared to me inconclusive, and where further experimental questioning has not resolved the doubt, I have fairly confessed my inability to settle the matter. This course I have adhered to in every such instance, thinking it better to state the known uncertainty thus created than to run the risk of strewing my path with errors in the garb of seeming truths.[7]

This statement is characteristic of Mitchell. In all his writings there was this large respect for fact and for honest statement. There was no pretense of knowing more than he knew. In his fiction as in his science, whenever he seemed to know something, he did know something. He did not use imagination as a substitute for knowledge, but only within the limits of his knowledge.

As for the antivivisectionists, he simply went ahead in spite of them. Certainly his experiments were hard on the animals he worked with. To test the effect of snake venom he encouraged snakes to bite pigeons, frogs, rabbits and dogs. He dissected animals impregnated with venom and cut off the heads of live snakes to study their glands—all in the spirit of a man too concerned with obtaining knowledge to be deterred by sentiment for the little animals that had to suffer and die.

Mitchell's study of rattlesnake venom was a strictly scientific work. It described with precise detail the anatomy of the venom apparatus in the rattlesnake, the physiological mechanism involved in the bite of the rattlesnake, the physical and chemical characteristics of the venom, its toxicology, its action upon warm-blooded animals, its action upon the tissues and fluids of the body, and finally its effect on man.

For many years after the publication of this work, Mitchell

---

[7] *Ibid.*, p. 1. In reading present-day psychiatric writings, so full of positive and extreme statements contradicting one another, I have often wished this practice of Mitchell's were more followed.

continued his studies of snake venom. He employed assistants who reported to him regularly, even when he was away. On one occasion, failing to get an expected report, he sent a petulant little note: "I don't hear of or from Hinsdale and I can't hear if the snakes are milked. What else on earth can be as momentous."[8]

Several years later Mitchell published another study of rattlesnakes and, referring to the work of 1860, explained the spirit in which it had been conducted, defending in particular his treatment of animals. His statement indicates how deeply a part of his moral and emotional fiber was his devotion to the scientific outlook:

> The present investigation has also been conducted at the cost of a large expenditure of the lives of birds, dogs and rabbits, for which I am responsible to my own conscience, and to the Maker, who has endowed us with the will and the power to search into the secrets of His universe. To men of science, I need not say that the torture inflicted has been used with all possible thoughtfulness, while at the same time I must add that it was usually impossible, in these experiments, to avail myself of chloroform, which would have introduced into my investigation new and obscuring elements. I have said these few words in apologetic preface, only because I respect the motives of the many ignorant and well meaning persons, who have recently sought to take away from us the chief aid of the modern physiologist.[9]

It might be added here that, aside from their importance to Mitchell's development, these studies of snakes had a value of their own as a contribution to knowledge. They were considered epoch-making in their day and are still highly regarded.[10]

8 Unpublished letter to Taylor (undated) in the College of Physicians of Philadelphia. Other unpublished letters there indicate the same enthusiasm.

9 S. Weir Mitchell, "Experimental Contributions to the Toxicology of Rattlesnake Venom," *New York Medical Journal,* VI (January, 1868), pp. 290-291. Later the same year Mitchell published two essays on snake and other poisons in the *Atlantic Monthly.*

10 Mitchell himself assessed his early contributions in the beginning of the work just referred to:

"In the year 1860 I published, through the Smithsonian Institution, a paper of 117 quarto pages, upon the Anatomy, Physiology and Tox-

It was not long before Mitchell's scientific work became chiefly concerned with human beings. With the advent of the Civil War he took a part-time post in an army hospital on Filbert Street in Philadelphia. Soon he became interested in wounds of the nerves. They were hard to treat, and most doctors, knowing little about such cases, were glad to transfer them to Mitchell's ward.

Again, as in the study of rattlesnakes, the reluctance of other men to attack a problem, presented Mitchell with an opportunity. When Doctor William A. Hammond, the Surgeon General, learned of Mitchell's interest, he created a special hospital for nervous diseases, and turned it over to Mitchell and his associates. There Mitchell received cases of "amazing interest," epileptics, palsies, choreas, stump disorders, and "every kind of nerve wound." He and his associates would often work till late at night, taking endless pages of meticulous notes, and then walk home discussing the work of the day. They developed new understanding of such wounds and new methods of treatment, contributions recognized today as milestones in the history of American neurology. Often they were cheered by the response of their patients. "It is such a pleasure," wrote Mitchell, "to see men who have drifted hopeless and helpless from hospital to hospital, with dead limbs moveless below the waist, to see them walking about and grateful even to tears."[11]

Soon they began publishing their findings and in 1864 they issued their major work, *Gunshot Wounds and Other Injuries of Nerves.* "Never before," they explained in the preface, "has there been collected for study and treatment so remarkable a series of nerve injuries," and they went on to describe the background of their investigations:

The great bulk of our patients has consisted of men who

---

icology of the Venomous Organs of the Rattlesnake. From the days of Fontana, 1781, no researches of any moment had added to our knowledge of the poison of serpents; and I had, therefore, the pleasure of contributing a large amount of completely new information to the modern history of animal poisons." *Ibid.,* p. 289.

11 *Ibid.,* p. 110.

have been shifted from one hospital to another, and whose cases have been the despair of their surgical attendants. As the wounded of each period of the war have been cured, discharged, invalided, or died, every large hospital has had left among the wards two or three or more strange instances of wounds of nerves. Most of them presented phenomena which are rarely seen, and which were naturally foreign to the observation even of those surgeons whose experience was the most extensive and complete.[12]

Along with the very considerable knowledge they accumulated, the investigators noted some curious facts:

In wounds of the neck, involving directly or not the brachial plexus, the wounded man sometimes feels pain which is distinctly referred to the elbow or to some other portion of the arm.[13]

Some phases of the study were directly concerned with the psychology of the individual, with his feelings. Mitchell and his collaborators described the "first impressions" of individuals receiving severe nerve wounds, the reactions at the moment of wounding:

By far the larger number felt, when shot, as though some one had struck them sharply with a stick, and one or two were so possessed with this idea at the time, that they turned to accuse a comrade of the act, and were unpleasantly surprised to discover, from the flow of blood, that they had been wounded.[14]

In some of his other studies of this period, too, Mitchell was led from physiological to psychological observations. In his article "Paralysis from Peripheral Irritation" he discussed a curious situation: paralysis of organs which showed no physical fault. When, after searching, he could not find even remote physical causes, he looked for less tangible, yet wholly natural ones, which is to say, he looked for psychological causes. Finally he concluded that the "constitutional condition at the

12 S. Weir Mitchell, George R. Morehouse, and William W. Keen, *Gunshot Wounds and Other Injuries of Nerves* (Philadelphia, 1864), p. 10.
13 *Ibid.*, p. 14.
14 *Ibid.*, p. 14.

time of the wounding, as to excitement, mental and physical, may possibly have to do with the resultant paralysis."[15]

Thus by pursuing his scientific method, by searching for a cause of paralysis, he was led away from purely physiological phenomena into the field of psychology, and was led to consider a new type of relationship, a paralysis in the body to be explained by a condition of mind or emotions.

Eight years after the first book on gunshot wounds Mitchell alone published a more extensive work, *Injuries of Nerves and Their Consequences*. While this study, too, was primarily a careful, detailed piece of medical research, Mitchell was again inevitably led into peculiar aspects of the human personality:

> The following case is a singular example of the effects of a punctured wound of a nerve in a child of hysterical temperament. . . . while she was playing in the street, a lad accidentally ran a small penknife blade into her right hand. . . . The injury seemed trifling, and gave no further trouble until thirty-six hours later, when she became sick, and began to suffer excruciating pain in the right hand, arm, sternum, and back, with fever, rigors, nausea, and slight convulsions, without loss of consciousness. The hand and arm were slightly swollen, and the head was drawn backward, while there was also tremor of the jaw and dysphagia.[16]

How explain this extensive and complex physical reaction to so "trifling" a cause? It was impossible to do so without going beyond the realm of physiology into psychology. Mitchell, recognizing this fact, classified what he observed as a case of hysterical temperament. He was thus discovering early how large a part psychological factors can play in the production of obviously physical symptoms.

In thus working at the boundary between physiology and psychology, he was learning new things about both neurology and human behavior, bringing into the sphere of science aspects of personality hitherto outside, and finding that the human

[15] S. Weir Mitchell, "Paralysis from Peripheral Irritation," *New York Medical Journal*, II (March, 1866), p. 422.

[16] S. Weir Mitchell, *Injuries of Nerves and Their Consequences* (Philadelphia, 1872), pp. 164-165.

personality is subject to the laws of science, to the orderly sequence of cause and effect. As a result of these studies he had knowledge of human behavior unknown before him—unknown not only by writers but by doctors too. His book *Injuries of Nerves and Their Consequences,* which incorporated some of this knowledge, provided the basic material for his unique story "The Case of George Dedlo."

Chapter III

"THE CASE OF GEORGE DEDLO": A STORY BASED ON MITCHELL'S STUDY OF NERVE INJURIES

THE FOURTEENTH and last chapter of *Injuries of Nerves and Their Consequences* carried Mitchell directly into an unusual psychological study—into an area which he declared had been "almost entirely neglected."[1] This chapter, "Neural Maladies of Stumps," is a careful and often detailed description of the reactions of the amputee to his condition, and particularly of the hallucinations which afflict him. Before publishing this material in his book on nerve injuries, Mitchell published it elsewhere in the form of a short story, "The Case of George Dedlo."

Mitchell knew, even as he wrote the story, that some of the material in it contributed to medical knowledge and that he would later publish the same observations in a scientific paper. The fictional young doctor, George Dedlo, telling the story in the first person, declared at the outset that he was printing it then "with all the personal details," and that later he would publish it elsewhere in the "dry shape" of a "psychological statement."[2] At the opening of the story George Dedlo joined the army of the North. Soon afterward, undertaking a lone

---

[1] S. Weir Mitchell, *Injuries of Nerves and Their Consequences*, p. 342.
[2] S. Weir Mitchell, "The Case of George Dedlo," *The Autobiography of a Quack and Other Stories* (New York, 1903), p. 83.

mission, he was wounded in both arms. Mitchell's description of his injuries and of his reactions to them is informed and meticulous:

> I staggered to my horse and tried to mount; but, as I could use neither arm, the effort was vain, and I therefore stood still, awaiting my fate. I am only conscious that I saw about me several graybacks, for I must have fallen fainting almost immediately.
>
> When I awoke I was lying in the cabin near by, upon a pile of rubbish. Ten or twelve guerrillas were gathered about the fire, apparently drawing lots for my watch, boots, hat, etc. I now made an effort to find out how far I was hurt. I discovered that I could use the left forearm and hand pretty well, and with this hand I felt the right limb all over until I touched the wound. The ball had passed from left to right through the left biceps, and directly through the right arm just below the shoulder, emerging behind. The right arm and forearm were cold and perfectly insensible. I pinched them as well as I could, to test the amount of sensation remaining; but the hand might as well have been that of a dead man. I began to understand that the nerves had been wounded, and that the part was utterly powerless.[3]

The wound in the right hand became particularly troublesome and Dedlo described at length not only his pain but the conditions which aggravated it and those which relieved it. When finally the arm had to be amputated at the shoulder, he described his sensations before, during and after the operation.[4]

Soon after this loss of his right arm Dedlo was wounded again, in both thighs, and another operation was required. Of particular interest was his reaction when he came out of ether:

> I got hold of my own identity in a moment or two, and was suddenly aware of a sharp cramp in my left leg. I tried to get at it to rub it with my single arm, but, finding myself too weak, hailed an attendant. "Just rub my left calf," said I, "if you please."

3 *Ibid.,* pp. 86-87.
4 It may be of interest to compare Mitchell's treatment of this operation with Melville's marvellous description of an amputation in *White-Jacket.* Mitchell, with his intimate knowledge, was able to present the experience from the point of view of the patient.

"Calf?" said he. "You ain't none. It's took off."

"I know better," said I. "I have pain in both legs."

"Wall, I never!" said he. "You ain't got nary leg."

As I did not believe him, he threw off the covers, and, to my horror, showed me that I had suffered amputation of both thighs, very high up.

"That will do," said I, faintly.[5]

Dedlo, already stripped of three limbs, developed gangrene in the wound in his fourth, his left arm, and when this was amputated at the shoulder he became a living torso.

Mitchell's narrative throughout these events remained scientific in tone and quite free of sentiment. "I have dictated these papers," said Dedlo at this stage in the story, "not to shock my readers, but to possess them with facts in regard to the relation of the mind to the body."[6] He proceeded then to consider this relationship. What happens to the personality of a man so cut down physically as George Dedlo? What are his thoughts and feelings? Mitchell applied himself strictly to these questions, and with no effort to exploit the emotional appeal of his unfortunate character. As a torso Dedlo was removed to Philadelphia, to a place known appropriately as "Stump Hospital,"[7] where he studied and reported not only his own reactions, but those of others:

I found that the great mass of men who had undergone amputations for many months felt the usual consciousness that they still had the lost limb. It itched or pained, or was cramped, but never felt hot or cold. If they had painful sensations referred to it, the conviction of its existence continued unaltered for long periods; but where no pain was felt in it, then by degrees the sense of having that limb faded away entirely.[8]

5 *Ibid.*, p. 93.

6 *Ibid.*, p. 94.

7 "Stump Hospital" was an actual place which Mitchell personally knew. "Toward the end of the great rebellion there existed in South Street, Philadelphia," he wrote, "a hospital of several hundred beds, which was devoted altogether to the lodging and care of men in need of artificial limbs. It was known as the 'Stump Hospital.' " See S. Weir Mitchell, "Phantom Limbs," *Lippincott's Magazine*, VIII (December, 1871), p. 563.

8 S. Weir Mitchell, "The Case of George Dedlo," p. 95.

Dedlo attempted to account in physiological terms for the strange fact that the missing limb still seemed to be present, causing sensations:

> I think we may to some extent explain this. The knowledge we possess of any part is made up of the numberless impressions from without which affect its sensitive surfaces, and which are transmitted through its nerves to the spinal nerve-cells, and through them, again, to the brain. We are thus kept endlessly informed as to the existence of parts, because the impressions which reach the brain are, by a law of our being, referred by us to the part from which they come. Now, when the part is cut off, the nerve-trunks which led to it and from it, remaining capable of being impressed by irritations, are made to convey to the brain from the stump impressions which are, as usual, referred by the brain to the lost parts to which these nerve-threads belonged. In other words, the nerve is like a bell-wire. You may pull it at any part of its course, and thus ring the bell as well as if you pulled at the end of the wire; but, in any case, the intelligent servant will refer the pull to the front door, and obey it accordingly.[9]

Dedlo's observation of the illusion became quite detailed. He noticed not only that an amputee often received sensations as though from the missing limb, but that these sensations seemed to come not from the whole missing limb, but from the extremity only, the foot or the hand:

> Where the leg, for instance, has been lost, they feel as if the foot were present, but as though the leg were shortened. Thus, if the thigh has been taken off, there seems to them to be a foot at the knee; if the arm, a hand seems to be at the elbow, or attached to the stump itself.[10]

At the time he wrote about Dedlo, Mitchell was studying actual cases of amputees, the very phenomena he was describing fictionally. When he later published his *Injuries of Nerves and Their Consequences,* he set down again the same observations. He noted, for example, the same strange fact as in "The

9 *Ibid.*, pp. 95-96.
10 *Ibid.*, p. 97.

Case of George Dedlo": The amputee had sensations not from the whole missing limb, but from the extremity only:

> The limb is rarely felt as a whole; nearly always the foot or the hand is the part more distinctly recognized.[11]

In some cases after amputation, Dedlo noted, the nerve ends do not heal, but remain in a constant irritation which results in neuralgia. The pain, in such cases, Dedlo continued, is

> usually referred by the brain to that part of the lost limb to which the affected nerve belonged. This pain keeps the brain ever mindful of the missing part, and, imperfectly at least, preserves to the man a consciousness of possessing that which he has not.[12]

Mitchell had studied just such cases in his medical practice:

> When a limb has been removed, the stump which forms is liable to certain nervous disorders, which are often intractable. . . . My own information on the subject is derived from the careful study of ninety stumps, and from the statements of fourteen persons who have consulted me on account of neuralgia or choreiform movements of their stumps, as well as from dissections of such parts.[13]

George Dedlo became the victim of a nervous disorder of the stump and felt pain in a limb that was missing:

> Before leaving Nashville I had begun to suffer the most acute pain in my left hand, especially the little finger; and so perfect was the idea which was thus kept up of the real presence of these missing parts that I found it hard at times to believe them absent. Often at night I would try with one lost hand to grope for the other. As, however, I had no pain in the right arm, the sense of the existence of that limb gradually disappeared, as did that of my legs also.[14]

Here again Mitchell's fiction paralleled his experience, for he was observing such sensory hallucinations in his medical study:

---

[11] S. Weir Mitchell, *Injuries of Nerves and Their Consequences,* p. 350.

[12] S. Weir Mitchell, "The Case of George Dedlo," p. 96.

[13] S. Weir Mitchell, *Injuries of Nerves and Their Consequences,* pp. 343-344.

[14] S. Weir Mitchell, "The Case of George Dedlo," p. 97.

No history of the physiology of stumps would be complete without some account of the sensorial illusions to which persons are subject in connection with their lost limbs. These hallucinations are so vivid, so strange, and so little dwelt upon by authors, as to be well worthy of study. . . .

Nearly every man who loses a limb carries about with him a constant or inconstant phantom of the missing member, a sensory ghost of that much of himself, and sometimes a most inconvenient presence, faintly felt at times, but ready to be called up to his perception by a blow, a touch, or a change of wind. . . .

Even in those who are least conscious of the missing part I have amazed them by suddenly recalling it with the aid of a faradaic current applied to the nerves of the stump. . . .

I recently faradised a case of disarticulated shoulder without warning my patient of the possible result. For two years he had altogether ceased to feel the limb. As the current affected the brachial plexus of nerves, he suddenly cried aloud, "Oh, the hand, the hand!" and attempted to seize the missing member. The phantom I had conjured up swiftly disappeared, but no spirit could have more amazed the man, so real did it seem. Very many have a constant sense of the existence of the limb, a consciousness even more intense than exists for the remaining member. "If," says one, "I should say I am more sure of the leg which aint than the one which are, I guess I should be about correct." . . . The sufferer who has lost a leg gets up in the night to walk, or he tries to rub or scratch it. One of my cases attempted, when riding, to pick up his bridle with the lost hand, while he struck his horse with the other, and was reminded of his mistake by being thrown. Another person, for nearly a year, tried at every meal to pick up his fork, and was so disturbed emotionally at the result as frequently to be nauseated, or even to vomit.[15]

Mitchell's descriptions of the reactions of an amputee to his missing limb are still valid, and referred to in present-day medical studies.[16]

15 S. Weir Mitchell, *Injuries of Nerves and Their Consequences*, pp. 348-350.

16 See Atha Thomas and Chester C. Haddan, *Amputation Prosthesis* (Philadelphia, 1945) , pp. 59-60, 68. The description these authors make

After a few months at Stump Hospital Dedlo was removed to the United States Army Hospital for Injuries and Diseases of the Nervous System. In this new place, said Dedlo, were "some three hundred cases of epilepsy, paralysis, St. Vitus's dance, and wounds of nerves."[17] The words seem like a description out of Mitchell's own experience during the Civil War when he had worked in a special hospital for diseases and injuries of nerves.[18]

As Mitchell indicated in the opening words of "The Case of George Dedlo," there is much in the story, "personal details," not present in his medical reports on amputees. In particular there are the more general reactions of Dedlo to his extraordinary condition, the absence of all four limbs. While no doubt Mitchell relied to some extent on his imagination, he depended most of the time and was guided always by his own substantial information. He knew how amputees felt, and he was able to describe from his own knowledge those reactions which Dedlo shared with other amputees. But when it came to describing the reactions peculiar to a man like Dedlo, Mitchell had to call upon his imagination, for he never had a patient who had lost all four limbs, as he himself indicated in describing the amputees of the Civil War:

> There survive, however, a considerable number of men who have lost both arms and one leg; one, at least, who lost both legs and an arm, and several who have parted with the two upper extremities or the two lower. One instance is known —and perhaps there are others—of the loss of all four limbs: that is to say, of both feet and both hands; but, so far as we are aware, no one survived the removal of all four limbs above the elbows and the knees, although such a case is said to have occurred in the Napoleonic wars.[19]

By the various operations performed upon him Dedlo had

---

of "phantom limbs" indicates how accurately Mitchell described a condition which still presents a "formidable" problem.

[17] S. Weir Mitchell, "The Case of George Dedlo," p. 98.
[18] See p. 19 of the present work.
[19] S. Weir Mitchell, "Phantom Limbs," p. 564.

lost four-fifths of his weight. As a result he needed much less food, and much less sleep. "I needed only that rest," he declared, "which was necessary to repair such exhaustion of the nerve-centers as was induced by thinking and the automatic movements of the viscera."[20] His heart beat slowed from seventy-eight per minute to forty-five. About half of the sensitive surface of his skin was gone, and "thus much of the relation to the outer world destroyed." As a result "a large part of the receptive central organs" were idle and "the great central ganglia, which give rise to movements in the limbs, were also eternally at rest."[21] The general health of the man, however, remained good.

The psychological changes that Dedlo noticed in himself were remarkable:

> I found to my horror that at times I was less conscious of myself, of my own existence, than used to be the case. This sensation was so novel that at first it quite bewildered me. I felt like asking some one constantly if I were really George Dedlo or not; but, well aware how absurd I should seem after such a question, I refrained from speaking of my case, and strove more keenly to analyze my feelings. At times the conviction of my want of being myself was overwhelming and most painful. It was, as well as I can describe it, a deficiency in the egoistic sentiment of individuality.[22]

For the last part of the story Mitchell added a melodramatic scene. Dedlo, invited by another patient, visited a spiritualist meeting to seek proof of the ability of the dead to speak to the living. At the meeting Dedlo, looking around him, described

---

[20] S. Weir Mitchell, "The Case of George Dedlo," p. 99.

[21] *Ibid.*, pp. 100-101.

[22] *Ibid.*, p. 100. The loss in sense of identity described by Dedlo seems much like the feelings of depersonalization reported in recent psychiatric literature. "One of the principal aspects of a depersonalization," writes Mandel Sherman, "is the realization by the individual that he has in some way lost his identity." Mandel Sherman, *Basic Problems of Behavior* (New York, 1941), p. 157. T. A. Munro, to give but one example, describes a patient who, along with his other symptoms, feels that "even his own body" appears "changed or unreal." T. A. Munro, "Depression and Mania," *Modern Practice in Psychological Medicine*, ed. by J. R. Rees (New York, 1949), p. 283.

the people present, particularly those who were a more intimate part of the proceedings. The descriptions certainly implied Mitchell's own disparagement of spiritualists. There was
a quack doctor; there was a female patient of his who had
deserted her husband "to follow this new light";[23] and there
was a female authoress of "two somewhat feeble novels"; the
others were strangers who had come out of curiosity. The
medium, looking anything but spiritual, wore a "good deal of
jewelry." He was "a shrewd-visaged, large-nosed, full-lipped
man, formed by nature to appreciate the pleasant things of
sensual existence."

When Dedlo's turn came and he was asked to think of a
spirit, a "wild idea" came to him, and in accordance with this
idea, not one, but two spirits identified themselves, and instead
of giving names gave numbers: United States Medical Mu-
seum, Nos. 3486, 3487.

"Good gracious!" exclaimed Dedlo, "they are *my legs—my
legs.*"[24] Mitchell added a further touch of melodrama when
Dedlo suddenly felt a return of his own full identity, staggered
across the room on invisible limbs, and then sank to the floor,
once more upon his stumps.

The reader unacquainted with Mitchell might be puzzled by
this ending. The whole story up to that point had been told,
for the most part, with such factual precision that one might
not be prepared for the sudden shift in the author's attitude.
Surely, however, there was such a shift. Mitchell undoubtedly
wrote this melodramatic ending merely as fictional entertainment, and with no intention of imposing upon the credulity
of his readers. He did not expect them to accept as plausible
the medium's supernatural knowledge nor Dedlo's sudden
ability to walk on legs he did not have. However, the story was
misinterpreted and Mitchell felt obliged to clarify his position.

[23] In some of his later writings Mitchell pictured the devotees of spiritualism in the same unfavorable manner. One of the worst of his women
characters, for example, the scheming Mrs. Hunter, twice brought Kitty,
whom she was trying to influence, to spiritualist meetings. See S. Weir
Mitchell, *Circumstance* (New York, 1903) , pp. 224, 267.
[24] S. Weir Mitchell, "The Case of George Dedlo," p. 108.

In his signed article "Phantom Limbs," published in the *Atlantic Monthly,* he referred to the story of Dedlo, clarifying its meaning, without however admitting authorship of the anonymously published story:

> Some years ago an article was published in the *Atlantic Monthly* which purported to be the autobiography of an officer who had survived the loss of all of his limbs. This sketch gave an account of the sensations of men who have lost a limb or limbs, but the author, taking advantage of the freedom accorded to a writer of fiction, described as belonging to this class of sufferers certain psychological states so astounding in their character that he certainly could never have conceived it possible that his humorous sketch, with its absurd conclusion, would for a moment mislead anyone.[25]

Even without this explanation, however, the meaning of the Dedlo story would be clear to the reader acquainted with Mitchell. Mitchell was never a mystic, neither before nor after his "Case of George Dedlo." Nowhere in his writing is there anything but skepticism or disdain for spiritualism, or for any form of mysticism.[26] The melodramatic ending apparently appealed to Mitchell's sense of humor. It was so fanciful, so absurd as to produce incredulity in the thoughtful and a laugh at the expense of spiritualism.

While the ending of "The Case of George Dedlo" may seem somewhat ambiguous until one views it in the light of Mitchell's point of view, the story as a whole remains an impressive accomplishment. It contains some of the virtues which were to characterize much of Mitchell's later work, particularly his informed treatment of abnormal characters. Dedlo's experiences were set down with such factual precision that many readers assumed the story was the report of a true case, and

---

25 S. Weir Mitchell, "Phantom Limbs," p. 564.

26 Mitchell expressed his disdain plainly and often through Dr. North, his fictional counterpart in *Characteristics* and in its sequel, *Dr. North and His Friends.* See *Characteristics* (New York, 1903), pp. 204-206. See also *Dr. North and His Friends,* pp. 96-97, 218, 262-263, 274 ff. Mitchell himself took part in the exposure of spiritualism conducted by the Seybert Commission. See Earnest, *op. cit.,* pp. 110-112.

sent money for Dedlo. A few even visited "Stump Hospital" to see him.[27] The story showed, too, Mitchell's ability, as Quinn puts it, "to project himself into the feelings and emotions of his characters."[28]

[27] See Arthur H. Quinn, *American Fiction* (New York, 1936), p. 306.
[28] *Ibid.*, p. 306.   This ability, Quinn declares, made Mitchell a "great novelist."

Chapter IV

MITCHELL'S CASE STUDIES OF NERVOUS AILMENTS: MATERIAL FOR FICTION

DURING HIS career Mitchell wrote a great deal of fiction which, like "The Case of George Dedlo," grew out of his scientific viewpoint and his specific medical knowledge. After completing the story of Dedlo (1866), however, he wrote little fiction of importance for eighteen years, until 1884, when his first novel, *In War Time,* appeared.[1] During this long interlude Mitchell continued his special studies begun during the Civil War and became a specialist in injuries and diseases of the nervous system. He gave up his busy general practice, which at one time included fifty-two calls a day, and devoted himself almost exclusively to nervous disorders. As physician to what was probably the first clinic for nervous diseases in the country, he brought in several very able assistants, including William Osler and his own son, John K. Mitchell, and he instituted new procedures in the treatment of patients and in the per-

[1] While Mitchell's "Autobiography of a Quack" (1867) concerns the medical profession, it depends little upon unique psychological insight. "Hephzibah Guiness" (1860) does have such insight, but it is a novelette. Important elements in the story were later elaborated, as Professor Lyon N. Richardson has pointed out, in the novel *Roland Blake* (1886); see his "S. Weir Mitchell at Work," *American Literature,* II (March, 1939), pp. 58-65.

formance of research.[2] As a result of his work in this clinic Mitchell not only published many original contributions, but became famous for his treatment of the nervously ill.

This medical experience was to prove of great value when he turned to writing novels. His work as physician carried him into hitherto unexplored regions of mental illness. The distressing problems of his patients not only demanded psychological studies the layman would never think of undertaking, but presented him also with the human material and the conditions necessary to such studies. In attempting to solve the problems, Mitchell acquired important new insights into human behavior. He not only made direct use, in his fiction, of some of this medical experience, but was influenced by it indirectly, in his attitude toward the human personality, and in his literary style and method. A brief review, therefore, of some of his medical background will enable the reader to understand better how Mitchell came to use psychiatry in his novels, and what he accomplished in his fictional studies of mental illness.

Many of the medical problems Mitchell faced as a specialist in nervous diseases took him straight into the field of psychology or psychiatry, and led him to consider the total personality of his patient. Men sometimes came to him, for example, with no other symptoms than plain, general nervousness. He felt obliged, in prescribing treatment for them, to study in detail the individual personality of each patient:

> The mental attitudes of the nervous man demand of his physician the most careful attention, nor can we afford to disregard anything in his ways of life or his habits of thought and action. We must determine for him how far and how much he shall use his mind; whether or not it is well for him to continue his work, whatever it be, what his amusements should be. The careful student of such cases will find in the individuality of his cases the need for the most minute of such studies, and, above all, he will learn that the more fully he commands the confidence of his patient the more can he effect. Such people are greatly helped by a word or

[2] See Earnest, *op. cit.*, pp. 76-77.

two of decisive promise or of reassurance, and since a part of the treatment of the acquired habit of nervousness must consist in mental and moral training, it becomes needful at times to make the patient comprehend that he himself has some control over his symptoms, or, at least, that constantly to yield to them is to insure defeat, and that constantly to struggle in a manly way is sure to bring nearer the day of perfect self-conquest.[3]

He wanted his nurses, too, to take full account of the individuality of the patients. In his *Hints to Nurses* he gave the following instructions:

To do your work properly, you must consider each patient as a new study, with character, disposition, and ways that must be learned by you and considered by you if you are to succeed.[4]

Many women came to Mitchell suffering from various forms of paralysis—but with no discernible physical causes. He was at such times inevitably led to search for psychological causes, and to consider the total personality:

We see here among the ill-fed, needy, and worried, a good many cases of hysterical loss of power, and I meet a yet larger number among women of the upper classes, where the disease is caused by unhappy love affairs, losses of money, and the daily fret and weariness of lives, which passing out of maidenhood, lack those distinct purposes and aims which, in the lives of men, are like the steadying influence of the flywheel in an engine.[5]

The cases of physical disabilities without apparent physical causes included not only paralysis, but many other symptoms, such as tremors, respiratory disorders, loss of hearing, gastrointestinal disorders, and a variety of aches and pains. Peculiar

3 S. W. Mitchell, "Nervousness in the Male," *The Medical News*, XXXV (December, 1877), p. 183. In this article Mitchell declared that the most common cause of nervousness in the male was tobacco, and that the worst cases he had seen "were those of sexual excess in the young." p. 181.

4 The printed leaflet is among the Mitchell papers in the College of Physicians of Philadelphia.

5 S. W. Mitchell, "The True and False Palsies of Hysteria," *Medical News and Abstracts*, XXXVIII (February, 1880), p. 65.

and baffling cases they often were, the despair of the doctors who sent them.

In 1881 Mitchell published some of his observations, including case histories, in *Lectures on Diseases of the Nervous System, Especially in Women*. In the preface he indicated the original nature of his contributions:

> The lectures which compose this volume deal chiefly with some of the rarer maladies, or forms of maladies, of women. Many of them are original studies of well-known diseases, and others deal with subjects which have been hitherto slighted in medical literature or which are almost unknown to it.[6]

In attempting to treat these unusual cases Mitchell seldom resorted to the easy expedient of drugs, but searched rather for the obstinately hidden, the intangible causes. Such disorders, he declared, "are to be met, not by mere symptomatic therapeutics, but by a full and clear comprehension of underlying causes, and by such treatment of these, whether they be moral or physical, as shall destroy the soil in which hysteric phenomena flourish."[7] Most of these cases were baffling because the causes seemed so obscure. The most careful examination of the disabled organ or part, such as a paralyzed limb, revealed nothing wrong, no sign at all of why the patient was unable to use it.

At this stage of the diagnosis most doctors in those days would give up in despair. The patient wasn't really ill, but only imagined he was, and that's all there was to it. The very effort to search for causes in this area was in itself a distinction which Mitchell shared with but a few of his contemporaries. The results of his search were noteworthy—although it must be added that, from the point of view of present-day knowledge, his limitations seem as impressive as his accomplishments. While he looked for all causes, he was too inclined to empha-

---

[6] S. Weir Mitchell, *Lectures on Diseases of the Nervous System, Especially in Women* (Philadelphia, 1881).

[7] S. Weir Mitchell, *Lectures on Diseases of the Nervous System, Especially in Women*, 2nd ed. (Philadelphia, 1885), p. 267.

size the remote physical causes of hysterical illness and to neglect the psychological causes, particularly those associated with sex. Furthermore, when he investigated the physical, he attempted to narrow his search precisely; when he investigated the psychological, he seemed content to point to a general area, such as an "emotional shock." Apparently it never occurred to him, at such times, to look for the specific content of the experience and probe it precisely.

In searching for causes Mitchell was much influenced by his own past training, especially during the Civil War. He had worked with known physical causes then, gunshot wounds, and had seen their far-reaching effects, such as paralysis of parts far removed from the wound. In his study of nervous disorders he reversed the process, beginning not with the known causes, but with the known, obvious effects and setting out to discover the causes, however remote. When he could find no physical cause, even at some distance from the disabled organ, he looked for a psychological cause, turned from an examination of the body to an examination of the life history. In the events of the patient's life he often found his answers. In one case of paralysis he found the explanation in a series of emotional shocks:

> Miss L., a fine, large, ruddy woman of 26 years of age, owes her hemipalsy to the shock of a fall from affluence to the need to support herself by giving lessons in music. Then a succession of deaths fell upon her household; and at last, one day, while engaged in teaching, she fell asleep, as it were, abruptly, at about 9 A.M. She was aroused enough to be taken to bed, and there remained thirteen hours, in what seemed to be profound slumber. After this unusual trouble she grew more and more hysterical, and at last came under my care.[8]

Mitchell found, as he acquired more and more experience, that all sorts of physical disabilities were due to psychological experiences. He found some remarkable cases of spasms: one woman, while crossing a room, would suddenly rotate furi-

8 *Ibid.,* pp. 29-30.

ously to the left;[9] another would hold her leg rigidly at right angles to her body, continuing steadily so for months, even in sleep.[10] He had patients who experienced unusual symptoms upon retiring for sleep, when they would suddenly hear loud noises, see flashes of light, or feel blows. A particularly odd case was the two hundred pound woman who involuntarily tossed in bed, her body jerking up high and descending violently.[11] He found vasomotor disorders of hysterical origin, as in the woman who, after passing water, suffered chilliness, twitching of the face and extreme palpitation of the heart. He found respiratory and circulatory disorders of hysterical origin, as in the girl who at the mention of certain odors would go into a faint, her pulse dropping rapidly until she lay in seeming death for two, three, or four days, her pulse too weak to be felt. He encountered a woman who would swell as in preg-

9 "At other times," continued Mitchell, "an irresistible power seemed to drag her up on to her tiptoes, where she would remain a moment, as it were, fixed. At this time she could walk, or even run, backwards, but a forward movement was beset with difficulties." The "great variety of the forms assumed by Miss L. P.'s attacks, and the temporary limitation of the disorder to partial groups of muscles," Mitchell continued, "would, I think, entitle us to suspect hysteria as a cause; and, when we learn that no attacks ever took place in the street, and that pleasant surroundings lessened the likelihood of the occurrence of the spasms, while all depressing and enfeebling agencies were apt to bring them on, no further doubt should exist as to the parentage of the disorder." Mitchell admitted that he failed in his treatment of this case. See *ibid.*, pp. 99-102.

10 Concerning this case Mitchell wrote: "A multitude of therapeutic experiments ending always in failure, and the abandonment of the case, had been made by several physicians; nevertheless, I undertook the treatment with a certain amount of hope, such, in fact, as I always have, when an hysterical case is taken away from her own home and social surroundings, and subjected to new and revolutionary influences." See *ibid.*, p. 125.

11 "The patient was one of those stout, ruddy women, with good ovaries, and uterus where it should be, and yet hysterical to an exasperating degree. She weighed over 200 pounds, and was unhappily subject to what she called 'fish-flaps,' which were really remarkable, because her body would be thrown up from the bed so high, and descend with such violence owing to her weight, that it was not rare to find the slats of the bed giving way. She grew better as her hysteria lessened, but is, I believe, still subject at times to these unpleasant and undesired gymnastic symptoms." *Ibid.*, p. 181.

nancy, others whose bodily joints failed to function.[12] He found various cases of intestinal and related disorders of hysterical origin, such as inability to chew, to swallow, to hold food, to defecate, to refrain from defecating.[13]

One of the most striking of all was a case of aphonia, which Mitchell described at length. It illustrates, perhaps better than any other single case of his, how various and complex can be the symptoms of an underlying hysteria:

> The patient before us today is a very notable illustration of the pranks which may be played by hysteria. I read you her history, and as you hear it I think you will see that almost at any time a resolute man, whom she trusted and who understood her disorder, could have saved her and her family from long years of suffering. Her case will enable me to point out to you, as I have done very often before, that the natural history of many of the forms of hysteria is still an open study. One reason for that is, I presume, the disgust with which the general practitioner encounters this malady. It is hysteria, and with that seems to end all need for observation of details and varieties of symptoms, such as more manageable disorders obtain.
>
> Mrs. R., aet. 31, from New Jersey, was brought up among people of narrow means and larger wants. A rather frail constitution and nervous parents doubly prepared her for the ills which were, perhaps, only hastened by an attack of ague, followed by pneumonia, in September, 1870. Soon

[12] Concerning one such case Mitchell wrote: "This was purely a hysterical joint and nothing more. Massage and induction-currents were used to awaken the unused muscles, bandage and crutch were put aside, and after a few words of kindly advice she was ordered to walk. In a week she could walk five miles and went home to have, I trust, no relapse." *Ibid.,* p. 219.

[13] Mitchell described one such case: "A long stomach-tube was carried six or seven inches up the bowel, and half a pint of olive oil injected; then followed one quart to three of flaxseed tea. During the use of the enema one person was occupied in compressing the anal opening . . . . the patient . . . . was shrieking with pain. The whole affair took two to four hours, and the patient was, I thought, the least exhausted of those concerned. . . . I endeavored to get this girl out of the control of her family, but I did not succeed; and I believe that her hysteria is now firmly established." *Ibid.,* pp. 260-261. Note how uninhibited Mitchell was in his medical writing compared to what some might call prudish restraint in his literary work.

after recovery a day of fatigue and some worries ended in hysterics, with retention of urine. A more violent fit followed an attempt to do some rather hard work. From this time the Pandora's box of hysteric ills was opened, and they came almost without limit. Remaining in bed, fit followed fit, until, when a little better, she chanced to smell musk, upon which she fell into a state of stupor, and was thought to be dying. Then the voice fell to a whisper, and so came and went for five years, and at last failed so utterly that for the last five years she has uttered no sound. Meanwhile she stayed in bed till 1872, and had, in succession, general paresis, right arm and hand paralyzed, enormous swelling of hand so as to resemble an abscess, and a variety of hyperaesthesias; on one occasion a blow on the hand caused retraction of the head, followed abruptly by recovery of previously lost power. Soon afterwards there were in succession repeated attacks of hemiplegia, renewed hysterics, paralysis of left leg, and swelling of foot, with exquisite hyperaesthesia of the whole skin. In September, 1872, a slight effort brought on palsy of the left arm, so that she had finally loss of power in both hands, with loss of voice. This was followed by anuria, and then by complete absence of saliva, so that for a time the mouth was absolutely dry. Meanwhile speechless, and with paralysis of all her limbs, she could only call anyone by seizing the handle of a small bell in her teeth and shaking her head. After a year and a half the use of induction-currents seemed to have a good effect, and she was soon able to use her hands, and to walk. At this time and for seven years the right hand swelled enormously before each menstrual flow, and at the close of the week the skin came off in large patches. In 1876, she had violent retro-spasms of the head and motor ataxia of the legs. In 1877, she had hysterical convulsions, photo-phobia, a variety of pains, glossitis, with great swelling of the tongue, long attacks of coma, hysterical vomiting, and two weeks of nearly complete fasting, and spasmodic ptosis.

You will, I think, agree with me that a more miserable catalogue of ills could hardly be made out. Within a year the active troubles have faded away, and we have before us only a weak, pale, sensitive woman, with complete loss of voice.[14]

[14] *Ibid.*, pp. 208-210.

In recording his case histories of nervous women Mitchell revealed, along with his merits, important limitations. What he was able to see as a doctor describing his mentally ill patients, and what he failed to see—both were reflected in his fiction dealing with the mentally ill. The understanding he could show as a novelist was limited by the understanding he had gained as a doctor.

One of Mitchell's cases reveals quite well both his skills and his limitations, the case of Miss B., aged nineteen, a college girl. She had worked hard at her studies, had become sick with headaches and with vomiting, and had at last refused all food. At the end of forty-five days of almost total fasting her breathing became labored, her vision, voice, and memory failed, and she became delirious and unconscious. Food had to be administered by enema; there was involuntary escape of urine and feces. For a time, she got better, went to the country, and then again became worse. At this stage she was brought to Mitchell. According to his description she was then a pathetically disabled creature, her knees drawn to her chin, rigid and immovable, and her pupils dilated, almost without vision; she suffered pains in her feet, constant headache, and loss of memory. In his treatment he concentrated on the physical symptoms. He straightened her limbs with the help of surgery; to enable her to sit up in bed he had her strapped to a board which was raised inch by inch three times a day. In this manner, Mitchell wrote, he achieved a cure. But one wonders how long the cure lasted, and what was the subsequent history of the case. To a present-day psychiatrist the background of this case, the specific psychological problems which oppressed the girl and led her to hysteria as a solution, would have seemed of the utmost importance.[15] He might suspect that Mitchell had not come to

[15] Psychoanalysts carry this background study far into the past. Charles Berg in his *Deep Analysis,* a detailed study of a single case treated by psychoanalysis, declares: "Thus anything more than the most superficial and transitory amelioration necessitates a tracing of the conflict down to its original infantile patterns." See Charles Berg, *Deep Analysis* (London, 1946), p. 24.

grips with the main psychological cause behind all the complex physical disabilities. Just as this girl seemed once before to have been cured only to suffer relapse, he might ask, will she not suffer another relapse, or acquire some new symptoms as long as the psychological distortion remains active? It is true that Mitchell declared he would have liked more information concerning the background of the case; but nowhere in his works is there any indication that he would have used such information to battle the illness at its source. In fact, he seemed quite satisfied with the "cure."

The same limitations are well illustrated by his treatment of Miss C., the young lady whose leg stood out rigidly at right angles to her body. He attacked her symptoms directly, using hypodermic injections and hanging gradually increasing weights upon the outstretched limb, forcing it back slowly to its normal position.[16] While he did show concern for the psychological factors, removing the girl from her home environment, he made no effort to probe into the precise psychological cause and base his main treatment upon it.

Mitchell again revealed the same shortcomings when, in his case histories, he referred to dreams. There was, for example, the unmarried woman of forty who sometimes, while dreaming, suffered from spasms in the toes:

> During the early months of the case there were at intervals attacks of athetoic spasms. Usually these came and went without appreciable cause. At other times emotion, especially

[16] Concerning this method, treatment of symptoms, Berg, in the psychoanalytic study already mentioned, declares: ". . . . it is a mistake to identify the symptoms with the illness.

"If we can see only the superficial manifestations of a deep-seated trouble we may try to cure these manifestations alone, thinking that they are the disease. When their shape alters, as it has probably altered several times in the course of the individual's life, we find that the *form* in which they were at first presented to us has disappeared and we may proclaim a cure as misleading and illusory as was our first superficial conception of the illness to be cured." *Ibid.*, pp. 15-16.

Freud, though he came but a few years after Mitchell, far surpassed him in the search for precise psychological causes.

terror from her sensory dreams, seemed able to occasion them.[17]

While Mitchell recognized the woman's symptoms as hysterically inspired, he failed to go further, to search for detailed causes in her personal background and experience. Whether she was married or unmarried, for example, seemed of no particular interest to him. Indeed the factor of sex, which carries so much weight in the analysis of present-day psychiatrists, seemed of little importance to Mitchell. There are few references to sex in his books and articles on nervous diseases in women, nor is there much appreciation of the role of sex in normal behavior.[18] In one of his few references to the subject, it was the importance of excess rather than repression that interested him:

> The history of the sexual life of the patient is also of great importance. Sexual excess, and especially abnormalities in the performance of the sexual act. . . . are definitely related to various functional and organic nervous diseases. Further, disease of the sexual apparatus, such as strictures of the urethra in men or organic disease of the ovaries and tubes in women, react profoundly upon the nervous system.[19]

Not only was Mitchell unconcerned about the marital status of his patient who suffered from hysterical spasms, but in his

[17] S. Weir Mitchell, *Lectures on Diseases of the Nervous System, Especially in Women,* 2nd ed., p. 112.

[18] This limitation is reflected in Mitchell's fiction, perhaps most clearly in his portrayal of Hephzibah Guiness and Ann Wendell, spinsters excessively devoted to their unmarried brothers. The questions which would shriek aloud to some modern interpreters, Mitchell ignored, showing no inclination to probe the love lives of his characters.

While Mitchell was relatively indifferent to sex as a factor in mental health, he did recognize the extraordinary influence certain women could exercise because of their sexual attractiveness, as his descriptions of Constance Trescot and Kitty Morrow indicate. Professor Quinn has commented on this matter in his *American Fiction,* p. 316.

[19] S. Weir Mitchell, "General Considerations," *Nervous Diseases,* ed. by F. X. Dercum (Philadelphia, 1895) , p. 19. Most practitioners then were still unprepared to consider seriously the role of sex. Freud describes the reaction of members of the Vienna Neurological Society and other doctors to his lectures given at about that time: "I treated my discov-

reference to her dreams he showed no more than a general interest. Beyond the fact that they frightened her he described almost nothing of their content. He made no effort to translate the symbols of her dreams into the realities of her life.[20] He revealed this same failure to exploit the content of dreams in his study on "Some of the Disorders of Sleep," where he discussed such matters as nightmares.[21]

In dealing with symptoms caused psychologically Mitchell showed more interest in the symptoms than in the causes. In his *Lectures on Diseases of the Nervous System, Especially in Women,* he classified his patients mainly according to their symptoms.[22] There is, for example, a chapter on cases of hysterical paralysis, another on cases of hysterical aphonia, and another on cases of hysterical joints. However, in his last chapter, on treatment, in classifying hysterically ill patients, he gave some consideration to causes.[23]

---

eries as ordinary contributions to science and hoped that others would treat them in the same way. But the silence which followed my lectures, the void that formed about my person, and the insinuations directed at me, made me realize gradually that statements concerning the role of sexuality in the etiology of the neuroses cannot hope to be treated like other communications." Sigmund Freud, "The History of the Psychoanalytic Movement," *The Basic Writings of Sigmund Freud,* tr. and ed. by A. A. Brill (New York, 1938), p. 943.

[20] A particularly interesting example of such an effort is furnished by a recent fictionalized study based upon a case history that terminated successfully, the chief clues being provided by the dreams of the patient as described to the psychiatrist. See John Coignard, *The Spectacle of a Man* (New York, 1937). For a rather early attempt by Freud to utilize the symbols of dreams in the study of hysterical illness, see Sigmund Freud, "Fragment of an Analysis of a Case of Hysteria (1905)," *Collected Papers,* Vol. III (London, 1925), pp. 13-146.

[21] S. Weir Mitchell, "On Some of the Disorders of Sleep," *Virginia Medical Monthly,* II (1876), pp. 769-781.

[22] In his later writings on nervous disorders, including his book *Clinical Lessons on Nervous Diseases* (Philadelphia, 1897), Mitchell's approach remained quite unchanged, revealed the same skills and limitations.

[23] S. Weir Mitchell, *Lectures on Diseases of the Nervous System,* 2nd ed., pp. 265-269. In describing one of the classifications he used the apt phrase, "couch-loving invalids," which I have borrowed for the title of Chapter VII.

In his analysis of psychological causes Mitchell was influenced by his physiological training, and perhaps by the belief he shared with Rush that mind and body were essentially one. In pursuing a psychological cause he was inclined to take a physiological direction. "I look upon most cases of confirmed hysteria," he wrote, "as finally dependent on physical states or defects which may first have been directly or indirectly due to moral causes. . . ."[24] He was quite impressed with his inability to discover precisely "what constitutes the physical basis of the disorder we call hysteria."[25] Apparently it never occurred to him to investigate the psychological causes more precisely. However, as long as he did not know such causes he could not operate against them. His psychological treatment could be no more specific than his analysis. It is not surprising, therefore, that the main psychological elements in his treatment were rather general. Mitchell's famous rest cure was a standard procedure, employing with some variations the same technique upon all patients receiving it. The treatment, to summarize it briefly, consisted "in an effort to lift the health of patients to a higher plane by the use of seclusion, which cuts off excitement and foolish sympathy; by rest . . . . by massage . . . . and by electrical muscular excitation. . . ."[26] In its psychological phase one of the most important principles was the seclusion of the patient. The patient who delighted in securing an audience while she expatiated on her hysterical pains could be sharply discouraged in this unwholesome practice. With Mitchell in control there was no coddling. ". . . .I tell the patient her pains will be well when she gets well, and then cease to allow them to be further discussed."[27] Mitchell's rest cure meant

24 *Ibid.*, p. 267.
25 *Ibid.*, p. 237.
26 *Ibid.*, p. 270. For a detailed description of this treatment see S. Weir Mitchell, *Fat and Blood* (Philadelphia, 1877). See also S. Weir Mitchell, *Lectures on Diseases of the Nervous System*, pp. 265-283.
27 *Ibid.*, pp. 263-264. In his efforts to suppress the patient's self-sympathy Mitchell resorted to whatever measures would help, at times even calling upon clergymen: "If I fail to dispel vain fears by reason,

the breaking up of old habits . . . . the cutting off of many hurtful influences; but, above all, it means the power of separating the invalid from some willing slave, a mother or a sister, whose serfdom, as usual, degrades and destroys the despot, while it ruins the slave.[28]

In his rest cure Mitchell recognized, too, the moral uses of enforced rest:

With this first sense of ease comes the precious chance of the doctor for moral medication. He can now point out that, however hard it was with failing powers to control emotions and suppress nervousness, it is easy to do all this when the physical condition is improving.[29]

Aside from the general psychological aspects of the rest treatment, there were specific psychological elements, as in fact there were in all Mitchell's treatments. He understood hysterical people well enough to be able, at times, to outwit them. He described, for example, the case of a "very charming young girl" who suffered from spasms, and how he used his ingenuity when he became convinced the cause was not organic:

When I first saw her she was lying on the bed, with her knees drawn up, her feet not extended as is usual, but flexed. I was told that when she awoke in the morning, they were straight, but were almost immediately drawn up into the state in which I saw them. After going over her whole system and not discovering evidences of organic disease, I finally made up my mind that it was a case for one of those bold experiments which sometimes succeed when more

to make someone realize how certain attitudes of mind degrade character and how full of peril is the selfful attention to symptoms; if I fail thus, I see no reason why. . . . I may not call in the help of some one who can better make this forcible appeal . . . . the physician who has never sought in such cases the aid of the clergyman must have missed some valuable assistance." S. Weir Mitchell, "The Treatment by Rest, Seclusion, etc., in Relation to Psychotherapy," *The Journal of the American Medical Association,* L (June 20, 1908) , p. 2036.

28 S. Weir Mitchell, *Lectures on Diseases of the Nervous System,* 2nd ed., pp. 270-271.

29 *Ibid.,* p. 276.

timid action fails. After inducing her mother to leave the room, I suddenly straightened one of the girl's legs. I met with no difficulty until I had partially attained my object, and this proved to me with certainty, that it was a willed spasm with which we had to deal, and not one controlled by volition. I then said to her, "I have straightened one of your limbs, straighten the other for me." She said, "I cannot, but perhaps you can." I straightened it with but little difficulty. I then said, "Sit up on the side of the bed." She replied that she had not sat up for years, but I finally got her seated with much trouble, and then, picking up a gay cravat, and tying it around her neck, I said, laughing, "Now you are all dressed for a walk, how amusing it would be to meet your mother at the door." To my surprise she yielded, seeming to enter into the fun of the idea, and with a staggering gait (such as you would expect from one long confined to bed) she advanced with me to the door, where she met her astonished parent who was just coming into the room. She never went back to bed again permanently, and in a few weeks afterwards was able to ride on horseback.[30]

One of the most dramatic examples of such firmness is recounted by Mrs. Burr in her biography of Mitchell. When a hysterically ill female patient refused to get out of bed to walk, claiming physical inability, Mitchell threatened to get in bed with her. He started to disrobe, but by the time he began unfastening his trousers, the startled lady got out of bed and walked.

Among Mitchell's virtues as a psychologist was his recognition of the value of confession, the relief the patient could get by describing his problems to the understanding listener, particularly to the doctor.[31] But he never developed this procedure into a systematic technique. He had no thought of pushing the patient's memory back to the crucial psychological

[30] *Ibid.*, pp. 130-131. The above case is one instance where Mitchell's literary skill, his ability to imagine a situation, aided his medical work.

One may wonder what Mitchell had in mind in distinguishing between *willed* and *controlled by volition.* Judging from the context of this quotation Mitchell apparently meant to distinguish between what is unconsciously willed and what is controlled by conscious volition.

[31] Not only in his medical writings, but in his novels, too, Mitchell frequently commented on this relief by confession.

causes of hysteria—and fighting out the battle by forcing the patient to re-examine those experiences. He recognized, in a general way, the importance of up-bringing and training, and the effect of early conditioning experiences in producing mental illness. But he had no procedures, such as those based on psychoanalysis or the conditioned response, for confronting those experiences and undoing their effect. In general, as it has been indicated, Mitchell concentrated his attack not on the original causes but on the symptoms. As a result, one must suspect that many of his "cures" were temporary. The symptoms which he relieved—often with astonishing success—were likely to return, or to reappear in another form, so long as the underlying cause of the hysteria remained untreated. Mitchell himself had misgivings about some of his cures. His concluding comment on the case of aphonia already discussed[32] is one of several such recognitions:

> Under the use of tonics, rest, and full feeding, with vocal lessons, and a continued order not to speak at other times, she has continuously improved. Whether or not she will relapse depends a good deal on her surroundings. Such cases are only too prone to fall back.[33]

Mitchell's own general point of view on treatment, in spite of his limitations, was scientific. It was the same approach he developed and applied in his study of rattlesnakes, of gunshot wounds, of nerve injuries. He tried, as always, to discern the cause and effect relationship, even though his picture of the cause was often only general.

When Mitchell came to write fiction he inevitably made some use of all the knowledge and experience he had gained as a doctor treating nervous ailments, studying his patients, relating their ills to their backgrounds, talking with them, and observing them in their contacts with nurses, relatives, and friends. It is true he made less direct use of this material than one might expect. Reading his fiction with his medical

[32] See pp. 40-41 of the present work.
[33] *Ibid.*, p. 216.

case histories in mind, one is more impressed by what he failed to use than by what he did use. He created no characters exhibiting the more spectacular forms of hysterical illness such as he described in his medical writing. It may be that he felt professionally bound to withhold such cases from his novels lest he trespass, or seem to trespass, the privacy of his patients. What he could write in studies addressed to his medical colleagues, he felt would be unsuitable in novels addressed to the general reader. However, he did make considerable use of his medical experience. Three of his best character creations, for example, are women who suffered physical disabilities without the corresponding physical causes. Furthermore, his medical experience affected Mitchell the novelist in a number of other important ways, particularly in the development of his scientific attitude toward people, his habit of looking upon his fellow men as creatures ruled to a large extent by forces they could not control, and subject in their thoughts, feelings, and actions to definite causes.

Mitchell's two careers as doctor and novelist were not separate but complementary. Each made easier and better his work in the other, for in both his chief merit was the same: his unique understanding of the human personality and particularly its nervous disorders.

Chapter V

MITCHELL'S SCIENTIFIC ATTITUDE TOWARD HIS CHARACTERS

THE MAN who looked at so many sick women, studying their nervous ailments and personalities, quite naturally retained his scientific attitude and applied his specific conclusions when, as a novelist, he put these and other people into his fiction. By his professional training Mitchell had become a student of character, interested in personalities of all sorts. At the outset of his autobiographical *Characteristics,* speaking through his alter ego, Dr. North, he explained:

> Whatever value this irregular account of myself and my friends may have is due to the care with which I have watched the developmental growth of character.[1]

Later in the same book Dr. North described a game based on character study which he used to play in his youth:

> My favorite amusement was to recall men I had known, and to construct for them in my mind characters out of what I had seen or heard of them under the varying conditions of camp, battle, or wounds. This would lead me to anticipate what their future lives would be and how in certain crises of existence they might act. I did this for myself over and over, until it seemed to me that I could be sure of

[1] S. Weir Mitchell, *Characteristics,* p. 1.

51

my precise conduct under any and almost every variety of circumstance.[2]

While Mitchell no doubt took great pains with some of his plots, he retained all through his career in fiction this primary interest in character. Near the end of his life, in describing his last novel, he wrote to Mrs. Mason:

> There is no plot in the sense of drama's need. It is *character, character,* in the war conditions and the influential relations of strong distinct personalities; people I came to love and disliked to dismiss.[3]

Mitchell took particular pride in the understanding of people he acquired as a physician. In *Dr. North and His Friends,* in referring to women, he wrote: "I was rather proud of knowledge born of many years of varied contact with the sex."[4] In the same novel he described a conversation at a social gathering of Dr. North and his friends: "The talk ranged widely, the novelist speaking with envy of the physician's opportunity of seeing character as we see it."[5] At a later date in a letter to Mrs. Mason, he wrote:

> I think I know something of women; I think I know more about women than most people do; I think also that I have an uncommonly large knowledge of women of the leisure class; and I will add that no man knows much about women who has not had under his care a good many sick women. Nothing differentiates the sex as much as sickness.[6]

Mitchell's approach to the study of character was quite similar to that of the scientist dealing with chemical or physical

[2] *Ibid.,* pp. 10-11. Mitchell made another reference to this same habit in writing of Anne Lyndsay, a character in another novel: "She shared with her friend, the Dr. North, the fancy for imagining what certain persons, real or unreal, would do under circumstances which she contrived for them." S. Weir Mitchell, *When All the Woods Are Green* (New York, 1903), p. 321.

[3] A copy of the unpublished letter, dated March 30, 1913, is in the possession of Mitchell's granddaughter, Mrs. S. W. Macdonough.

[4] S. Weir Mitchell, *Dr. North and His Friends,* p. 75.

[5] *Ibid.,* p. 279.

[6] A copy of the unpublished letter, dated November 22, 1912, is in the possession of Mrs. Macdonough.

bodies. Once the main properties of characters were known one could fairly well predict, as with other natural phenomena, how they would behave under given circumstances. The results of his "excursions into the puzzleland of character," he wrote, were "insights" which "used to startle" him:

> What it left with me was an unusual fondness for the study of men and women, and this I take to be a rare taste, because although people make guesses at character, and novelists and dramatists are presumed to study it for a purpose, and some men of affairs have an almost instinctive appreciation of what a man in contact with a given matter may do, the tendency to study character for its own sake from a naturalist's point of view is most uncommon.[7]

In the sequel to *Characteristics,* Mitchell described again his interest in character, and in terms which make more clear than ever his scientific approach:

> I have always had a fancy for the study of character. Novel social contacts offer fresh opportunities for such study. A new situation becomes a laboratory in which one may consider the reactions of one man upon another. If people are diverse, yet positive, the results are the more apt to be distinct and valuable.[8]

In his discussions of the characters in his fiction, Mitchell tended to use scientific analogies and metaphors, and to apply the same terminology used in describing natural phenomena. Concerning the troublesome Mrs. Grace he wrote: "Her life had been a feeble acetous fermentation."[9] In describing Alice Westerley, who had just made a most shocking discovery about the man she intended to marry, he explained: "Great moral catastrophes, like physical shocks, disturb or even obliterate in some minds the memory of the lesser events which follow them."[10] Speaking of the frustrated young Olivia, he commented: "The moral and mental machinery may, like the

---

7 S. Weir Mitchell, *Characteristics,* p. 11.
8 S. Weir Mitchell, *Dr. North and His Friends,* p. 107.
9 S. Weir Mitchell, *In War Time* (New York, 1903) , p. 207.
10 *Ibid.,* p. 404.

muscular mechanism, become disordered from lack of chance to develop."[11] Concerning memory, he wrote:

> If I shut my eyes and lay still . . . . and then seized firmly on some remembrance of verse or prose or events, by degrees it seemed to aggregate other memories long forgotten. It was like a process of crystallization—to stir up the fluid is apt to disturb the formative action.[12]

Elsewhere he again wrote of memory:

> We set an idea before us, and by and by we are amazed to find how many ghosts of things apparently forgotten are summoned by this steady call upon associative memory. It is as when you drop into a solution of numberless salts a crystal of one of them. The formed solid begins at once to gather for its increase all the atoms of its kind.[13]

Mitchell compared three of the characters in *Dr. North* to chemical agents; Vincent, the highly cultivated lawyer; Crofter, the rough entrepreneur; and Clayborne, the scholar:

> Here were three very definite people. Each of them was typically peculiar. In the laboratory certain agents which come in contact chemically decline to alter or to be altered, and remain neutrally indifferent. This idea was in my mind as I watched Vincent and Crofter.[14]

Continuing this description, he developed the chemical analogy:

> Would these two prove too socially neutral? It seemed likely to be so. Once or twice I tried to come in as the third reagent, which in a chemist's solution of inactive compounds has the capacity to cause abrupt and interesting interchange of the constituent elements. I had no such luck.[15]

Pursuing the analogy, Mitchell noted that perhaps the artist,

---

[11] S. Weir Mitchell, *Roland Blake* (New York, 1903), p. 209.
[12] *Ibid.*, p. 10.
[13] *Ibid.*, p. 172. Mitchell's view of memory here is very similar to the view held by psychoanalysts today. The psychoanalytic process is used to summon back to consciousness "things apparently forgotten."
[14] S. W. Mitchell, *Dr. North and His Friends,* p. 107.
[15] *Ibid.*, p. 108.

St. Clair, would prove an effective addition to the other men: "I made up my mind that here was the reagent needed to disturb this solution of neutral elements. I was not mistaken."[16] A moment later, watching the process, Vincent speaking in calm sharpness, Crofter's face stern with anger, and St. Clair's temper rising, Mitchell concluded the analogy: "My social chemistry seemed to me about to result in a disastrous explosion."[17]

He not only used scientific metaphors and analogies in his descriptions of people, but he looked upon people themselves as the subject matter of science. A human being in action was to Mitchell a physiological mechanism, worth describing as such. His views concerning the unity of mind and body— outlined in the previous chapter—encouraged him always, whether he viewed a person smoking a pipe or suffering an emotional crisis, to see the physiological aspect of what was happening. When, for example, Dr. Wendell settled back to enjoy a smoke, Mitchell wrote:

> He was rapidly coming to a state of easier mind, under the effect of the meerschaum's subtle influence upon certain groups of ganglionic nerve cells deep in his cerebrum. . . .[18]

When the attractive Hester in *In War Time* fainted and the devoted young Edward watched, Mitchell described the circulatory changes and their relationship to the nervous system:

> Then he saw for a moment the white sweep of the girl's neck and shoulders, flushed with moving islets of blood that came and went, the signals of a nervous system shaken by a storm beyond its power to bear.[19]

Later in the same novel Mitchell pictured Dr. Wendell in an embarrassing situation, and again considered the physiological aspect of the man's behavior:

> This added blow fell with but little weight on Wendell.

16 *Ibid.*, p. 114.
17 *Ibid.*, p. 116.
18 S. Weir Mitchell, *In War Time*, p. 18.
19 *Ibid.*, p. 256.

Capacity to feel anxiety has its limits in mysterious failures of response in the brain cells, and in some people convulsive explosions of emotional torment make impossible for a time the normal activities which an intellectual conception of a difficulty or trouble should awaken.[20]

Mitchell not only stressed the physiological aspect of behavior, but he also often showed how physiological conditions affected the total character. In describing Major Morton, who had been long ill, he wrote:

All that was worst in Morton was being accentuated by sickness, and, like most people on the rack of pain and weakness, he was undergoing the process of minor moral degradation which chronic illness brings to so many. Acute brief disease may startle us to better and graver thoughts of our aims and our actions, but prolonged illness makes more noble but a rare and chosen few.[21]

Again, in *Characteristics,* he observed how health influenced character: "I learned also how much of character is a question of health, and this too has had for me its value in life."[22] Mitchell made the same observation, only more specifically, in the novel *Circumstance:* "Illness may leave men in a condition which for a time lessens the power to control emotion, or to summarily dismiss unwelcome memories."[23]

Sometimes Mitchell brought over into his analysis of a character principles he had observed as a doctor studying physical ailments, as in his description of Darnell, shocked at the exposure of his treacheries:

The surgeon's idea of a "shock" as a result of sudden physical injury should be imported into the domain of criminal psychology. The ball which crushes a joint stops or weakens the distant heart, or palsies a remote limb, or enfeebles the whole frame. In the sphere of mind and morale the abrupt shock of fear or shame may in like manner affect distant nerve-cells and thus deaden memory, palsy

20 *Ibid.,* p. 390.
21 *Ibid.,* p. 87.
22 S. Weir Mitchell, *Characteristics,* p. 22.
23 S. Weir Mitchell, *Circumstance,* p. 269.

the organs of reason, annihilate for a while the power to love or hate, and even reduce a man for a time to the verge of inert idiocy.

Under such a blow . . . . Darnell found himself all day incapable of thought, stupid and indifferent.[24]

In discussing characters in literature, Mitchell suggested a scientific approach. In *Dr. North,* when the conversation turned to *Macbeth,* he recommended that the authenticity of the queen's behavior in the sleepwalking scene be checked against the actual practice of sinners:

> The fact that the queen was seen washing her hands for a quarter of an hour at a time is very interesting. Was it in the day that this was to be seen, or only at night? If in the day, it implies a disordered mind, something more than— shall I say?—normal remorse, a possession akin to insanity. I cannot even mildly match in my professional memory the night-walking horror. I have often meant to ask some prison warden if murderers ever speak of their crimes in their sleep, or dream of them.[25]

Having posed the problem Mitchell partially answered it from his own experience, giving some justification to Shakespeare:

> There is a form of mental disorder marked by a never-ending sense of being unclean. If let alone, these people bathe repeatedly and wash their hands many times a day, and feel that they are continually being contaminated. This disease takes many forms and is very lasting. I have only spoken of so much of it as has relation to the case of Lady Macbeth.[26]

Mitchell himself could have passed the sort of test he proposed for Shakespeare, for his abnormal characters were drawn from experience and behaved in real life as he represented them in fiction.[27]

24 S. Weir Mitchell, *Roland Blake,* p. 345.
25 *Ibid.,* p. 280.
26 *Ibid.,* pp. 280-281.
27 Mitchell took pride, as many of his comments indicate, not only in the accuracy of his observations of people, but also in the accuracy of his

Because of his training, Mitchell developed the habit of considering people as part of the subject matter of science. He tended to look upon not only their overt actions, but their subtlest impulses too, as the product of causes. While his attitude is implicit throughout all his novels, he occasionally made explicit statements. On several occasions he stated his general belief that man was a product of nature and circumstances. In one of his earliest stories, in describing Hephzibah Guiness and her brother, he wrote: "Theirs were richly contrasted natures,—each a compound of what Nature and a creed had made."[28] In the same work he described Elizabeth Howard: "Nature had here formed a remarkable character, and circumstance had given it a strange part to play in the drama of life."[29] Why did Elizabeth and Hephzibah dislike one another? They "were made by Nature to dislike and respect one another."[30] In his later novels, too, Mitchell expressed the same view. The intelligent Susan commented on Constance and George Trescot: "Both of you are what nature and the chances of life have made you."[31] Mitchell explained his view in a somewhat different manner in his novel *When All the Woods Are Green:*

> The lives of men are lived under the limited monarchy of circumstance. Within this, men's instincts and personal qualities—in a word, character—decide how they deal with the stringency of events, or meet the despotism of changeless natural laws.[32]

observations of nature. Pardy, a character in *When All the Woods Are Green,* rated some famous poets upon the accuracy of their observations: "And there is some nonsense in the notion that poets are very close observers of nature. They vary, of course. Take Wordsworth, he was a mere child in minute observations compared to Shakespeare. Tennyson is better, too,—oh, by far; and any clever naturalist sees far more than any of them." S. Weir Mitchell, *When All the Woods Are Green,* p. 88.

28 S. Weir Mitchell, "Hephzibah Guiness," *The Autobiography of a Quack and other Stories,* p. 131.

29 *Ibid.,* p. 135.

30 *Ibid.,* p. 137.

31 S. Weir Mitchell, *Constance Trescot* (New York, 1905) , p. 35.

32 S. Weir Mitchell, *When All the Woods Are Green,* p. 352.

A few lines later Mitchell referred to "the fatal meshes which circumstance spins in the way of human flies, or which character weaves when the fly is his own spider."[33] The author summed up his discussion by declaring that "instincts, character, and circumstance combine to determine the fates of men."[34]

Man acts, according to Mitchell's view, not out of an uncaused volition, but as a result of causes he cannot control. Mitchell explained this view most effectively, perhaps, in his novel *In War Time:*

> In morals and social action, as in physics, it is common to find that we act under the domination of a number of influences, and submit in our decisions to what the physicist calls a resultant of forces.[35]

It should be added here that Mitchell did not adhere with absolute consistency to so thoroughgoing a determinism as this statement might indicate. He never elaborated a complete statement of his views on the mind-body problem, nor on the related problems of free will and determinism. In general, however, he emphasized the many outside forces that acted upon an individual and made his actions, to a large extent, the outcome of causes he could not control.

This scientific point of view made Mitchell feel how often helpless men were. It moved him to understanding and sympathy toward even the worst of his characters. At the end of his novel *Roland Blake,* after the villainous Darnell had gambled away his sister's money, betrayed her trust, tried to pressure an unwilling girl into marriage, blackmailed a helpless old lady, and, worst of all, betrayed his own fellow soldiers and his own flag in the Civil War—after a whole novel of such treacherous actions, Mitchell expressed his final verdict on the man: "He is to be pitied."[36] That is the tone he took toward all his villains. In his later novel *Constance Trescot,*

33 *Ibid.,* p. 353.
34 *Ibid.,* p. 354.
35 S. Weir Mitchell, *In War Time,* p. 202.
36 S. Weir Mitchell, *Roland Blake,* p. 336.

there is John Greyhurst, who had murdered the benevolent husband of Constance and ruined her life. Mitchell expressed his attitude through Dr. Eskridge, a kindly man of large understanding and with special experience in the treatment of nervous disorders. Dr. Eskridge had

> a fund of pitiful charity, kept full by sad personal experiences and by the physician's vast explanatory knowledge of the lives of men and women, which accepts heredity, education, and environment as matters not to be left out of the consideration of disease or of the motives of men's actions. . . .
> The contrasts of Greyhurst's life interested him. . . . He felt how vain it was to judge of human actions without the largest knowledge. . . .
> He lighted his candle and went up to bed, more than a little pitiful for the woman who suffered, and for the man who had caused her to suffer.[37]

Mitchell considered himself a religious as well as a scientific man. In his attitude toward human character he found both his religion and his science leading him in the same direction: to understand, to forgive, and to help.

[37] S. Weir Mitchell, *Constance Trescot*, p. 318, 323-324.

Chapter VI

DETERIORATION OF CHARACTER

Dr. Wendell

In some of his novels Mitchell presented vivid case histories of deterioration of character. He concerned himself with one particular pattern, but in doing so he cast light on elements commonly occurring in various patterns of deterioration. There is a definite sequence in Mitchell's case histories: A character has at least one weakness which events play upon; acting out of this weakness, the character does wrong; he does not honestly face his wrong action and see it for what it is; having committed and rationalized one wrong, he finds it possible to commit and rationalize ever greater wrongs;[1] finally he commits gross misdeeds which others become aware of; as a consequence, losing the esteem of those for whom he cares most, he finds himself oppressed beyond his tolerance and breaks down.

Mitchell's most complete study of deterioration concerns

[1] Mitchell applied this same principle in his medical practice when he enabled an hysterically ill woman to sit up in bed by adjusting her into a sitting position an inch at a time, or when he enabled another hysterically ill woman to bring into normal position her rigidly extended leg by hanging gradually increasing weights upon it. (See Chapter IV.) The same principle has been expounded and applied by I. P. Pavlov and others in their work on the conditioned response, their studies of the learning and unlearning of habits. See Chapter V, "Inhibitory Conditioning," in E. R. Guthrie, *The Psychology of Learning* (New York, 1935).

61

Dr. Wendell, the chief character in the novel *In War Time*.[2]
The portrait is based upon a doctor whom Mitchell knew in
real life, as he indicated in a letter to his friend Mrs. Mason:
"The doctor, yes, I drew him from life, but of course it is like
taking a man with certain characteristics and putting him in
a new position."[3] Not only was Dr. Wendell drawn from life,
but the hospital where he worked was really a description of
the Filbert Street Hospital, where Mitchell himself served as
an army surgeon during the Civil War.[4]

At the outset of the story, Dr. Wendell was a fairly capable,
upright and ambitious young doctor, an intelligent and quite
sound individual. At the end he was psychologically broken
down, unable to carry on his professional practice even after
he had escaped to a new environment. A large part of the
novel is devoted to the details of the transformation.

Early in the story Mitchell revealed a weakness in Wendell,
though the reader could hardly suspect at first how crucial it
was to become. In his first appearance in the story, Dr. Wendell was walking with his sister Ann to the army hospital
where he was employed. Though already quite late, he stopped
to observe a tree trunk which had distracted him. He had seen
this tree many times before, yet became so engrossed his sister
had to remind him to hurry. As we learn more of Wendell we
realize this weakness was customary: he often failed to meet
his obligations as well as he might. He lacked the drive to
carry out not only the duties imposed by his work, but even
the ambitions which he set for himself. Habitually he allowed
himself to be overmastered by his feelings, always finding some
reasons to justify himself. People like Wendell, Mitchell ob-

[2] By the time Mitchell completed this novel, his first, he was fifty-five
years old, and well enough established as a doctor to dare sign his own
name. "Feeling that I could not be injured by literary success," he
wrote, "and trusting the good sense of the American people to know
whether I was any the less a good doctor because I could write a novel,
I continued to thus amuse myself." Burr, *op. cit.*, p. 127.

[3] A copy of the unpublished letter, dated July 19, 1912, is in the possession of Mrs. S. W. Macdonough.

[4] Burr, *op. cit.*, p. 104.

served, "call to their aid and comfort whatever power of casuistry they possess to support their feelings, and thus by degrees habitually weaken their sense of moral perspective."[5] Speaking the language of the determinist, Mitchell declared that Wendell "was designed by nature to illustrate, soon or late, the certainty of failure where, although the machine be competent, its driving power is inadequate."[6]

The chief events acting upon Wendell's weakness involved matters of finance. Wendell's income was not great. For his work in the Philadelphia military hospital he received eighty dollars a month, while his private practice in Germantown, a few miles away, was only in its beginnings. Under these circumstances he took on an unexpected responsibility, the upbringing of the daughter of a patient, the Confederate Captain Gray. The Captain, shortly before dying, had asked Wendell to take care of his daughter, and Wendell, unable to refuse, had taken the girl home where he lived with his sister Ann. By a strange circumstance the burden was not to fall on him alone. A union officer, Major Morton, had shared the hospital quarters with the Confederate Gray. The two wounded men, lying near each other on cots, had exchanged conversation, and discovered that they had both been wounded in the same battle. In fact, it seemed quite possible that Gray had received his mortal wound from the gun of Major Morton. Gray himself certainly believed this and accused Major Morton bluntly of having fired the shot. Because of this circumstance, Mrs. Morton, who could well afford to do so, volunteered to pay to Wendell the expense of rearing Hester, Gray's daughter.

After Hester had been living with the Wendells for some time, Mrs. Morton, wishing to send the girl away to school, offered her first check, to pay the expenses. This offer was the first important event to play upon Wendell's weakness; his response was his first act along the road to calamity, a slight act which made progressively grosser acts possible. Wendell ac-

5 S. Weir Mitchell, *In War Time*, p. 19.
6 *Ibid.*, p. 235.

cepted the money without compunction, seeing nothing wrong or compromising in doing so. Mitchell, however, made it clear that he regarded this acceptance as an expression of weakness, however slight. He pointed this up by sharply contrasting Wendell's behavior with his sister's. Ann, who had herself been giving Hester instructions, was not in favor of the offer. It seemed like charity to her. She had "the admirable dislike of the hardy New England mind to being assisted by money."[7] She felt unhappy about Wendell's acceptance in spite of his explanation that the Mortons wished to help and there was nothing to do but accept. Even after the matter seemed settled, she did not use the check until reminded of it more than once.

Another event soon played upon Wendell's weakness, and this time his reaction was more clearly wrong. Again the event concerned the acceptance of money for Hester's education— this time from a cousin of Hester's, Henry Gray, a Southerner whom the Mortons had met in England. He sent $10,000 to Dr. Wendell, asking him to invest it for Hester and safeguard it for her future education. When the war was over, he added, he would come for Hester and take her away with him.

Again Wendell failed to meet his obligations as well as he might. He lacked the force to break past his own inclinations. He was growing to like Hester, wanted to keep her, and therefore decided not to show her this letter. Mitchell emphasized how wrong this was by contrasting once again his attitude with Ann's, who was "always just." Ann urged Wendell to show Hester the letter, asking, "Wouldn't it be wrong not to?" Wendell, always putting off the unpleasant duty, said he would think about it. He yielded complacently to this new situation, himself the possessor of $10,000 of Hester's money which Hester herself knew nothing about, a dangerous situation which could lead Wendell to do more and greater wrong. However, for the time being, he invested the money in government bonds, an investment which proved to be profitable.

At this stage in Wendell's career Mitchell had already ex-

[7] *Ibid.*, p. 159.

posed the chief elements of the catastrophe. There was Wendell with this sum of money in his possession. There was this same Wendell, an indulgent spender, careless of his finances, not too well off, and not too strict in meeting his obligations. Surely, it would not take much to place him in the way of temptation. The character and the situation were taking shape before the reader, following their own logic to the inevitable outcome. From this point on the story moved largely on its own momentum. There were no sudden deaths, no wondrous effects of weather, no remarkable coincidences to break into the logic of events. Mitchell faced his problem through to the end at the scientific level at which he had posed it. Wendell was confronted by a situation resulting largely from his own character deficiencies and he had to meet it with what strength he could muster. Mitchell would not save him—nor escape pursuing the logic of the situation—by the sudden intervention of extraneous or irrelevant agencies.

Wendell was not yet prepared to commit the wrong which was already within his power, to tap secretly some of Hester's money. He was an honest man. However, his weakness was making him ever more vulnerable. Victim of his inclinations, he kept living beyond his means, buying whatever appealed to him, fancying he needed what he wanted: lenses, expensive books, rare engravings. If he indulged himself when it came to spending money he was equally inclined to do so when it came to working for it. When his schedule of hours at the military hospital was changed, he found the new hours inconvenient and wanted to give up the post even though it paid eighty dollars a month, which he badly needed. His sister urged him to keep the job, knowing the loss would be a very serious matter, but, commented Mitchell, the doctor regarded "his personal convenience" as "far more important."[8]

Yielding to his sister, Wendell kept the job but continued living beyond his means. He justified some of his expensive purchases on the ground that he needed them for research—

[8] *Ibid.*, p. 231.

but he was not really accomplishing any research, for he lacked the energy and persistence to overcome the difficulties he inevitably met, and he lacked, too, the stern honesty to see his own shortcomings. Thus he merely talked of his grandiose plans while he continued to bow to his expensive inclinations.

But a day came when Ann, unable to meet the daily expenses of the household, had to say to him, "I must have more money."[9] To Wendell this news was surprising. He couldn't understand where the money went, certainly he himself spent very little. When Ann reminded him of his recent expensive purchases, a microscope, lenses, encyclopedia, he dismissed the whole matter casually, "I have a good many bills, and I can jog the memory of one or two patients."[10] Mitchell observed that this was more wish than fact, that Wendell "made things so easy with his comfortable outlook."[11] Mitchell exposed the real situation even more clearly through a question of Ann's, "Is your practice growing?" "I—I guess so," replied Wendell, "I am told I have been unusually successful, for a newcomer. People do leave one, you know."[12] Wendell's answer revealed quite plainly his refusal to see the direction he was traveling.[13] When he couldn't honestly answer that his practice was growing he turned away from this crucial fact and took refuge in the irrelevant: others think he is proving successful—as though they knew more than he about his own practice. In this connection Mitchell gave the reader facts which Wendell apparently didn't make clear even to himself, his serious shortcomings as a doctor:

9 *Ibid.*, p. 232.
10 *Ibid.*, p. 233.
11 *Ibid.*, p. 233.
12 *Ibid.*, pp. 233-234.
13 Mitchell here, as on a number of other occasions, emphasized his point by adding a comment of his own: "But a man must be very blind indeed not to recognize sometimes that he is drifting from the course he meant to take. . . . There come to most of us, in fact, times of unpleasant illumination, when we are forced to see things as they would appear to an uninterested or abler observer; but some men are always so near their moral mirror that their breath obscures the image they ought to see." *Ibid.*, p. 235.

He was in every way an agreeable and amusing visitor, but when he had to sustain the courage of the sick and satisfy watchful friends through grave illness he failed. For some reason, he did not carry confidence to others; perhaps because he was unable to hide his mental unstableness, which showed in too frequent changes of opinion. Moreover, his love of ease made impossible for him the never-ending daily abandonment of this moment of quiet, or that little bit of tranquil home life, which every wise physician counts upon once for all as a part of the discomforts which he must accept if he means to win success.[14]

Wendell's failure to see his own actions honestly made his progress along the road to deterioration easier and faster, for it saved him the need to struggle. As long as the weakness was unrecognized, he could feel free to indulge it.

Wendell was not yet ready to dip his hands into Hester's money; he had to be prepared by other less obviously wrong acts. His next step was to borrow money from Major Morton's invalid son, Edward. While the Mortons were in Europe, their invalid son, a young man of kindly character, stayed with the Wendells. The doctor found it tempting and easy to borrow small sums from Edward. Again he failed to face the facts. The debt steadily mounted, but "somehow the weight of this gathering debt seemed to Wendell to be of little importance."[15]

All the while his finances were getting worse, Hester's were improving. The money he had invested for her in government bonds was producing a good profit. At first he had given no thought to this money, but gradually he began to feel that he was entitled "to some share in her good fortune." This thought was only a small step toward wrong, for Gray, who gave Wendell the money, did want him to get something for his trouble. Furthermore, Wendell only thought of Hester's money. He was not yet morally prepared to dip into it, to take the "first positive practical step." That was something he could not do until urged "by unrelenting circumstances."[16]

14 *Ibid.*, pp. 234-235.
15 *Ibid.*, p. 236.
16 *Ibid.*, p. 236.

His next act, however, did prepare the "unrelenting circum-stances." It was as small a step, apparently, as Mitchell could make it. Wendell touched not Hester's money, but someone's closer to him, his sister Ann's. And even that wasn't so very bad, for it was money which he himself owned jointly with her. More than that, he did not pocket or spend the money, but merely reinvested it without her knowledge or consent. Observing how profitable his investment of Hester's money had been, he decided, after much hesitation, to invest the $6,000 which he had inherited jointly with Ann. Keeping the matter to himself, he took the money, which had been safely put away in a secure mortgage, and invested it in a railroad which, he thought, would yield a more "brilliant return." While his intentions were still honest, this was definitely the most clearly wrong act he had so far committed. The money was only partly his—yet, without consulting Ann, who had a right to know, he had invested this money. The investment turned out badly.

When the time came to give Ann the usual semiannual in-terest on their mortgage, he did not have the means. Yet he would not confess the truth to her. The one way out was to take some of Hester's money. "I should do an interesting but weak nature a wrong," declared Mitchell, "to presume that it cost him nothing to reason himself into borrowing enough of Hester's capital to enable him to give to Ann the money she had habitually received."[17] The phrase "reason himself into" is worth noting. As Mitchell observed, Wendell committed the act without clear understanding of what he was doing. He ra-tionalized, made it appear to himself as less offensive than it really was.

At first he could feel that the money he was taking from Hester was partly his own, was merely part of the profit his fortunate investment had earned for her. The "excess seemed almost as much his as Hester's." Then, too, he persuaded himself that he was merely borrowing. He made a note of the

17 *Ibid.*, p. 237.

amount taken and put it in his little box of private papers. Soon, when he "borrowed" again, he added a second receipt. He never asked himself just where he was going to get the money to pay this debt. His ability to turn away from the true nature of events played an important part in his deterioration. These receipts were what his mind dwelled on:

> . . . . these papers were, in some fashion, a comfort to the troubled man, who by habit dwelt within an ever-widening horizon of hopeful possibilities, as inexhaustible as the growing zone of successive mornings. Like all who tread this evil path, he honestly meant to replace what he took, and nothing could have surpassed the force of his conviction that he would do so; indeed, to have been told that he would not would have been felt by him as the deepest insult.[18]

Had he faced his prospects sensibly he would have seen that they were all too likely to grow worse, for his part-time army job as contract surgeon, bringing him eighty dollars a month, could not go on much longer. When, however, the army hospital, carrying out its expected cut, released Wendell, it was a blow he had not prepared for. "It had to come, of course," said Wendell. "Soon or late it had to come."[19] But all the while Wendell had continued piling up the acknowledgments he had somehow expected to fulfill, and "had already used, little by little, fifteen hundred dollars of Hester's money,— borrowed it, he said to himself."[20] Each step had been a little one, but eventually Wendell had moved a fearful distance. The loss of his hospital job was a sort of climax, a shock. Until then he had been easygoing, rationalizing the uncomfortable thoughts out of his mind. Now the facts were suddenly too gross to be ignored. As long as he had been able to ignore them he had been optimistic about his problems. Now that the shocking facts had struck home, Wendell became suddenly as distressed as he had been easygoing, his cheer giving way to despondency and mental torture.

[18] *Ibid.,* p. 237.
[19] *Ibid.,* p. 252.
[20] *Ibid.,* p. 252.

Though he still intended to repay the money he had taken from Hester, he had a sense of guilt for what he had done. He had "a clearer sense of his own moral degradation," and he could feel the pull of horrible temptations. One easy way out of his financial difficulties kept forcing its way upon his attention. There was Alice Westerley, the charming widow. His friendship with her was deepening and she had money.

Here Mitchell added his own comments, describing Wendell's feelings and preparing the reader for his future behavior:

> Do what he would,—and the thought immeasurably distressed this sensitive being,—he kept thinking about Mrs. Westerley's money, and how surely it would rescue him, and how often it had come before him that now he need have no fear as to repayment of what he had borrowed from Hester's means. There was a fiend's cruelty in the conception that a noble, honest creature like Alice was ignorantly making it easy for him to do a shameful thing, and not suffer for it. If she should ever come to know of his guilt, what then?[21]

Wendell, we see, was very sensitive to the opinions of those he cared about. What would happen to him if he stood out as the thief he was becoming, stood exposed before his sister Ann and before Alice Westerley?

Events which he might have anticipated continued to pressure him into ever greater wrong. A day came when Gray informed Wendell he desired to take $9,000 of the $10,000 he had sent for Hester, and to invest it in the South where he felt it would yield a greater profit. Apparently he was unaware of how fast the power of the Southern states was crumbling. The other $1,000 of the original sum, Gray said, Wendell was to keep for his trouble. The letter caught Wendell painfully unprepared. He was $3,000 short. What was he to do? The thought came to him that he could refuse the request, that he could say he ought to refuse it in order to protect Hester. In a way, the money, to be sure, was Gray's, but if Gray should put it in Confederate bonds, as seemed likely, the money

21 *Ibid.*, p. 253.

would be thrown away. Then what would happen to Hester?

If Wendell refused the money on such grounds, he asked himself, how would his position appear to others? He tested an old gentleman of his acquaintance, Mr. Wilmington, and met an emphatic rebuff. The sternly honest old gentleman made it plain that the money ought to be returned immediately upon request. When Wendell pressed his own arguments, Mr. Wilmington stated his position even more sharply, his suspicions beginning to stir. As a result of this interview Wendell felt a mounting pressure to marry the wealthy Mrs. Westerley. The fact that he really did love her added new pain:

> . . . . the thought was ever present to him that he loved Alice Westerley purely and for herself, and must marry her to be clear of his pecuniary load. He wanted to marry her, and yet not to have to think he had or might have a bad background of urgent motives.[22]

But what could he do? Admit to Gray, to everybody, that he had taken Hester's money? The thought was unbearable. He could hardly imagine facing even his adoring, forgiving sister Ann. "Death would be easier than to face Ann's pure face, and say, 'I have stolen, I am a thief.' "[23]

It was the fear of the opinion of others that troubled him most, and especially the fear of Mrs. Westerley. He was beginning at last to see himself more plainly; and he found the picture unpleasant, not because it failed to measure up to his own stern standards, but only because it could not come up to the standards of others. Wendell lacked the independent strength even to judge himself by his own moral principles. The sense of guilt which he felt, came not from himself but mostly because of Mrs. Westerley. "It cannot be said," wrote Mitchell, "that this sense of degradation was altogether the growth of honest hatred of his weakness and sin. . . ."[24] Wendell tested his ways against the purity of the woman he loved,

22 *Ibid.*, p. 293
23 *Ibid.*, p. 293.
24 *Ibid.*, p. 339.

Alice Westerley. There were times when he felt like going away and writing to her that he was unworthy of her love and trust, but he lacked the strength to carry out such inclinations. In fact, he did nothing at all until finally Mr. Gray came for the money. In this new crisis Wendell turned to Edward, the invalid son of the wealthy Mortons. Edward was generous and kind, and Dr. Wendell had treated him well as both patient and friend. Edward could help. It was unnecessary, in fact, even to ask him, for he suspected Wendell's financial troubles and offered whatever amount was needed. When Wendell explained that a loan of $5,000 would solve his problems Edward promised to get him the money, graciously making much of his obligations to Wendell and belittling the money. Because he was too confined as an invalid to arrange the loan, Edward informed his mother of the whole arrangement in order to get her assistance. Before the matter could be accomplished, however, an accident occurred, not something from out the clouds transforming the situation and saving the author the job of working out the inevitable logic of events, but an accident which grew out of the situation and hastened it toward its own logical climax. While he was in Edward's bedroom Wendell, suddenly called away, instructed Arthur to give his brother Edward some medicine, but in his hurry Wendell pointed to the wrong bottle, which contained the poisonous tincture of aconite. Arthur administered this medicine, and in a few moments Edward was dead. At the outcry Wendell, not yet out of the house, returned to the room, tasted the spoon Arthur had used and realized his own responsibility for what had happened. Arthur in alarm asked, "Did I make a mistake?"

Wendell, seeing his own peril, decided on the instant to consider the death due to Edward's illness, not to any medicine. To save himself, he said there had been no mistake. But these selfish words, spoken in front of Mrs. Morton and Mrs. Westerley, were misinterpreted. Knowing nothing of the hasty directions Wendell had given Arthur, they assumed he was trying to protect Arthur, to keep him from knowing he had killed his own brother. Wendell's dishonesty and cowardice they mistook for generosity, and he was all too willing to let their opinion be. At this point Mitchell described vividly the turmoil of Wendell's thoughts and feelings, his desperate efforts to make himself blameless in his own eyes, to devise some honorable motive to explain the act which really grew out of his cowardice:

> He was annoyed that he could not steadily control his own logical processes. He tried to feel clear that he was not entirely to blame for Edward's death, and then essayed with some ease to persuade himself that Arthur was the person most blamable, and yet that even if he himself has been hasty or careless he was bound to protect Arthur, and that to speak frankly would never so entirely clear Arthur as to be of any use. Still, no sooner had he seemingly satisfied himself than thoughts which rose unsummoned, like ghosts, startled him, and filled his mind with new and horrible suggestions of future risks and dangers. Vivid and terrible images of the fatal moment of haste came before him, and with a memory of his physical recoil he saw again the dead, and his own hand stretched out to close the open eyes. It was growing dark. He rose and lit the gas. . . . He sat down, with his face in his hands, and gave way to a strange sense of mental confusion, a valueless jostling of incongruous thoughts and memories and fears, which seemed to come and go on the stage of consciousness, until at last the giddiness which sometimes follows great emotional tension made him stagger to the bed, on which he fell heavily.[25]

Mitchell continued his analysis, exposing sharply Wendell's attempts to rationalize, and describing, too, the useful role that self-deception can play in an individual's adjustment: "Many people are helped at such times by their incapacity to think clearly."[26] In fact, by his twisted thinking Wendell was able to suppress from his mind some important and unpleasant facts. He was able to conclude that the proper course was for him to remain silent about the exact details of Edward's death, ignoring, at least for the time being, the fact "that in hiding the truth he was allowing an innocent person to bear his

25 *Ibid.*, pp. 388-389.
26 *Ibid.*, p. 391.

guilt, even if only in the minds of Mrs. Morton and Mrs. Westerley."[27]

While Wendell was struggling with his new complication, his older financial problem suddenly became more pressing. Returning home from the Mortons, he received a letter from Mr. Gray asking for the return of $9,000 as soon as convenient. The death of Edward, who had promised him the money he needed, made Wendell's position seem hopeless, exposure certain. What he feared most of all was the opinion of the woman he loved, Mrs. Westerley:

> Too well he knew what sentence he might have to read in those eyes, whose light would be to him as the sheen on the blade of the angel of judgment. For the time the nearness of this peril routed all other terrors. . . .[28]

The world of reality was becoming intolerable to him. He took some whiskey to put himself to sleep. The next morning, the day after Edward's death, he took refuge in illness, and "felt it an inconceivable relief not so soon again to have to enact his part before Mrs. Morton, and possibly Alice."[29] But meanwhile he had to perform a little task which he found most distasteful, "a sin against the moral code of his profession."[30] Writing the formal attestation of Edward's death, he gave as the cause, not the truth about the poisoning, but the concealing phrase, "paralysis of the heart." He signed his name in a most unhappy mood. The following day he received a note from Mrs. Morton. Edward had told her, she said, of his intention to send Wendell money. She thanked him for all he had done for Edward and in accordance with her dead son's wishes, enclosed a check for $5,000. The relief Wendell experienced was as brief as it was sudden. Mrs. Morton informed the fastidiously honorable Alice Westerley of what she had done. "My God, how horrible!" was Mrs. Westerley's reaction. It was an insult, she thought, to Dr. Wendell. He had honor-

27 *Ibid.*, p. 391.
28 *Ibid.*, p. 391.
29 *Ibid.*, p. 392.
30 *Ibid.*, p. 393.

ably shielded Arthur, withheld from him the terrible truth that his mistake had killed his brother. He would never take money that could be construed as payment for such an act, as a bribe for continued silence. Alice's view, as it is presented so briefly here, may seem strained, but as Mitchell presented it, against the full background of her character and of the circumstances, it is entirely credible, in fact, the only possible view she could take. Mrs. Morton, of course, defended herself against the charges that she was insulting Wendell with a bribe. She showed Alice his reply which thanked her profusely and requested her to say nothing about the letter to Alice Westerley.

> Alice took the open note; and reading it, life grew black before her. Its sweetness went out of it, and belief in man, and trust in God.[31]

This letter left Alice with no choice: all thought of marriage to Wendell was out of the question. "I must decide," she said to herself. But Mitchell the scientist knew better, knew that a character such as hers compelled but one answer:

> In fact, from the instant that she read Wendell's note to Mrs. Morton she had made up her mind; nay, all the habits and sentiments of a life of truth and purity and honor made it up for her. When seeming to hesitate she was only cheating love's sweet patience with the semblance of indecision.[32]

The next day the unsuspecting Wendell called upon the woman he hoped to marry. In the dramatic scene that followed, Mrs. Westerley confronted him with her devastating questions. At first he lied in desperation, making matters even worse, until at last, having no other hope, he confessed the full story of his weakness and wrong. "Help me to do what seems right to you," he pleaded, an abject figure of a man. But the reaction of Alice to his humility was disgust and the great pain of most shocking disillusionment. "And you won't desert me,

31 *Ibid.*, p. 399.
32 *Ibid.*, pp. 403-404.

Alice?" he asked pathetically. "I could not marry a man I do not respect," she replied.

"Then it is all over."
"Yes, it is all over,—all but the shame and the bitterness of it. And I loved you! —oh, I loved you dearly; more than life, more than my soul! God help me, I would give it now, this instant, to be able to think of you as I once thought!"[33]

In this scene Mitchell showed what it was that Wendell found most unbearable: "And I must be to you of all men the lowest. . . . I cannot bear your scorn. I can bear the rest; *that* I cannot bear."[34] It was this loss of the esteem of the woman he loved, this more than all else, which broke Wendell. As he left, he could hear her last words: "Oh, my God—the shame of it! The shame of it!"[35]

The story of Wendell's deterioration was over. When he next appeared in the story he was a broken personality, his face "haggard and flushed," his voice "uninterested." Informed that Edward, in his will, had left him $10,000 he answered in a "monotonous voice" that he couldn't accept it. All he wanted was to lie down. Was he sick? "No, I am not sick; I am dead. But hell is alive. Go away, all of you."[36] He sought refuge away from people, in solitude and in opium. Soon he and his sister left the community abruptly, with no leave-taking.

Dr. Wendell appeared no more in the story, but Mitchell

33 *Ibid.*, p. 409. Mrs. Westerley, it might be noted here, was one of Mitchell's most outstanding character creations, and provided an example of his conception of a wholesome and admirable personality, a charming woman with noble principles, self-control and a deeply ingrained sense of humor. She was, Mitchell wrote in a private letter to his friend Mrs. Mason, not based upon any one he knew: "I think I may have stated to you before that I believe one gets into his first novel some of the freshness he never quite attains in the later books. Mrs. Westerley is a creation, not a portrait. I never knew intimately a woman just like her." From the unpublished letter to Mrs. Mason, dated July 19, 1912. A copy of the letter is in the possession of Mrs. S. W. Macdonough.

34 *Ibid.*, p. 410.
35 *Ibid.*, p. 411.
36 *Ibid.*, p. 415.

did add one final scene, set a year later, in which he informed the reader that Dr. Wendell was ill, penniless, broken in health and spirit, a victim of causes he could not control. Mitchell, with the mercy that grew from his scientific understanding, felt sorry for him and withheld the last blow. He did not permit Mrs. Westerley to marry Colonel Fox, who despised Dr. Wendell. Mitchell explained his feelings in one of his letters to Mrs. Mason:

> Your very interesting letter found me amply armed, as I had already recast the end of my story and decided that Mrs. Westerley could not marry the colonel. In fact, in my tale, she is only said to be about to do so. My trouble with the old lover is that I like him in spite of his being morally weak.[37]

In spite of the acute insights and general soundness of Mitchell's study in deterioration, there are definite shortcomings from the psychological point of view. The story of Wendell is incomplete. We have no sufficient hint of his earlier life.[38] When we first meet Wendell he is in his early thirties, and while the story may, of course, properly begin there, it can do so only with certain deficits. A man in his thirties is well along the way to whatever culmination his character may be

[37] The letter, which has not been published, is undated, but, it is clear, was written shortly before the publication of *In War Time* (1884). The "old lover," of course, was Dr. Wendell. A copy of the letter is in the possession of Mrs. S. W. Macdonough.

It might be added that Mitchell finally did permit Colonel Fox to marry Mrs. Westerley, although not in the novel *In War Time*. There is a reference to their marriage in a later novel, *When All the Woods Are Green*. One of the characters mentioned a Mrs. Westerley: "There was some queer story about her wanting to marry a country doctor who came to grief, or did some queer things, I forget what." Another character continued the reference: "Yes; she married Colonel Fox, at last." S. Weir Mitchell, *When All the Woods Are Green*, p. 304.

[38] Mrs. Westerley, as Mitchell pictured her, found it hard to understand Wendell's degradation without more knowledge of his earlier life. "How," she asked herself, "could a learned, scholar-like man, of gentle ways and refined tastes, suddenly fall so far! She shuddered. There must have been events in his life of which she knew not—horrible preparations for this final degradation." S. Weir Mitchell, *In War Time*, p. 403.

destined to reach. Mitchell told all too little about Wendell's past, the character-shaping elements of it; one would have liked at least a few revealing backward glances.[39]

From an artistic point of view Mitchell's shortcomings are more serious. While his story of Wendell's deterioration is clear and convincing, it is not so effective as it could be. Too often we learn of Wendell through the obtrusive intervention of Mitchell's own comments instead of by the words and actions of the character himself. One of the crucial events in the story, for example, was Wendell's first "borrowing" of Hester's money. We do not live through this scene with Wendell, this momentous downward step in his deterioration, but are merely told about his feelings:

> I should do an interesting but weak nature a wrong to presume that it cost him nothing to reason himself into borrowing enough of Hester's capital to enable him to give to Ann the money she had habitually received.[40]

The fuller picture, of course, would have required a much longer book than Mitchell's, or else a more restricted area of concentration. Too often one misses in Mitchell's story the sort of scene one gets, let us say, in Dostoevski's *Crime and Punishment,* where several pages are often devoted to one small act, recreating in detail the thoughts and feelings of the character. There are, however, some excellent scenes in Mitchell's story of Wendell's downfall, particularly near the end, where Mrs. Westerley confronted him with her judgment and accusations.

In spite of its shortcomings the story of Wendell's downfall was an outstanding accomplishment, and made a deep impression upon some of Mitchell's most distinguished contemporaries. The great English novelist George Meredith, for exam-

39 For a recent study of the background, the predisposing elements—as well as the immediate cause—of a criminal action see Frederic Wertham, *Dark Legend* (New York, 1941). In this fictionalized study, which is essentially a case history, the author, a psychiatrist, told the story of a young man who murdered his mother.

40 S. Weir Mitchell, *In War Time,* p. 237.

ple, was much impressed with the entire novel, and wrote his praise in a letter to Mitchell:

> I have at last read the book, and I find it a piece of psychology wrought into a production of art. The story is excellent; and you have done what I constantly protest should be done to give a fruitful repast to cultivated readers. You have evolved the story from the characters. I look about me in my country vainly for an author who is up to that high-water mark of fiction. The characters are so clearly drawn as they are forcibly conceived, and for that reason the crux of the position between the young medicus and Mrs. Westerley, (to whom my heart is vowed) has the stamp of highest nobility.[41]

RICHARD DARNELL

Richard Darnell, an important character in *Roland Blake*, is another, though less complete study in deterioration. He had already, at the beginning of the novel, gone far along the path of wrongdoing. When we first meet him it is as a traitor to his own army, a Confederate soldier who had sold military information to the North. In the first scene in which he appears, after he received his money, he tried from the safety of ambush to shoot in the back the northern officer who had just paid him. He was still, however, a man of ambition and evil strength, by no means a broken personality such as Dr. Wendell at the close of *In War Time*, or such as Darnell himself was to become.

During the course of the novel Darnell committed new crimes which led to his downfall. Mitchell not only described these crimes in some detail, but he cast long glances back at Darnell's earlier life, and thus indicated, as he did not in the case of Wendell, the origin of traits which led to the man's downfall. The study of Darnell that emerges, however, is similar in essentials to the study of Wendell, for both men follow the same general pattern of deterioration.

[41] Burr, *op. cit.*, p. 212. William Dean Howells, too, was much impressed. See Earnest, *op. cit.*, p. 99.

Darnell's downfall, like Wendell's, began with an important weakness of character: he was accustomed to having his own way by merely demanding it and without giving a thought to the interests of others. How he acquired this weakness Mitchell indicated by a clear discussion of Darnell's boyhood days:

> The strange beauty of the boy Darnell had been a curse to him. There are guards about a girl's attractiveness which a lad lacks. Some honest ancestor had given the young Virginian large, soft, brown eyes, ingenuous in expression, but had failed to endow him with the combination of moral qualities which, as time went on, should have given reality to what in childhood was but picture. The crown of curls around the head, the lips bold and clearly modeled in lines which approached those of feminine type, the masterful vigor of look and carriage, had won from a foolish mother that fatal form of worship which as years go on is apt to make an iconoclast of the idol's self.
>
> Death saved her from seeing this, and a nervous, sensitive, adoring sister took up the evil task of despoiling a life by flattery and indulgence of its best chances. The firmest rule would have found him difficult to save; the weakest treated him as a toy, and insured his ruin. What was good in him failed to crystallize in definite habits of good. He grew up amidst slaves and women, lawless and fearless,—a character in a state of solution. Good women and thoughtful men found in their relations to the slave a self-education which helped to evolve many noble characteristics by reason of the awful responsibilities which the position of master created. To a man like Darnell plantation-life was fatal.[42]

When, early in the novel, Darnell visited his sister Octopia, the final phase of his deterioration began. As with Wendell, his wrongdoing arose from constant need for money. He had no income nor any intention of looking for honest work; he had only wild schemes, or plans for gambling. Like Wendell, he indulged his impulses as though reality would somehow adjust itself to him. He did not face his problems honestly, for that would have meant surrendering his schemes and disciplining himself to concentrate at some honest occupation. It was easier

42 S. Weir Mitchell, *Roland Blake*, pp. 116-117.

and more pleasant, for the time being at least, to borrow from his sister the money to dissipate in gambling and dishonest projects.

On the very first day of his visit to Octopia he asked her for money to buy quinine, which he would smuggle into the South, where it could be sold at a huge profit. "Once already," commented Mitchell, referring to events preceding the opening of the novel, "he had ruined his sister's fortunes, and he meant now again to use her savings."[43] In her great adoration for her brother, Octopia could refuse him nothing, even though she knew he was a spendthrift. Bit by bit he borrowed and spent her money until she had little left to give him.

But there was on hand a larger source of money than Octopia's. His sister lived in the home of her young cousin, Olivia, and the girl's grandmother, Mrs. Wynne. Olivia was not only attractive but was to inherit a fortune from her grandmother. Darnell deliberately set out to captivate this young lady for her fortune, but in the process became intensely attracted to her. He wished to do things for her, to give her luxuries and pleasures now beyond his means; he regretted his own past evil actions and was glad that on a certain night the shot he fired from ambush failed to kill. He "felt that his love was nobler than his nature."[44] When he proposed marriage to her, he said sincerely, "God knows you would make me better."[45]

Olivia did not accept his proposal, but he retained his interest and was prepared to try again. However, his romantic feelings toward her did not keep him from designs on her grandmother's money. He realized he was exhausting his sister's funds; yet at the rate he spent, he remained constantly in need. "I am at my wit's end," he declared to his sister, "I must live. I can't work."[46] His plan was blunt and simple. His sister had once vaguely hinted to him that she knew confidential,

43 *Ibid.*, p. 121.
44 *Ibid.*, p. 146.
45 *Ibid.*, p. 148.
46 *Ibid.*, p. 242.

unpleasant facts about Mrs. Wynne's dead son and that this knowledge could have value. Darnell proposed blackmailing the elderly lady for ten or fifteen thousand dollars even while he continued to court her granddaughter. "Mrs. Wynne," he said, "has far more than she can need; you and I have nothing."[47] When his sister appeared shocked[48] at his proposal, he continued to rationalize: "As to the Wynnes, they have treated you disgracefully, and I do not see why you need to be so careful of their feelings. I at least do not mean to be."[49]

Though his sister pleaded with him, he refused to say he would not attempt blackmail, but promised only that he would do nothing for a week or two. Meanwhile he made a desperate effort to win Olivia, only to learn that she was in love with another man. He threatened to kill the man—until he learned that it was Roland Blake, who had once saved his life. Darnell had enough decency to feel the obligation, even though Blake now treated him coldly.

However, after this episode, Darnell's position seemed desperate. He was pressed for money and no longer had hopes of marrying into Olivia's fortune; he was defeated in love by a man he detested; and yet because this man had saved his life he could not satisfy his passion for revenge. Darnell was frustrated.

> His self-esteem was hurt. . . .
> Having never been taught self-control or mental discipline, his consciousness was now like a madhouse in which the mutinous insane range unchecked without a keeper. At such moments crime is in the air, murder at the elbow.[50]

In this mood Darnell was approached by Blake who, fearing he might harm Olivia and the grandmother, asked him to leave

[47] *Ibid.*, p. 241.

[48] His sister remembered him before his moral deterioration had progressed this far, as Mitchell indicated: Octopia "respected her fixed conception of her brother's sense of honor, little knowing to what deeps of degradation he had fallen since she had last seen him." *Ibid.*, p. 121.

[49] *Ibid.*, p. 243.

[50] *Ibid.*, pp. 329-330.

the resort where they were all gathered. When Darnell refused, Blake identified himself as the northern officer to whom Darnell gave military papers, and threatened to expose Darnell's treachery unless he would leave. Such a threat, explained Mitchell, meant much to Darnell:

> As Blake spoke, Darnell recoiled, his face a livid mask, his jaw dropped. He was ruined. The one thing he yet valued —the opinion of men of his own caste—was lost.[51]

On more than one earlier occasion Mitchell had prepared the reader for this moment:

> Darnell had but one cowardice,—the fear of the public opinion of the caste to which he belonged. He had imperiled himself in this direction more than once, but had never come to complete wreck.[52]

In this crisis Darnell had no choice: he promised to leave.

Mitchell set this whole episode in the perspective of his own philosophy, the outlook of a humane, scientific student of human behavior. Through Blake he expressed more than once a certain type of sympathy for Darnell, the sympathy that came from understanding that Darnell himself was a victim of forces outside his control. "He is to be pitied," said Blake. Darnell, too, had insisted—with bad grace, it is true—that a man's life is not in his own hands, that he himself was spoiled by his early training.

Hurt though he was by Blake's knowledge of his treachery, Darnell was not yet utterly broken. He was sustained by Blake's promise to tell no one. By the next morning, just before leaving, he was ready for one more desperate effort. He visited Mrs. Wynne and tried to blackmail her with pretended knowledge about her son. When this seemed to fail, becoming excited, he seized her arm and spoke so harshly she became alarmed and cried out for help. At her outcry, into the room came Darnell's sister and the woman he loved, Olivia. This was the situation which broke Darnell. He had always

51 *Ibid.*, p. 333.
52 *Ibid.*, p. 277.

been more averse to certain wrongs than to others. He had been troubled by the "petty meanness" of his borrowings from his sister. He had always had "some educated disinclination to oppress the weak or take small dishonorable advantages." He had always been proud of his courage, and hated to tell a lie because it partook of cowardice. Now, with all the others in the room staring at him, he was in an unbearably humiliating position, threatening a weak, old lady until she had called aloud in terror for help. He was exposed in an act despicable even in his own eyes, exposed indeed—before Blake whom he hated, before his devoted sister, and before Olivia, the girl he still loved and admired as a creature better than himself.

At this moment he looked at his sister, who "threw herself on the lounge in an agony of sobbing."[53] He turned and saw Olivia, an "awful pity" in her eyes. Then, said Mitchell, indicating the pity he himself felt toward the man, Darnell "caught her by both hands and looked and looked in her eyes,—a stare of yearning love, blurred by tears."[54] As Darnell left the room, determined what to do, he spoke low, "Octopia—my sister—you will understand."[55]

Mitchell added a scene which made even more emphatic the final cause of Darnell's breakdown. Blake, understanding that Darnell intended to kill himself, rushed after him to forestall the act. Catching up with the desperate man, Blake made it clear that if it was money Darnell needed, he would supply that. No, it was not lack of money which was driving him to suicide, Darnell indicated. He was beyond the help of money. Like Wendell, he had lost the esteem of those for whom he cared, and that was unendurable. "There are things a man can do," explained Darnell, "and keep his place, and some he can't do; and these are known. If they had not been, I should not have cared. Even the worst of women likes the semblance of covering. Mine is gone. I am sin-naked."[56] He turned away, toward suicide.

53 *Ibid.*, p. 351.
54 *Ibid.*, p. 352.
55 *Ibid.*, p. 352.
56 *Ibid.*, p. 356.

Chapter VII

THE COUCH-LOVING INVALIDS

OCTOPIA DARNELL

THE DOCTOR who had observed the many nervous women described in *Lectures on Diseases of the Nervous System* had acquired not only a considerable medical knowledge but a knowledge of people as well. In his close daily contacts he learned how these women looked, talked, felt, and behaved toward doctors, nurses, and relatives. Utilizing this experience he created a new character in American fiction, Octopia Darnell, the couch-loving invalid, and later, two similar characters, Constance Trescot and Ann Penhallow. Octopia Darnell seems to have stepped out of the pages of *Lectures on Diseases of the Nervous System,* a lean, pale woman, ever complaining, yet really free of organic disease. Mitchell has described her type again and again in his medical writings, and practically always in a satiric tone. It was such a woman, he declared on one occasion, who inspired him to devise his famous rest treatment:

> Some years ago I saw a woman who was like half a dozen any of you can now recall,—a pallid, feeble creature, who had menstruated irregularly until two years before, and then stopped at the age of thirty. She was the type of a class. Everything wearied her,—to walk, to read, to drive, to sew. She was the woman with a back, and a shawl on her shoulders, and a sofa for a home, and hysterics for a diversion. She had tired out the doctors, and exhausted drug-shops and spas and travel, and outlived a nurse or two. The deformity

85

man had found a spinal curvature and put on a brace; the gynecologist had had his turn; the quacks had had their share; and she wore blue glasses to keep out the blessings of daylight. She was five feet four, and weighed ninety-four pounds, and had as much figure as a hat rack, and had no more bosom than the average chicken of a boarding-house table. Nature had wisely prohibited this being from increasing her breed. How many of you have stood helpless before this woman! Like you, I had had my failures with such cases, and I was driven to reflect as to what new device I could try.[1]

Octopia Darnell, while having her own individual qualities, belonged to the same general class as this woman. Mitchell pictured her with consistency, understanding, and imagination. She was just as credible as she was unique. We first meet her when her distant cousin Olivia opened the door to her room:

The room was darkened by partly-drawn curtains, and was luxuriously comfortable with a heavy-piled Turkish carpet and easy chairs. On a long reclining chair, and covered with a silken down-lined coverlet, lay the long and attenuated figure of Octopia Darnell. She had the singular pale-golden complexion of a woman originally dark-skinned and now lacking blood.[2]

In this very first description Octopia exhibited several of the peculiar characteristics of the couch-loving invalid. Like the women already described as the inspiration for Mitchell's rest cure, Octopia favored the reclining position and shunned light. Furthermore, she was thin and lacked blood, two of the outstanding characteristics of women needing the rest treatment, as Mitchell explained in his book *Fat and Blood,* his first extensive explanation of his method. At the very outset of this book, in describing such patients, Mitchell referred to them as "nervous women, who as a rule are thin, and lack blood."[3]

[1] S. Weir Mitchell, *The Annual Oration before the Medical and Chirurgical Faculty of Maryland*, pp. 13-14. Mitchell has given differing accounts of the origin of the rest cure, Ernest Earnest points out in his *S. Weir Mitchell: Novelist and Physician*, p. 81.

[2] S. Weir Mitchell, *Roland Blake*, p. 42.

[3] S. Weir Mitchell, *Fat and Blood*, p. 7.

"The loss of fat," he continued, "nearly always goes along with conditions which impoverish the blood."[4]

Octopia's first words after inviting Olivia to enter were a petulant complaint:

> Why do you make so much noise, dear Olivia? And please not to keep me waiting, I am so weak today. You are young, dear, and death does not seem as near to you as it does to me. There! don't make so much noise.[5]

The most minute noises troubled her. She could not bear the sound of Olivia's shoes which "creaked," nor of her dresses, which "rustled." In this first scene she revealed her habit of appealing for sympathy and attention. "Don't desert me," she pleaded to Olivia, "I am so lonely, and the days are long,— very long. . . . Read to me a little while; I want to hear the wretched war-news. And don't read the comments. You will be careful, love, won't you? I cannot stand what they say about the South. . . . And don't move about so."[6] In this first scene we learn too of the extreme physical sympathy she demanded, kisses and petting from Olivia, who found the task becoming ever more nearly unbearable.

In this same scene Mitchell implied that Octopia's complaints were without organic basis. "An analysis," he declared, would yield "reasons for doubt, disbelief, or refusals."[7] Later in the story he referred sarcastically to Octopia "surrounded with an invalid's armament of cushions, shawls, and smelling-salts." Women of her type, he went on, "are heart-misers; they like to have constant touch and sight of the gold of love."[8] In this first scene with Octopia, Mitchell continued to develop the reader's suspicions concerning her illness by describing her through the eyes of Olivia:

> As Olivia seated herself, she saw her cousin's long hands rising and falling on the coverlet, and said, gently,—

[4] *Ibid.*, p. 11.
[5] S. Weir Mitchell, *Roland Blake*, p. 42.
[6] *Ibid.*, p. 43.
[7] *Ibid.*, p. 45.
[8] *Ibid.*, pp. 157, 158.

"You are suffering, cousin; can I help you?"

To an experienced eye the movements would have seemed too regular to be the expression of pain.

"Yes, I suffer; I cannot bear these struggles with you, Olivia. You are like all young people; you have no real sympathy. When I am dead you will remember me and wish in vain you had done more to help a pain-broken woman. I don't want you to answer me; I cannot talk long, and I have something to say."

Olivia watched the sallow face, with its look of languid inaction, noticing for the first time, being a clever but undeveloped observer, that the lips spoke without the other features appearing to take any expressive interest in the thoughts thus uttered.[9]

In this first scene, too, Mitchell showed how Octopia behaved when crossed, the characteristic behavior of the hysterical patient, hysterical, as he used the term, to describe a patient having a physical disability without its corresponding organic cause. When Octopia tried to arrange a match between her brother Richard, whom she adored, and Olivia, who was to inherit a large sum of money, she found her young cousin recalcitrant. Olivia refused to send pictures of herself to Richard, whom she had never met, declaring that she had, in fact, destroyed them. When Octopia tried threats and they failed, she resorted to her favorite and most effective weapon, an appeal to sympathy. She gave forth a "wailing cry":

Olivia! dear Olivia! . . .

Try not to trouble me; I am sick and irritable. And you will be kind to my brother. And shut the door gently, love. I can bear no more.[10]

Octopia had her way of breaking down any resistance of Olivia's to her wishes: she became "hurt or nervous, or both, or else, when defeat was near, gave way to such distressing symptoms as commonly routed Olivia. . . ."[11]

When the usual appeals to sympathy failed, Octopia be-

9 *Ibid.*, pp. 45-46.
10 *Ibid.*, p. 50.
11 *Ibid.*, p. 51.

haved in an extreme manner, as Mitchell indicated in picturing another quarrel between Octopia and her young cousin. On that occasion Olivia failed to respond very readily to an appeal for sympathy and when, as the scene seemed about to end, Octopia commanded, "Kiss me good-night," Olivia refused. Octopia then resorted to one of her most desperate measures:

> "How can you hurt me so, Olive? There! I knew you would upset me, soon or late." Her pupils dilated, and beginning to tremble, she threw herself on the sofa, and with her hands extended in rigid spasm. "Send Judith, and go— go away; you have done enough."
> Her distress and terror and pain were evident, and the glance of reproach she cast at her cousin was pitiful.
> Olivia was disarmed, knowing well that these symptoms usually meant days of suffering for her cousin. She promptly called the old black woman, and, with wrath and pity and a hideous sense of puzzle in her mind, left the room and descended the stairs.[12]

Olivia was being worn down by the behavior of Octopia. Particularly difficult were the incessant calls for kissing and petting:

> This was a daily trial to Olivia. The close, ill-ventilated room, the obscurity, the sallow woman with a constant atmosphere of strong scents about her, were alike harmful to the very organization of the honest, wholesome maiden, and this final annoyance—the kiss and the little physical pettings —was becoming almost impossible to be endured. . . .
> She had yielded so often to the sick woman's plea of weakness, of loneliness, and of multiple disabilities, that the claim upon her sympathies had in time developed easily in one at the plastic age a habit of docile submission. It could not be said that she was ever unwilling; her momentary impatience was due to the craving of her physical nature for air and movement. All that was noblest in the girl made her incline towards tender helpfulness. Each revolt caused her intense self-reproach.[13]

12 *Ibid.*, p. 72.
13 *Ibid.*, pp. 44-45.

Olivia's entire health was deteriorating:

> The exactions of her nervous, sickly cousin were surely
> sapping the wholesome life of the younger woman, and as
> surely lessening her power of self-restraint.[14]

At last, worn out by the exactions of the sick woman, Olivia
approached the breaking point:

> Her head ached, and with the consciousness of constant
> fatigue, the outcome of a life of strain and repression, began
> to come its certain result, irritability. . . .
> Her power of self-government was fast deserting her, and
> her reason was rapidly going over to the part of mutiny. . . .
> She began to hate Octopia at times, in little fractions of
> hatred.[15]

Mitchell's comments on Olivia's deterioration were certainly
based upon his medical experience, particularly his knowledge
of how hysterical patients wear out their nurses. The comments in *Roland Blake* are paralleled by similar observations
scattered through his medical writings. There are several such
observations in *Lectures on Diseases of the Nervous System*.[16]
In his book *Fat and Blood* he described even more fully the
relationship between the couch-loving invalid and the victim
who nurses her, a picture very similar to the relationship
between Octopia and Olivia:

> Nothing is more curious, nothing more sad and pitiful, than
> these partnerships between the sick and selfish and the sound
> and over-loving. By slow but sure degrees the healthy life is
> absorbed by the sick life, in a manner more or less injurious
> to both, until, sometimes too late for remedy, the growth of
> the evil is seen by others. Usually the person withdrawn
> from wholesome duties to minister to the caprices of hyster-

14 *Ibid.*, p. 50.

15 *Ibid.*, pp. 111-112. It might be added here that in a personal letter to
Mrs. Mason, written while he was working on the novel, Mitchell described
Olivia as "a woman who is nearly wrecked by the claims on her feelings
and body by a sick woman's exaggerated crave for sympathy and help and
'glutinous' affection." A copy of the unpublished letter dated September
24, 1885, is in the possession of Mrs. S. W. Macdonough.

16 See S. Weir Mitchell, *Lectures on Diseases of the Nervous System*, pp.
66, 270-271. See also earlier in this present work, pp. 46-47.

ical sensitiveness is the person of a household who feels most for the invalid, and who for this very reason suffers the most. The patient has pain, a tender spine, for example; she is urged to give it rest. She cannot read; the self-constituted nurse reads to her. At last light hurts her eyes; the mother remains shut up with her all day in a darkened room. A draught of air is supposed to do harm, and the doors and windows are closed, and the ingenuity of kindness is taxed to imagine new sources of like trouble, until at last the window-cracks are stuffed with cotton, the chimney stopped, and even the keyhole guarded. It is easy to see where this all leads to,—the nurse falls ill, and a new victim is found. I have seen a hysterical, anaemic girl kill in this way three generations of nurses.[17]

Did Octopia know she was really cruel, and showed so little sympathy for others? In supplying the answer to this question Mitchell again drew upon his medical experience. He knew that such women as Octopia, despite all their cruelty, actually considered themselves kind; they were too absorbed in their own ailments to notice the harm they were doing to others. Mitchell created a scene which reveals this blindness of Octopia's. With her young cousin she was watching a group of northern soldiers marching, when Olivia, overcome with thoughts of the danger facing these boys, exclaimed, "Oh, the pity of it!" "You foolish child!" answered Octopia. "They get paid for it." Spurred by anger Olivia cried out, "You have no heart for any sufferings but your own!—None! none! You are heartless." Octopia's reaction was characteristic:

"I? I?" said Octopia, "I?—no heart?" She was honestly amazed at the charge. Intensity of attention to her own ailments had given them for her a dangerous capacity, and she was simply shocked that any one should fail to believe with her in their seriousness. "When," she added, "you have lived through such years of pain as mine, you will learn to feel for another's ills."[18]

Octopia reacted just the way hysterically ill women gener-

17 S. Weir Mitchell, *Fat and Blood*, pp. 29-30.
18 S. Weir Mitchell, *Roland Blake*, pp. 69-70.

ally do when accused of cruelty, as Mitchell described them in his medical writings. One may recall his comments concerning those patients who wear out the relatives who attend them, particularly his reference to the hysterical, anemic girl who killed three generations of nurses. Does such a patient realize what she is doing, how unkind she really is? "If you tell the patient she is basely selfish," wrote Mitchell, "she is probably amazed and wonders at your cruelty."[19]

But such patients were indeed selfish, and Octopia was no exception. Her sickness was ever related to her convenience. She knew how to become ill at the opportune time. When, for example, her brother finally was to come for a visit, Octopia, wanting him to meet her young cousin alone and have full opportunity to make a good first impression, suddenly became too ill to meet him and sent a note to Olivia saying so. "These notes on the smallest occasions," observed Mitchell, "were a part of the trivial incidents of Octopia's life; and whenever she desired to settle a matter without chance of appeal, she resorted to the device of a note."[20] Olivia was inclined to accept these communications at their face value, but her old grandmother, who had a sharper understanding of Octopia, scoffed at her niece for believing such notes. Octopia, Mrs. Wynne said, "is well enough when she pleases to do anything."[21]

After approximately the first third of the novel, one has a fairly clear picture of Octopia—but the basic cause of her condition remains vague. How did she ever acquire the hysterical sickness in the first place? Before proceeding very far into the second third of the novel, the reader is given some definite insight into this question. It seems that at some time before the opening of the story, Octopia had been of real service to the elderly Mrs. Wynne, whose son, Olivia's father, had been sick; Octopia had nursed him during the last week of his life, which ended in his suicide. Octopia kept this suicide a secret, but her

19 S. Weir Mitchell, *Fat and Blood*, p. 30.
20 S. Weir Mitchell, *Roland Blake*, p. 100.
21 *Ibid.*, p. 110.

implied threat of revealing it gave her power. She would occasionally remind Mrs. Wynne of the past: "I am sick and feeble; I have never recovered my health since that awful week with Cousin Arthur. I have paid for your security from the discomfort of publicity with my lost life."[22]

This very significant statement provides a key to the interpretation of Octopia, for it indicates just what she had to gain from her illness. By being ill *as a consequence* of serving Mrs. Wynne, she had a claim upon the lady, a claim she used to the limit. By implication, if she got well her claim would diminish.

Thus Octopia could hardly afford to get well. She lived in the home of the old lady, a pampered invalid, supplied with excellent board and room, and with sums of money, too, from time to time. "For years she had secured a home and luxury by gently-urged claims which amply sufficed to keep Mrs. Wynne in a state of obedience which she found insured her comfort."[23] Nevertheless, Octopia considered herself a woman of moral integrity, and had persuaded herself that her claims were justified. With the appearance of Darnell in the story, she began to make new demands upon a different level. Finding Olivia stubborn, unwilling to marry Darnell, Octopia called upon Mrs. Wynne to urge her granddaughter to accept the marriage, and added to her demand a vague threat of exposing the suicide of Arthur Wynne if Olivia continued her refusal. Octopia could hardly justify this threat even to herself; it was too grossly wrong, and so remained vague, even in her own thoughts:

> The marriage of Olivia to Richard Darnell was a scheme of recent growth. Her plan had always for her a certain vagueness which seemed to prevent her from seeing it in a true and unpleasant light. Octopia had always said to herself, "I am only using and shall only use my knowledge to secure to me and to them a mutual relation which will be of service to them." As to going further she had no intention. To

22 *Ibid.*, p. 153.
23 *Ibid.*, p. 156.

proclaim what she knew, would be, she was well aware, an act of dishonor, which she set aside as for her impossible.[24]

Olivia defiantly rejected all pleadings, threats, and pressures of Octopia and of her grandmother as well. Nothing could bend her to agree to a marriage with Darnell. The increasing pressure became ever more intense, and finally produced a crisis. When Octopia went away on one of her brief, habitual pilgrimages for her health, Olivia persuaded her grandmother that they ought to go away for awhile, escape to some place where Octopia would not find them. The two ladies packed their baggage and hurried away, leaving no trace for Octopia to follow.

When Octopia returned, her birds had flown. She was quick to grasp that this was clear and open rebellion. Her security was threatened. If Olivia and her grandmother should succeed in making the separation permanent, Octopia would be deprived of her home, her source of income, and all the tokens of sympathy and affection as well. How would she behave under the circumstances, this weak, helpless invalid, this woman who could not stand the daylight nor the least noise of the rustle of a dress, who was so delicate she could not read a newspaper nor bear to hear unpleasant aspects of the news, who needed constant attention, sympathy, and kisses? Would she not collapse utterly under the impact of desertion, of learning so bluntly that she was not wanted? The answer to that would depend upon the nature of Octopia's illness. Mitchell had indicated that her illness was not a fixed, inflexible element. It could grow only in a suitable environment, where there were sympathetic persons ready to be impressed. But now there were no such persons around. The author emphasized in his medical writings the harm that can be done by too sympathetic an audience. The reader may recall Mitchell's explanation, quoted earlier, of how he handled a patient who had physical pains of psychological origin: "I tell the patient her pains will be well when she gets well, and then cease to

[24] *Ibid.*, pp. 156-157.

allow them to be further discussed."[25] The reader may recall also his comment upon introducing one of his most elaborate and complex cases of hysterical disorders: "I read you her history, and as you hear it I think you will see that almost at any time a resolute man, whom she trusted and who understood her disorder could have saved her and her family from long years of suffering."[26] In his famous rest-cure treatment he again stated his view that the hysterical patient must be cut off from "foolish sympathy." This treatment consisted, as has been described, of rest, substantial feeding, and "passive exercise obtained through the steady use of massage and electricity."[27] But there was, in addition, the important psychological element which induced the hysterically ill woman to want to get well, her isolation. Was she too weak to work? Did she love to lie in bed indulging her weakness? Then Mitchell would prescribe rest indeed, would order it sternly enforced until she was surfeited with it and welcomed a firm order to do the things she once felt she could not do:

> To lie abed half the day, and sew a little and read a little, and be interesting and excite sympathy, is all very well, but when they are bidden to stay in bed a month, and neither to read, write, nor sew, and to have one nurse,—who is not a relative,—then rest becomes for some women a rather bitter medicine, and they are glad enough to accept the order to rise and go about when the doctor issues a mandate which has become pleasantly welcome and eagerly looked for.[28]

Mitchell explained in his medical writing that such women as Octopia had to be cut off from the sympathies of their customary environment, that such separation was a necessary part of their recovery:

> It is needful to disentangle them from the meshes of old habits and to remove them from the contact with those who have been the willing slaves of their caprices. . . . Once sep-

[25] See p. 46 of the present work.
[26] See p. 40 of the present work.
[27] See S. Weir Mitchell, *Fat and Blood*, p. 7.
[28] *Ibid.*, pp. 40-41.

arate the patient from the moral and physical surroundings which have become part of her life of sickness, and you will have made a change which will be in itself beneficial, and will enormously aid in the treatment which is to follow. . . . I am speaking chiefly of the large and troublesome class of thin-blooded emotional women, for whom a state of weak health has become a long and almost, I might say, a cherished habit.[29]

Octopia was certainly one of those "thin-blooded emotional women" for whom illness had become "a cherished habit." Her illness was cherished because it served a purpose, satisfied her need for security and affection. It had no value in itself, but only in its effect upon Olivia and upon her grandmother. She had been ill for them. Now that they had gone away, Octopia's illness was useless, could no longer bring her comfort. In fact, as Mitchell explained, it became an obstacle in her path:

Octopia at once rose to better health and large possibilities of action, as do such sick persons in the presence of an emergency which threatens their comfort.[30]

At this stage in the story the reader is given the glimpse he may have been waiting for. Why had Octopia not obtained her security and affection in the usual way, through marriage? Certainly she had been physically attractive enough. Mitchell answered the question directly: "A foolish, wilful desire to show her power had lost her long years back a good man's love."[31] And this loss was a bitter memory, for she had loved the man ardently and admired him too.

Left alone, Octopia determined to find her cousin and the elderly Mrs. Wynne. There was only one person who knew where they were, Mr. Pennell, a man who was courting Octopia with little success. However, he had promised Olivia to keep her whereabouts a secret, and he remained adamant in his honor. Despite his intense wish to please Octopia he would

[29] *Ibid.,* pp. 34-35. See also *Doctor and Patient* (Philadelphia, 1889), p. 130.
[30] S. Weir Mitchell, *Roland Blake,* p. 180.
[31] *Ibid.,* p. 181.

not betray the secret, not even when she pulled out her old tricks and appealed to his sympathy. "Have you no pity for me, who am left by a girl's whim stranded, a sick, suffering woman?"[32]

After this vain appeal to Pennell, Octopia continued rising to the occasion, acquiring the new vigor necessary to pursue her vanished victims:

> With her recent shock of discovery that her victims had fled, some of her former energy had come back. Vigorous motives for action had been, as usual, potent moral tonics, and had influenced no less her physical condition. She smiled to see that she was not so thin as formerly, and that there was more color in her cheeks.[33]

Mitchell gave an interesting picture of the struggle she had to go through to adjust, to resist the old behavior patterns and act more independently. But, urged on by her strong motives, she was able to summon the necessary power:

> Already she missed Olivia. Now there was no one on whose little charities she could call, no one whom she could drag within the morbid circle of her own demands for sympathy. She felt the results of her talk with Pennell and with her brother in an attack of intense fatigue of mind and body and in a desire to give way to one of her volcanic emotional explosions. Having no one to summon as audience, she controlled herself; but a fierce feeling of having been wronged arose in her mind, and the demon of wrath at last expelled all his lesser brethren and remained in sullen possession.[34]

As Octopia, cut off from her usual audience, made these successful struggles, she continued to improve:

> Her recent need to think of others had beneficently taken

[32] *Ibid.*, pp. 184-185.

[33] *Ibid.*, pp. 188-189. Octopia's behavior here was similar to that of a girl described by Mitchell in his *Lectures on Diseases of the Nervous System.* She had been so ill, as a result of hysteria, that she could not walk. By supplying her with sufficient motives, Mitchell induced her to get out of bed and walk—much to the amazement of the girl's mother. See pp. 47-48 of this present work.

[34] *Ibid.*, pp. 191-192.

her outside of the slowly-narrowing circle of self-care and self-contemplation, and, by relieving her of some of the morbid habits of disease, had greatly bettered her physical condition. The mind rose in the scale of soundness with the body,—slowly, of course, as when one long crouching in slavery, straightening himself, tends to walk erect. To do right became more easy, because to see the right grew more possible. The changes were fractional and irregular; but surely when Olivia hurried her relative away she did Octopia a service of inestimable proportions.[35]

Octopia's immediate improvement was, of course, only partial. She still had her spells of nervousness and, in writing to the fugitive Olivia, she could still use the endearing terms of old, and express her craving for sympathy: "I miss . . . . your soft touch and the morning kiss."[36]

Octopia's next appearance in the story is toward the end. Her brother had caught up with the Wynnes at their resort hideout, and she had followed, arriving in time to witness his final degradation. What she had urged him not to do, she saw him do. The criminal blackmail of Mrs. Wynne, which had been vaguely in her own mind as a threat, a plan which she dared not look at in its true ugliness, she now saw her brother put into horrible action. She heard the old lady scream for help when Richard, threatening her for money, put his hands upon her. At the sight, Octopia was overcome, throwing herself on the lounge in an agony of sobbing.[37]

Under the stress of this blow, with Olivia nearby to give her sympathy, Octopia fell back temporarily into her previous behavior pattern:

She did not ask for her brother, nor did she even mention his name, but lay most of the time in a darkened room, holding Olivia's hand. . . .
   It was hard not to pity the tall, wasted, sick woman, with her refined face and her gentle claims to be soothed or caressed in her fits of self-abasement. When Olivia tried to

35 *Ibid.*, p. 254.
36 *Ibid.*, p. 273.
37 See p. 84 of this present work.

escape, she would say, "Don't leave me, dearest! I am so wretched!" and then her long arms fell around the girl and held her in a passionate embrace. As Octopia slept little and refused to eat, Olivia became alarmed, and proposed to send for a doctor; but this the invalid resolutely declined.[38]

But there was a new element in her sickness this time. Self-justification had given way to self-reproach. She had seen, in the horrible example of her brother, the inevitable outcome of the course she was pursuing. She had seen the facts of reality. To Pennell she confessed her new insight, brought to her so shockingly by the behavior of her brother:

> I think Richard tried to get money from Cousin Anne by pretending he knew something of Arthur Wynne's death.... Yes, it was so. Oh, I am sure it was so. I would give—oh, I would give my right hand to be sure it was not so. I—I—you know what I did for my cousins. Perhaps I overrated the service I did them. If I reminded Cousin Anne of it,—and I did; yes, I did,—it was because I wanted what they never gave me,—their love. They never really loved me, and I had helped them well. It is so hard to say! I wanted Olive to marry my brother, and the devil tempted me to show them what power I possessed....
>
> Don't touch me.... I am vile. How can you touch me? ... I boasted to Richard that I could have what I wanted; I told him that Mrs. Wynne was in my power; I played with the idea that one way or another I could rule Olivia; and then—oh, Mr. Pennell, when I found that he meant to make believe that he knew what I knew, when I grew sure that he was really going to do what I had only just thought of doing,—oh, then I saw! then I saw! I wish I had done it! Then he could not have been as wicked as I,—my beautiful boy-brother! Oh, I would have sinned in his place and saved him.[39]

This confession, as Mitchell recognized, gave Octopia a "strange relief." Furthermore, having so clearly looked upon the ugly truth of her own past actions, she was prepared to

[38] *Ibid.*, pp. 365-366.
[39] *Ibid.*, pp. 369-371.

change. At the close of the scene she vowed to Pennell, "So help me God, I will try to be a better woman."[40]

Within a few weeks Octopia was so altered Olivia noticed it and commented to her lover, Roland Blake:

> You do not know Octopia. She is very much altered, poor thing! . . .
> She was gentle and kind,—oh, quite too sweet,—except at times, when nothing pleased her. But she wanted all of everybody about her; and then as she had no serious work, she thought about herself and thought she didn't think about herself.

When Blake asked whether Octopia was really ill, Olivia replied, no doubt indicating Mitchell's own view of the case:

> Yes,—at times very ill. I think, Roland, that what must be the worst evil of half-sick people is the absence of regular work, of set duties,—things they have to do.

Roland emphasized the point by adding *"Must* is a noble tonic."[41]

Mitchell described Octopia once more as she appeared two years later. Having seen all too clearly the ugliness of her previous adjustment, having faced the unpleasant truth, she could not remain feeding upon Olivia and her grandmother. She could not any longer find there her source of economic security or of affection—aside from the fact that the situation was soon changed by the death of the elderly Mrs. Wynne and the marriage of Olivia to Blake. Because of her own change in outlook, Octopia had to find a new way to comfort. The most obvious way was to marry her ardent suitor, Pennell, to whom she had grown closer during the final events of the story, touched as she was by his devotion. To this remorseful, lonely woman he offered not only the affection she craved but the economic security she needed. There was practically nothing for her to do but marry him.

40 *Ibid.,* p. 373.
41 *Ibid.,* pp. 375-376. In his medical writings, too, Mitchell pointed out that hysterical illness is fostered by lack of set purposes and duties. See p. 36 of the present work.

Mitchell was too much the realist, however, to picture a complete reformation of Octopia. In her new adjustment in marriage she still remained true to herself. As an independent housewife, quite unhampered by externally-set duties, she was still free to consult her whims and to demand attention and sympathy from Pennell. Mitchell gives us one glimpse of her marriage through a letter written by one of the minor characters:

> I think she would like him to give up business and spend most of his time at home. He wisely resists, but I am of opinion will go to the wall soon or late. She has what I should call flabby obstinacy of purpose,—a sort of unsteady fractional persistency, which does not seem to have much fibre to it and yet is pretty sure to win. . . .
> Nevertheless, the man seems to like it, as a whole. . . . As for Pennell, he followed her about with a shawl and a scent-bottle, and says he has left the club and prefers the evening tranquility of domestic life.[42]

The final picture, while not detailed, is still revealing and consistent with all that has gone before. Octopia is a character quite unlike any that preceded her in American fiction, an achievement based to a large extent upon Mitchell's special knowledge and experience as a pioneer psychiatrist.

CONSTANCE TRESCOT

Constance Trescot, the central character in the novel that bears her name, devoted herself completely to the pursuit of revenge. At the beginning of the novel she was a physically healthy, passionate woman; at the end she had become, like Octopia Darnell, an anemic, couch-loving invalid, cultivating her incapacities. In his medical writings, as has been said, Mitchell set down many case histories of such women. In this novel, infusing his knowledge with his imagination, he undertook to present in detail one such case history. He himself

42 *Ibid.*, pp. 378-379.

considered Constance his best character creation, and the story
which she dominates his "best book."[43]

On various occasions he asserted that the story of Constance
was based on fact. "It is based on a woman's vendetta that
actually came under my observation,"[44] he told Beverley R.
Tucker. To Mrs. Mason he wrote:

> Yes, I knew Constance. A school teacher's husband, a meek
> foolish man, talked abolition loosely in a Southern town and
> was shot by a "prominent" citizen. The widow haunted him,
> and at last he fled. She became hysterical, and so—ages ago,
> I heard the tale. I know one—no two—women capable of
> what C. does, but to make her seem natural the book must
> be read.[45]

Although at the outset of the novel Constance was a physically healthy woman she already had deficiences which, under
the impact of events, were to lead to her deterioration. She
was too absorbed in her love for George Trescot, her fiance;
she showed no interest in anything but him, and desired an
equal devotion on his part. So unrestrained was her passion
that it appeared plainly to others, even to Trescot himself. As
he saw it, Constance had for him "a passion of affection" which
"seemed to take as small thought of the future as a bird might
do."[46] Soon he began to feel "more than was convenient
Constance's too steady call upon his time."[47]Constance's sister,
Susan, living in the same household, also noticed her sister's
unrestrained feelings: "This abandonment to love, so profound, so abrupt, shocked Susan. A man might thus exhibit
affection, not a woman."[48] Mitchell himself broke into the

43 He stated this opinion, for example, in his diary, April 2, 1906. The
diary, never published, is in the possession of Mrs. Macdonough.

44 See Beverley R. Tucker, *S. Weir Mitchell* (Boston, 1914) , p. 32. See
also Burr, *op. cit.,* pp. 277-278.

45 A copy of the unpublished letter, dated April 26, 1905, is in the possession of Mrs. S. W. Macdonough.

46 S. Weir Mitchell, *Constance Trescot,* p. 16.

47 *Ibid.,* p. 90.

48 *Ibid.,* p. 20.

narrative to describe the rare sort of passion shown by Constance toward her lover:

> Such a passion as possessed her with the power of a primal instinct was not yet in him victorious over all rational considerations. He knew little of women, and nothing of the woman who desires to absorb, so to speak, all of the thoughts and feelings of the one man, and who, as time goes on, becomes jealous of his friends, and even of his work, and, at last, of every hour not given to her. Such women are happily rare, but are now and then to be found. From the hour she first saw him, frail and pallid from suffering, a vast protecting eagerness arose in her mind. . . .[49]

At various later times Mitchell commented on Constance's obsessive passion:

> . . . the thought that to take him away even from his friends gave her a sense of such completeness of possession as filled her with joy. . . . She had all her life had a singular incapacity for generous division or sharing of her affection. Once it had been wholly Susan's. It was now George Trescot's, and this predisposition was reinforced by a passion deep, jealous, and exacting.[50]

Constance herself, too, was aware of the nature of her love:

> Life can ask nothing of me, large or small, which I would not give or be or do for you. . . . I am scared sometimes when I think of how all other love has shrunk to nothing, as if it had all gone to make up one great love for you. . . . I am half jealous of the company you find in your pipe.[51]

How Constance acquired this trait, how she became a person who would love in this manner, was outside the scope of Mitchell's inquiry. However, he did give the reader a brief glimpse of her childhood, indicating that she had even then characteristics similar to those in the adult woman. Her uncle in describing her to Trescot declared:

> This girl, this woman, is a creature of instincts. As a child

[49] *Ibid.*, p. 24.
[50] *Ibid.*, p. 60.
[51] *Ibid.*, pp. 43-44.

her temper was terrible; under my wise rule it has been tamed. She loves and hates with animal fidelity; and once she is set on doing anything, neither saint nor devil can change her.[52]

Aside from the exceptional nature of her love for Trescot, Constance at the outset revealed another characteristic: she had no religion.[53] Her uncle had deliberately brought her up with no creed, and had never allowed her even to set foot in a church. As a result, she grew up not only without religious beliefs, but ignorant of all religious knowledge.

George Trescot was aware of her condition and hoped that someday she would change: "Between us," he wrote to her, "There lies one large gulf of difference—and only one. That some day we shall bridge it over, I hope and believe. Meanwhile we shall trust each other's honesty in this, life's largest matter. . . ." In reading this letter Constance thought to herself: "No. . . . it is not for me life's largest matter. This human love is for me the larger. His religion, or any faith, is, compared to that, dim, misty, unsatisfying. . . . He is my religion."[54]

To Mitchell this lack of religion was a serious defect in personality. It had played an important part in the downfall of some of his earlier characters. Dr. Wendell, not fastened to any creed, was adrift and at the mercy of circumstances which overcame him. His sister, whose integrity of character and devotion to her brother stood all tests, derived some of her strength from her creed. "She was firmly anchored," wrote Mitchell in contrasting the two, "and he was carelessly adrift as to all spiritual beliefs."[55] Mrs. Hunter, victim of her own unscrupulous ambitions, was another character weakened by

52 Ibid., p. 12.

53 How serious Mitchell regarded this defect is indicated in a letter he wrote to Mrs. Mason: "The lesson of C. T.'s life is plain to read. She lacks motives. Women without religion suffer for it far more than men." See Burr, op. cit., p. 280.

54 Ibid., pp. 25-26.

55 S. Weir Mitchell, In War Time, p. 73.

lack of creed.[56] Constance, too, was to suffer from her deficiency.

The great test for Constance came when her husband was murdered. It happened in the South where they had gone to live shortly after the Civil War, while wounds were still new and feelings inflamed. George Trescot was administering the lands of Constance's uncle, the absentee northern owner, and enforcing the uncle's claims against the southern inhabitants. Personally, however, he was sympathetic toward the poor Southerners and exerting all the pressure he could to soften the stubborn old uncle toward them. Trescot's opponent in the legal contest that developed was John Greyhurst, an impulsive, quick-tempered lawyer who desperately needed to win the case. During the trial there were sharp personal words between the two lawyers. As Trescot was leaving the courtroom, winner of the case, he was handed a telegram: the uncle had died, leaving Constance and her sister Susan sole heirs. Trescot now could act as he wished, could settle all matters generously toward Greyhurst's clients. Walking toward his legal opponent, he reached with his lame hand into his pocket to show the telegram. But Greyhurst, bitter over his loss, pulled out a gun and fired, killing Trescot immediately.

Constance, witness of this act, walked swiftly to Greyhurst, indifferent to his gun, to everything but her own rage. "You have murdered an unarmed man," she cried. "Oh, coward! coward!"[57] She was pale, "motionless, unable to say more, her lips moving, her face twitching."[58] She fell at Greyhurst's feet, insensible.

After this event any novelist would have found himself confronted with the question: What will Constance do next? Mitchell too, of course, faced this question. But he asked particularly, what will Constance *be* next? In answering this he used, in some detail, his medical knowledge. To get across his views unobtrusively he brought into the story a physician, Dr.

---

[56] See S. Weir Mitchell, *Circumstance*.
[57] S. Weir Mitchell, *Constance Trescot*, p. 221.
[58] *Ibid.*, pp. 221-222.

Eskridge, who had special training in nervous disorders, and who "had been at one time in charge of the State asylum for the insane."[59] Dr. Eskridge attended Constance from the time she was brought home immediately after the shock until she could go about once more, and he commented frequently upon her condition, no doubt expressing Mitchell's own views. At first Constance was in a wild hysteria, knowing nothing. She would lie in a stupor, or she would talk and laugh about the unborn child she was carrying at the time of the shock. "It must be called George," she said, not knowing that it had been lost. Constance will improve, said Dr. Eskridge. "In a few weeks—perhaps abruptly—Mrs. Trescot will come out of this state, perhaps well, perhaps physically broken in health. Then she must go away and never return."[60] Constance's sister, Susan, then asked the doctor, "Do you think that if she recovers she will be in mind what she was; and can you . . . . form any idea of how this calamity will influence her life?" In reply Dr. Eskridge described the changes which he felt would take place in the personality of Constance:

> I think it likely that she will get well and be sound in mind and body. Unless misfortune wrecks us utterly and we become insane, after a shock like this we remain essentially what we were. New conditions, accidents, sorrow, may cause people to appear for a time alien from themselves. They are rarely so. The novel incident only evolves what might have remained unused, unknown, for a lifetime. She may surprise you, but it will be with the use of some quality you have never had occasion to see—or she to employ. Grief does not, as a rule, alter people radically.[61]

Mitchell did not, at this point, describe fully what Constance would be like when she recovered from the shock. Before doing so he allowed us to see the problem through the eyes of some of the other characters. Susan, imagining how she would react in her sister's place, declared:

59 *Ibid.*, p. 287.
60 *Ibid.*, pp. 227-228.
61 *Ibid.*, pp. 228-229.

I should go to the East—to Egypt . . . . I should try to forgive. Oh, I should try to save my soul alive; but then, doctor, I am an old maid, and cannot imagine what a woman like Constance feels or will feel.[62]

When Constance's gardener suggested that she might want to kill Greyhurst, Susan was horrified, "Oh, no, no!" she cried. "It is horrible—murder on murder. We are going away as soon as she is well enough. God will help her to forget, and she is young, and time is God's great peacemaker.[63]

Mitchell described Constance's convalescence meticulously, with a precision based on sound knowledge. Her recovery of her senses was slow and unsteady: "At times she sat up of a sudden with dilated pupils, staring, but silent. At other times she babbled of her home, her childhood, of Susan, but never of recent events."[64] One morning she called out imperiously for her husband, and when no one could explain where he was, she suddenly fell back, insensible.

> From this time she began to recover, as it were in fragments, her memory of the tragic past. For awhile she lost today such remembrances as yesterday had brought. A little later, the storm which had left her nervous system shattered passed away, and she began to piece together her recovered recollections.[65]

Nine weeks after her collapse Constance was quite recovered in mind, but still weak and wasted physically. It was then she learned for the first time that she had lost her child, and that Greyhurst had been tried and declared not guilty.

Upon hearing this news she decided at once what she would do, but concealed her thoughts from others. "I do not wish to die," she told her doctor. "I want to live." And she determined to get well.[66] She explained her new motive in life, revenge against Greyhurst, to no one except her gardener:

62 *Ibid.*, p. 229.
63 *Ibid.*, p. 230.
64 *Ibid.*, p. 230.
65 *Ibid.*, p. 231.
66 *Ibid.*, p. 233.

I want that man to suffer. I want him to suffer every day, every night, till he curses the day he was born. I don't want him to die, Tom; not yet—no, not yet."[67]

Mitchell was well aware that the intention of Constance was unusual. He made clear, through the reactions of the other characters, that most people in the same situation would have behaved differently. Not only were her intentions unusual, but there was, too, an important change in her physical condition, which we learn of through a letter of Susan's written while the sisters were in Europe:

Constance was, apparently, well again, but still thin and without a trace of her lovely coloring. The doctors said it was anemia, but one in Milan insisted that it was not want of blood, but some change in the nervous system. He had seen such cases and said that she would always be pale.[68]

The "doctor in Milan," of course, really represented Mitchell. The prediction that Constance would always be pale proved correct, for she remained pale as well as thin to the very end of the story. The psychological change had produced the physiological condition. The mind and body were one. The emotions, acting through the nervous system, had caused the anemia and loss of weight. Constance illustrated clearly some of the principles Mitchell had described in his medical writings.[69]

The course of revenge Constance undertook was the result not only of her passionate nature and her tendency to be dominated by primitive instincts, but also of her moral outlook. In this crisis she had no spiritual creed to which she could turn for comfort; in fact she would not even permit Susan to speak of religion. As a substitute for the comforts she might have found in religion she chose a harsher way, revenge—a decision which proved crucial. Even after the death of her husband, she repressed all her emotions except feelings of

[67] *Ibid.*, p. 238.
[68] *Ibid.*, p. 242.
[69] See Chapter IV of this present work.

revenge. Mitchell described in some detail one of the few times she was overcome by any other feeling. It was a year after the death of her husband, when she had just returned to St. Ann and to the house where she had lived. Amid the familiar surroundings, the old associations with her husband, she sat down and "for the first time in months broke into a passion of tears."[70] Utilizing his medical background, Mitchell described her futile efforts to recall the image of her husband's face, her longing to see him again as he was in life:

> The longing seemed to affect her whole strong young body, so that she felt her heart beat in her neck and down to her finger-ends.
> Suddenly she swayed to one side. She sat up, alarmed. A slight, abrupt sense of weakness, of want of control over her muscles, announced that to indulge in the remembrance of hours of passionate love, or of joyous comradeship, was perilous to such absolute self-command as she well knew she should need.[71]

By having Constance recall the warning of Dr. Eskridge, Mitchell was able to insert again his own remarks:

> He had said that to give way to emotion would for a long time to come be likely to bring about a fresh attack of loss of self-command.[72]

Bearing in mind the doctor's words, Constance determined to keep control of herself and to maintain her power to reason calmly. She went to bed and, after a deep sleep, awoke the next morning unrefreshed. Certainly she was troubled by her hatred of Greyhurst, and was losing her peace of mind; but, Mitchell implied, she might have fared even worse, for the shock of her husband's death might have produced an even more harmful reaction than her obsession with revenge: her "unsatisfied desire to make her husband's murderer atone in

70 *Ibid.*, p. 249.
71 *Ibid.*, p. 250.
72 *Ibid.*, p. 251.

suffering took the place of a more perilous form of mental activity."[73]

For awhile the reader may wonder just what was this "more perilous" activity, for he gets no outright explanation. He may recall, however, Susan's statement that were she Constance she would not care to live. He may recall, too, that Constance herself desired to live for only one purpose, revenge. Certainly the conclusion seems clear: revenge gave Constance her sole motive for living. The conclusion becomes even more apparent later when Constance declares that for a time she thought of suicide.[74] Thus Mitchell, in spite of his disapproval of her course of action, was still able to point out that it had its positive aspect, that it protected her from possible suicide.

For a moment only, Constance hesitated in her resolve to punish Greyhurst. Her husband, she knew, would have urged her to forgive, but the demands of her own nature were too strong. Everyone she knew tried to dissuade her from her obsession, but where the memory of her husband had failed no person could succeed. Mrs. Averil pleaded as a Christian: revenge was not only useless, but wicked. The reply of Constance was brief: "I am not a Christian."[75] A short while later, in speaking to her sister, she added, "I have no beliefs which teach me to sit down and cry and pretend to forgive."[76]

Having set her course, Constance pursued it with persistence and ingenuity. She directed that the tombstone over her husband's grave carry the inscription "Murdered on October 9, 1870, in St. Ann" (the order was refused) ; whenever she met Greyhurst she did not turn away as other women might have done, but looked straight at him with undisguised hatred; she sent him the telegram her husband had received the day of his death, spotted with blood from the fatal wound and with it enclosed a note on mourning-paper. "The enclosed

73 *Ibid.*, p. 251.
74 *Ibid.*, p. 279.
75 *Ibid.*, p. 257.
76 *Ibid.*, p. 280.

telegram was in the hand of the man you murdered at the moment he was going toward you to offer, as before he had no power to do, a friendly, and even generous, division of the lands at the bend. His blood is on it, as I trust it may rest on your own soul."[77]

She gave funds to a charity, and got Greyhurst's name erased from the board of managers; she sent him other notes, like the first, and with further evidence of her husband's generosity; she followed him, at times, at a distance as he walked along the street, making him feel her hate behind him at every step; she stood in his audience when he attempted a political speech, disturbing him with her presence; she overpaid for land near his in order to reduce the value of his holdings and ruin him financially; and finally, when she learned he was to be engaged, she wrote a bitter letter to the lady, describing Greyhurst as the cold-blooded murderer of her crippled husband.

Pursuing her revenge with such single-minded devotion was a great strain, and Constance felt obliged to seek the services of Dr. Eskridge. She spoke to him freely, giving way to her pent-up feelings. "We must confess to some one," commented Mitchell, "priest, or, better, to the large, wise charity of the doctor. It was a relief to the woman, who was indisposed to talk of her husband even to Susan."[78] The doctor, urging Constance to give up her obsession, explained that it was bad for both her physical and mental health:

> . . . . you are doing that which will surely end in ruining your health and making you useless. . . . The steady thinking on anything that involves emotion is full of peril to a woman like you; in fact, to any one, man or woman.[79]

Finding he could not change Constance, Dr. Eskridge did not become angry, but took the objective view so characteristic of Mitchell, free of praise or blame:

[77] *Ibid.*, p. 260. For a description of Greyhurst's reaction to Constance's campaign of revenge see pp. 174-177 of the present work.

[78] *Ibid.*, p. 288.

[79] *Ibid.*, pp. 289, 291.

I do not blame you. I shall say no more. I had far rather you left vengeance to Him who soon or late is sure to punish as man cannot. I see that I, at least, am unable to convince you. But take care; you are on a dark and dangerous way.[80]

Not long after this interview, Constance had reason to recall the doctor's warning. Grief overcame her one day in her husband's study, a room she kept just as it had been during his life, except now she secluded it from all but herself:

The room was full of him. She walked about, thinking of her dead, and, then, with another thrill of anguish, of the lost child. "And you would have had me forgive!" she cried. "Oh, George, George, how can I! You are dead; I shall see you no more. My baby is dead—and I am dead, too—oh, dead to love, to joy! And it gets worse and not better."
She sat down and rocked back and forward, clasping her head. "Perhaps to die were better." Her face twitched around the mouth, her jaw stiffened, and she recalled again the doctor's warning. Even the luxury of self-abandonment to lonely grief was not for her. She controlled herself, but not readily.[81]

As the doctor had warned, her too steady preoccupation with thoughts that involved emotion was wearing her down.

However, she continued thinking with "too habitual intensity" about her husband's death and revenge against Greyhurst until she lost all interest in books, flowers and all that had ever attracted her attention. All joy went out of her life; even her satisfaction from the misery she inflicted on Greyhurst was "not such as she had expected."[82] At last she experienced a rare moment of hesitation, but it disappeared at once. Her "obsession rose again dominant, and deprived her of liberty to reflect or to marshall the forces of reason."[83]

Under the pressure of her obsession Constance changed so definitely that Susan, too, observed the changes:

80 *Ibid.,* p. 292.
81 *Ibid.,* pp. 310-311.
82 *Ibid.,* p. 333.
83 *Ibid.,* p. 334.

In fact, my sister never was a great reader; and now she is too uneasy, too restless-minded, to sit down to a book. . . . My sister is evidently failing in health. She is becoming more and more silent, and she is gradually losing interest in the charitable work she did so well.[84]

Occasionally Mitchell made his own undisguised comments on the changes occurring in Constance as the result of her single-minded devotion to revenge.

It had become so despotic in its rule as to make all else secondary in value, and, as is the case with the domination of a fixed idea, to impair, in time, the competence of will and of reason. Thought is then emotionally disturbed, and, soon or late, mere indecision and indefinite craving replace resolute and well-considered plans of action. Constance was near the verge of such a condition, but still far enough away to feel alarmed at her lessened efficiency. She was irritable, spent more time alone, rode less frequently, and became indifferent as regarded her charities. . . . The pale face was thinner, the set look, as she stood at times listless and unoccupied, more intense.[85]

Eventually this too intense thinking brought on emotion, brought before her, unbearably vivid, the scene of her husband's murder:

Suddenly, as she sat down, she saw with vividness the man with the revolver, the little haze of smoke rising as he stood, the dead man, the dearly loved face, the crowd. She caught her head in her hands, clutching it in the agony of a hysterical vision which reproduced the anguish of life's darkest hour. Her hair fell about her, over the black dress. She staggered to her feet, and, swaying, dropped to the floor.[86]

In a day or two she quite recovered, "strangely eased by this riotous outbreak of emotion."[87]

The climax came at last, brought on by Greyhurst, who could endure no more. When Constance succeeded in break-

84 *Ibid.*, pp. 335-336.
85 *Ibid.*, pp. 340-341.
86 *Ibid.*, p. 348.
87 *Ibid.*, p. 349.

ing the marriage he had hoped for, he came to her house, gun in hand, and pointed it straight at her. She stood motionless. "Thank you," she said "I am glad—glad to die!"[88] Greyhurst laughed, called her a fool, and fired the gun at his own temple. When Constance realized he was dead, she showed no satisfaction whatever. "Take him away!" she cried and fell onto the lounge, dazed.

Constance was in the same situation, essentially, as Chillingworth in Hawthorne's *The Scarlet Letter*. Like him she had lived for but one purpose, revenge, and now that her victim, like his, was destroyed, there was nothing left to do. Chillingworth, deprived of "the very principle of his life," shriveled away "like an uprooted weed."[89] But Constance lived on, and we get a full view of her after the climax. Hawthorne dismissed his burned-out Chillingworth, but Mitchell had seen too many women disabled by the strains of life and could hardly resist presenting a picture of a condition he knew so well. He was not content merely to indicate the future semi-invalid condition of Constance, but prolonged the story past its climax in order to represent that condition.

When Constance awoke from her daze a few hours after the suicide of Greyhurst, she seemed to have but one thought: was the body removed? Assured that it was, she seemed to be at ease. "Although her mind was clear," wrote Mitchell, "she spoke little, and was apparently indifferent to everything."[90] For a month she remained apathetic, steadily losing weight and strength. Then she began to recover, but only to a limited degree, never becoming the energetic woman she once had been. She became, in fact, a creature very similar to Octopia Darnell, the couch-loving invalid in *Roland Blake*. Just as Octopia made demands upon her young cousin for attention, sympathy, affection, so now Constance turned to Susan. Like Octopia she seemed unaware of her own selfishness, and overestimated the affection she herself gave. Susan, in turn, was in

88 *Ibid.*, p. 378.
89 Nathaniel Hawthorne, *The Scarlet Letter* (New York, 1946), p. 250.
90 S. Weir Mitchell, *Constance Trescot*, p. 380.

the same unfortunate position as Olivia had been. Like Octopia's victim, she, too, found it hard to escape the greedy affection which permitted her no time of her own, cut down her independence and endangered her health. Mitchell analyzed the change that had occurred in Constance:

> As she slowly regained her strength she turned anew to Susan for the only society she cared to have, and by degrees taxed more and more heavily the time and attention of the self-sacrificing sister. She began at last to read, or liked better to be read to; but never returned to her music, and never spoke of the Averills. . . . Neither did she ever mention George Trescot. So long as she had been actively employed in thinking of means of ruining Greyhurst, she had asked of Susan no more attention and care than was easy and pleasant to give. When once her pursuit had ended, and one dominating idea had ceased to occupy her mind, she began to enlarge the boundaries of those despotic claims which the feeble or suffering sometimes make upon the unselfish.[91]

In his practice as a doctor Mitchell had himself often been frustrated by just such patients as Octopia and Constance. He had stood helplessly by, as described in his medical writings,[92] while such patients, indulging themselves, ruined the too-sympathetic relatives or nurses who attended them. But in his fiction he was free to treat these hysterically ill women, these semi-invalids, as he felt they deserved. Susan, like Olivia, rebelled against the demands of her oppressor. She saw only too well how she could ruin her own health in attempting to serve her sister's real and fancied needs:

> As the warm summer days came and went, Susan was made to feel more and more plainly that she was becoming the slave of exactions which had in them something morbid. To her alarm, she began also to suspect that incessant care of a depressed and too dependent woman might prove to be a dangerous tax on health, and recognized at last with some alarm that she herself was consciously losing vigor. . . .
> By degrees Susan also learned that Constance relied on

91 *Ibid.*, pp. 380-381.
92 See Chapter IV of the present work.

her misfortunes and her long illness to insure to her an excess of sympathetic affection and unremitting service. The discoveries thus made troubled the less selfish sister, and her good sense made plain to her that to permit limitless use of this form of devotion was to commit suicide of health and to sacrifice more than herself.[93]

Though Constance never suspected it, Susan was interested in a certain young man and resolved that her future with him was not to be sacrificed. At last she informed Constance of her engagement to Reginald Kent. "It is simply out of the question," cried Constance. "You must see that your duty lies with me. . . . I will never consent to it. Must I always be sacrificed?"[94]

Her plea was useless. Susan explained that it was beyond her powers to do what Constance wished. ". . . .you need more than I can give," explained Susan. "I mean to marry Reginald Kent."[95] For Constance there was nothing to do but look elsewhere for adjustment.

The story of Constance, with so much of Mitchell's understanding and effort in it, made a strong impression upon many of its readers. Before the book was ever published the poet R. W. Gilder, working as reader for the Century Company, wrote a glowing tribute to the publishers:

> I have re-read Constance Trescot—with my heart in my throat. It is a remarkable book—unique—a masterpiece by a literary artist who is also a "wise physician" and a psychological expert. It touches on the deep things of life. . . . The book is successively and progressively painful. It marches to its doom with trembling.[96]

With all its merits, however, the story of Constance has some serious shortcomings as a psychological study. Mitchell presented one major set of causes, the emotional shocks to which Constance was subjected, and their major result, her

93 *Ibid.*, pp. 381-382.
94 *Ibid.*, p. 384.
95 *Ibid.*, p. 384.
96 This unpublished letter, dated October 5, 1904, is in the library of the University of Pennsylvania.

hysterical, semi-invalid behavior. He presented the causes of a process and its final outcome, but he quite neglected the process itself; he gave us the beginning and the end of the psychological story concerning the transformation of Constance, but hardly the story itself. He did not recreate her thoughts and feelings as she suffered the change, nor did he show the particular path that she took to her ultimate condition. In general, emotional shocks can lead to all sorts of results, as Mitchell well knew, and as he pictured in his medical writings: spasms, aphonia, circulatory disorders and a variety of other symptoms. Constance gave way under the impact of events, but why did her distortion take the particular form it took, instead of some other form? That type of question Mitchell did not answer in his medical writings,[97] and he did not answer it in this fictional portrait of Constance. The shortcomings he revealed as a doctor analyzing disordered personalities he inevitably revealed in his novels, as in this portrait.

While shrewd insight and careful observation went into the making of Constance, she was, like Octopia, seen from the outside, understood as a skilled doctor might understand her—in some ways better than she could understand herself—but not with the same intimate knowledge. Mitchell's experience with such women was evidently limited. It seems he had few opportunities to observe them in their everyday affairs while they were becoming couch-loving invalids, and in his novels he made little effort to reconstruct the process. In the study of Constance we hardly see the invalidism coming on, but receive, at most, some statements by the author hinting at the condition to come. Suddenly at the end, the hysterical illness appears, quite developed, a transformation that seems to have occurred while the reader wasn't looking.

While Constance is Mitchell's most ambitious portrait, Oc-

---

[97] Modern psychiatrists frequently attempt to explain, in discussing a hysterically ill patient, just how the particular symptoms are related to the psychological background. See, for example, Samuel W. Hartwell, *Practical Psychiatry and Mental Hygiene* (New York, 1947), pp. 305-310.

topia is perhaps his most successful one. In Octopia he gave a more detailed portrait than anywhere else of the kind of woman he knew so well, the hysterically ill female. He never presented her before her illness and therefore was saved the problem of delineating the process of change. In Constance he began at an earlier stage and thus set himself a task which he did not adequately perform.

ANN PENHALLOW

Ann Penhallow, one of the chief characters in Mitchell's last novel, *Westways,* was an exceptionally fine woman, generous, kind, courageous, attractive in almost every way. Yet she became hysterically ill, at one time so ill she was confined to her bed for a month, grew thin and pale, and for brief intervals lost her sanity. She had one weakness which made her susceptible to the causes which combined to break her down: she had been spoiled by her husband, had been given her own way all too often.

Her husband, James, the wealthy owner of the estate where they lived, adored his wife too much to cross her. But he was a Northerner, sharing the outlook of the North, while she had come from the South and believed in slavery. As the Civil War approached, it put a strain upon their relationship; but they loved one another too much to quarrel over their differences, and refrained from discussing them. This repression of sentiment was unhealthy and played its part in the future illness of Ann.

The dissensions of the coming war put pressure upon Ann in other ways, too. She became involved, through no choice of her own, in the escape of a fugitive slave, an episode which proved an emotional strain not only because it was exciting, but because it tested so severely the creed in which she had been reared. There was in the town a Negro barber, Josiah, who had served Ann and her family in many ways, and had once injured himself saving her niece from a runaway horse. Learning that his master was about to discover him, and fearing that he would be punished for his escape, she sent word to him, and even signed a check so that he could get his life-savings from the bank before he ran out of town.

As a result of this episode Ann's health began to deteriorate. She slept badly, tired easily, became irritable and often lacking in her usual good sense. But the pressures of the times continued, and she was soon hurt again. One of her two brothers, Charles, deserted his ancestral creed and came out for the Republicans, and now neither brother would speak to the other. After that Ann could be seen at times with tears in her eyes—a rarity for her—and at other times she spoke sharply to her husband against the North. Once after such an outburst, so unjust she herself could see how wrong she was, she asked him to forgive her and laughed "half-hysterically."

When the war broke out, the strains increased. Young John Penhallow, their nephew who had been living with them, went off to the army of the North, and Ann feared that James too would soon be going. It had been hard enough before, with her brothers on opposite sides in this bloody struggle. So obsessed did Ann become with her new worries that she lost all interest in matters which ordinarily would have engrossed her. Even the imminent bankruptcy of her husband's mill—as a result of the war—failed to stir her interest. Not daring to talk to her husband about the war, she did not talk at all. She went about her household duties, while her repressed sentiments raged silently.

Her husband came to her one day with what he thought was good news. His financial worries were over. He had received a government contract to manufacture cannon. When he announced this news to her, her whole manner changed:

"And you—you are to make cannon—you—and I—and with my money!" she laughed hysterical laughter—"to kill my people the North has robbed and driven into war and insulted for years—I—I—" her voice broke—she stood speechless, pale and more pale.[98]

[98] S. Weir Mitchell, *Westways* (New York, 1914), p. 310.

Within a few moments this fit of hysterics had sent her into a faint.

When Ann awoke the next morning, after a night of deep sleep, she was still definitely ill. When she recollected the events of the day before she poured forth her feelings to her niece, who was at her beside.

> She broke into unnaturally rapid speech, reddening darkly, with ominous dilation of the pupils of her large blue eyes. "And so James Penhallow is to be made rich by making cannon to kill my people. . . . And with my money— it is easy to stay at home and murder—and be paid for it. Let him go and—fight. . . .
> Oh, those cannon! I hear them. He shall not do it—do you hear me? Now send me up a cup of tea—and don't come in again. I want James—tell him—tell him."[99]

How far Ann was carried by her hysteria may be indicated when one recalls that her most constant fear, which helped break her down, was the very thing that she was now perversely crying for, her husband's going away to war. Ann became so ill that for a whole month she did not leave her room.

Just what were the causes which brought on so severe an attack? In a number of passages Mitchell supplied hints and explanations. Dr. McGregor explained to Penhallow's niece some of the background causes:

> She had been living of late a life of unwholesome suppression. She has been alarmed by Penhallow's looks, hurt by her brothers' quarrels, and heartsick about the war and John. Then your uncle springs on her this contract business and there is an explosion.[100]

The immediate cause was, of course, a very strong one. Her husband was doing something which she most deeply desired

---

[99] *Ibid.,* p. 313.

[100] *Ibid.,* p. 314. In one of his letters to Mrs. Mason, Mitchell indicated that Ann's life had been too smooth to prepare her for the pressures she was now subjected to. He called her illness "the psychic disaster of a noble woman too hardly beset by cruel fate and a life without previous trials." A copy of the unpublished letter, dated March 30, 1913, is in the possession of Mrs. S. W. Macdonough.

that he should not do. How could she stop him from the out-rageous act? He himself seemed so happy over the contract. It meant so much to him, the difference between the loss of all he owned and prosperity. Mitchell implied that Ann was un-consciously using hysteria as a means of getting her way. Ann had been accustomed to obedience from her husband and this had spoiled her. "To the end of his days," Mitchell wrote of James, "he never suspected that to have been less the lover and more the clear-sighted outspoken friend would have been better for her and for him."[101] Dr. McGregor, understanding the situation clearly, and realizing how tempted James would be to yield now to his hysterically-ill wife, tried to put him on his guard. "Have no alarm about her health, my friend. It is only the hysteria of a woman a little spoiled by too tender in-dulgence."[102] He advised James to take Ann's share of the stock out of the business, but to yield no further than that. "What else you do," he added, "depends on her condition of mind and the extent to which you are willing to give way be-fore the persistency of a woman who feels and does not or can not reason."[103]

Mitchell was always ready to take up the challenge of a hysterical woman and defeat her at her own game. In the per-son of McGregor he again marshalled all available forces against the willful sick woman. McGregor not only encour-aged James to resist but, following the principles explained in Mitchell's medical writings, he ordered that the patient be quite isolated from too much sympathy. In spite of the fact that Mrs. Penhallow cried for her husband—no doubt to win her way by an appeal to his sentiments—indeed, *because* she cried for her husband, Dr. McGregor ordered James to keep away from her.

James Penhallow did keep away from his wife during the following weeks, and was thus "mercifully spared the sight of the drama of hysteria." It might be added that, unfor-

101 *Ibid.*, p. 311.
102 *Ibid.*, p. 311.
103 *Ibid.*, p. 312.

tunately, the reader too, sees little of this drama. After several weeks of this rest and relative isolation, Ann grew better, and Dr. McGregor permitted James to visit her. "Now Squire," he said, "you will be shocked at her appearance, but she is really well in body, and this thing has got to be set at rest. She talks of it incessantly."[104]

Even before the visit, however, Ann had won her battle. The thought alone of his sick wife, without the appeal of her wasted face or her words of entreaty, was enough to sway James Penhallow. He would give up his mill and the manufacturing of weapons for the North. He would do anything to set his wife at ease. "I shall end by accepting a command," he told his niece. "Now since her reproach I shall feel that war offers the bribe of ease and relief from care." Thus did James's own inclination to go to war reinforce his decision to yield to his wife. "Now I ought to thank Ann for making me see what I ought to do," he added.[105] His one worry, as he entered the room, was how to tell her that he had yielded completely, that he himself was going to become a soldier in the war. He determined to withhold that news until she was improved in health.

James walked into the dimly lighted room and tried at once to make the sick woman feel better. "I want to say to you, Ann, that having your power of attorney, I have withdrawn your fifty thousand dollars you had lent to the mills."[106] "And you are going on with the business?" Ann's voice rose as she asked this crucial question. She had unconsciously become ill in order to get the right answer to just that question. Would she have to remain ill, maybe even get worse, or could she, having won her point, continue the road to recovery? His answer would tell. But James, not daring now to inform her of his plans to join the army, refused to answer. "We will talk of that later, Ann. I was told not to let you talk long." But Ann was not to be put aside. "Do you think me unreasonable,

104 *Ibid.*, p. 317.
105 *Ibid.*, pp. 316-317.
106 *Ibid.*, p. 317.

James?" When he replied in the affirmative she looked up at him with her "great blue eyes . . . . in dumb appeal." Then she spoke, with a threat lurking behind her sweet voice, "Won't you think a little of how I feel—and—and shall feel?" When he hesitated, she spoke her threat more plainly. "It is a pity I did not die. . . . That would have saved you all this trouble."[107] He broke away and left the room, her plea unanswered.

Just what happened to Ann after that scene Mitchell failed to describe. We get no real picture of her psychological development following this meeting with her husband. What we do obtain are bits here and there which fail to achieve a complete picture. We learn that James continued to see her. What he said, what passed between them we are not told, except that he made no direct statement about his plans to give up the mills. Ann, however, continued to improve in health. She "ceased to dwell on the matter which had so disturbed her, and rapidly regaining health, flesh and strength, began to ask about the house and the village people."[108] Apparently she understood from her husband's manner that his solicitude was great, and that he would deny her nothing.

When finally James felt that Ann was strong enough, he told her of his decision. She accepted it bravely enough, but showed little understanding of the sacrifice he had made for her. It was largely to please her that he had sold his share of the mill at great financial loss. But so spoiled was she that it did not occur to her to consider what it had cost him to yield to her wishes.

After James volunteered for war duty and went away, Ann's health became again dangerously unsteady. The strains of the war, her worries over the men she loved, and over their opposing roles, combined to make things difficult. Once when Ann, with her niece Leila, heard some guns being tested, she became so startled Leila warned her, "Do be careful—you are

107 *Ibid.*, pp. 317-318.
108 *Ibid.*, p. 319.

getting . . . . hysterical."[109] This, commented Mitchell, was an effective warning:

> She could have applied no wiser remedy than her warning advice. No woman likes to be told she is nervous or hysterical and now it acted with the certainty of a charm. . . .
> She [Ann] had been scared at her own realization of her want of self-government and was once more in command of her emotions.[110]

Paradoxically, what really worked Ann out of her developing hysterical illness was another blow. When she received word that her husband was returning home wounded, instead of breaking down, she rose to the occasion. This was a blow not to be endured in helpless frustration, but requiring action. There were things to be done to prepare the household for James' homecoming. Like Octopia Darnell, who rose to accept a challenge, so now did Ann Penhallow. Until this challenge Ann had been steadily growing worse. She had allowed the management of her household to slip from her hands, had lost interest in all the duties that once absorbed her attention, and had lapsed into a weakness of mind and body. Mitchell commented in his own person upon the sudden change which came over her when she learned her husband had been wounded and was to return:

> Every physician of large experience must have seen cases of self-created, unresisted invalidism end with mysterious abruptness and the return of mental, moral and physical competence, under the influence of some call upon their sense of duty made by calamity, such as an acute illness in the household, financial ruin, or the death of a husband. The return of a wounded man and the need to care for him acted thus upon Ann Penhallow. . . . Like the pine-tree winning vigour from its rock-clasped roots, she gathered such hardening strength of soul and body from his condition as the more happy years had never put at her command.[111]

109 *Ibid.*, p. 361.
110 *Ibid.*, p. 361.
111 *Ibid.*, p. 387, p. 395.

So much did Ann change as a result of the new situation, that she not only surrendered her own willfulness, but she humored her husband "as she would a sick child."[112] When finally, against her opposition, he was operated on and cured of the brain injury which had impaired his mind, she saw her own willfulness more clearly than ever. "God forgive me," she exclaimed, "I have been a fool!"[113] With the causes that made her a hysterical invalid removed, and motives to wholesome behavior supplied, she gave up her hysteria and became a sound personality.

The portraits of Ann Penhallow, Octopia Darnell, and Constance Trescot are based in large part upon Mitchell's own psychiatric research and medical experience, and illustrate clearly principles described in his medical writing. In all three instances he exposed the subtle and often unconscious artifices of hysterically ill women. He revealed the relationships between their ill health and their wishes. He showed under what circumstances their hysteria flourished and under what circumstances they surrendered it to accept the responsibilities of honest adjustment. Certainly these women illustrate vividly some of the less obvious mechanisms of human behavior. In portraying them as well as he did Mitchell achieved something new in American literature.

112 *Ibid.*, p. 455.
113 *Ibid.*, p. 486.

Chapter VIII

DUAL PERSONALITY

MARY REYNOLDS

IN 1886 Robert Louis Stevenson published *The Strange Case of Dr. Jekyll and Mr. Hyde*. The story, of course, had never happened, never could have happened. The complete transformation in appearance that occurred when Dr. Jekyll became Mr. Hyde and vice versa was something outside nature. In spite of its impossible elements, however, the story did point to the strange psychological fact of dual personality.

Mitchell, too, was interested in this phenomenon. He wrote at some length upon the subject three separate times, once in a scientific paper, and twice later in fiction. While he never invested the subject with the appeal of Stevenson's famous story, he brought to it his own special qualities. His fictional reports as well as his medical one were sound, informative case histories, based on his close observation and his special knowledge.

Mitchell's first treatment of dual personality was a strictly scientific study. Among the papers of his father he had discovered a manuscript concerning the strange case of Mary Reynolds. The case had at one time attracted wide attention, and Mitchell, drawn by the manuscript, decided to look into the matter for himself. He found two nephews of Mary Reynolds still living, and they had considerable knowledge of their aunt, for she had stayed with them during the last twenty-five years of her life. From these nephews Mitchell was able to verify statements already published and to get new facts of his own.

Mary Reynolds provided a very clear example of dual personality. She was "two persons in one body—two distinct lives antipodal from every mental and moral point of view."[1] She had been a melancholy person until one day, when she was eighteen, she woke up as a quite different, cheerful person, unable to remember anything at all about her previous self. In the next several years she reverted back and forth between the two personalities, each one lasting for weeks at a time and having no memory of the other. When she was about thirty-five she reverted permanently, for the last twenty-five years of her life, to her second, cheerful personality. Mitchell summarized her condition during the years of her dual personality:

> The two lives which Mary Reynolds lived for many years were thus entirely separate; each was complete in itself, the fragments of which it was composed, though in reality separated by the portions of the other life intervening, sustained a due relation. Each state had its mental accumulations. The thoughts and feelings, the likes and dislikes, of the one state did not in any way influence or modify those of the other. . . .[2]

While Mitchell did not describe the cause of Mary Reynolds' condition, he did give some clues, particularly when he quoted her own words indicating how unhappy she had felt in her natural, original state. On one occasion, finding herself returned to that state, she described the change as a downfall "from the height of happiness into these nocturnal regions, where nought but sullen silence reigns and death-like inactivity slumbers."[3]

The modern psychiatrist regards the second personality as

---

[1] S. Weir Mitchell, *Mary Reynolds: A Case of Double Consciousness* (Philadelphia, 1889), p. 2.

[2] *Ibid.*, p. 14.

[3] *Ibid.*, p. 16. Of course Mary Reynolds could not, in her unhappy state, remember her other personality. Her picture of a contrast had to depend on what others told her of her happy condition.

a refuge from something unbearable to the first. Louis P. Thorpe and Barney Katz, for example, in their recent book on *The Psychology of Abnormal Behavior,* in discussing the cause of dual personality, give the following explanation:

> Unpleasant and painful ideas of guilt or shame are forced below the threshold of consciousness. To permit these ideas to come into consciousness would be distressing to the individual, since they constitute a continual threat to his self-esteem.

In such cases, the authors continue, the "individual flees . . . . to a different personality."[4]

While Mitchell offered no such analysis of Mary Reynolds, and consequently made no effort to discover just what in her original personality she was evading, he still presented some possible clues. He described, for example, the rather curious affection she had, in her new personality, toward her brother John:

> At the time of her first change her brother John was living in Meadville. Hearing of her remarkable condition he visited her at the old homestead. Of course she did not recognize him. But having been told of his relationship to her she soon became warmly attached to him, and her affection grew as he repeated his visits during her continuance in the second state.
> Miss Reynolds became very anxious to visit her brother in Meadville, but her friends did not think it advisable to give her permission.[5]

This affection seems even more worth investigating as one looks further into the case. There is extant an unpublished manuscript, written by one of Mary Reynolds' nephews, which describes an episode between Mary and her brother. In his published accounts Mitchell made no reference to the episode:

> My father used to go frequently to see her, on which oc-

4 Louis P. Thorpe and Barney Katz, *The Psychology of Abnormal Behavior* (New York, 1948) , p. 389.
5 S. W. Mitchell, *Mary Reynolds: A Case of Double Consciousness,* pp. 14-15.

casions he always treated her with the greatest kindness, and studied to please her. . . . In this way he won her friendship. On day, when he visited her, she requested him to walk with her, saying she had something to tell him. He did so. She led the way, along a blind path, some distance, till they came to a log. She then told him to sit down on a certain part of the log which she pointed out; and she herself sat down on another part of the same log. "Brother" said she, and then checking herself, she laughed—and continued—"They say you are my brother, but I know better than that. However, I like you better than I do the rest of the people here, because you are kind to me. . . ."

Then, according to the nephew's account, she told of meeting a lady at the very spot where they were now sitting:

"She sat down where you are now sitting . . . . she talked to me a long time, and was so kind, that I wanted to kiss her, but she would not let me touch her."[6]

This story, apparently, did not seem significant to Mitchell. He not only failed to mention or use it; he offered no explanation based on other facts to account for the strange behavior of Mary Reynolds.

MR. J. C.

A few years after publishing his paper on Mary Reynolds (1888), Mitchell presented a case of dual personality in one of his novels, *Characteristics* (1892). In this fictional portrait he drew very definitely upon the material he had presented in his medical paper. The character afflicted with dual personality occupied no central part in the novel but was rather the chief character in a short story within the novel. *Characteristics,* it should be understood, is a loosely constructed book concerning the versatile Dr. North—obviously based on Mitchell himself —and his cultivated friends. It is not so much their own undramatic actions that provide the interest of the novel, but the

6 The handwritten manuscript is in the Philadelphia College of Physicians.

play of their conversation, and the stories they tell one another. The dual personality was brought into the novel by Frederick Vincent, Dr. North's lawyer friend. A pretty, well-bred lady came to him, Vincent explained, for legal advice concerning her husband, who had suddenly disappeared. At the time of the marriage the husband was thirty, the wife was twenty and, incidentally, very rich. The husband, whom Vincent referred to only by the initials J. C., was "a man of refined and scholarly tastes, a student of Oriental languages."[7] Shortly after the marriage he failed in business, and they retired to their charming home in the country. Here he seemed generally healthy and gay, but subject, at rare intervals, to fits of depression, particularly when he had to be away from his wife and only child. In his youth the man had sometimes walked in his sleep. His father had died early of palsy.

One day J. C.'s wife received a check for twenty thousand dollars and endorsed it to him so that he could go to a nearby city and pay off a debt—the only debt remaining from his business failure. He arrived at the nearby city, wrote his wife that this debt had been the one burden in a life otherwise entirely happy, and then completely disappeared. When, through a coincidence, the woman was able to locate her husband, she found him a quite different person, in fact, the antithesis of what he had been: he was no longer a man of refined tastes and gentle manners, but was slovenly in his dress and morose and abrupt in temper. Replacing the refined wife ten years his junior was a new wife, a rough, uneducated, good-natured woman older than he was. Instead of cultivating his intellectual tastes as a scholar, he worked as a clerk in a dry-goods house and in his spare time frequented taverns.

Dr. North became quite interested in this account and arranged to see this man in Mr. Vincent's office. Under questioning by Mr. Vincent, the man confessed he could remember nothing of his life beyond seven months back. At that time, he said, he must have been sick, for he could not then write his

[7] S. Weir Mitchell, *Characteristics*, p. 142.

name, and when he had tried had written from right to left.
When the Oriental scholar he used to be was described, it
brought no recollection at all; he had never heard of him. No,
he had never heard of Sanscrit either. When his first wife was
brought into the room she too stirred no memory whatever;
he reacted as to a complete stranger. However, the story eventually had a happy ending. The man suddenly returned to his
original personality, forgetting completely the events of the
past several months. He resumed his life as it was before, with
his first wife. The second wife was informed that the man she
considered her husband was disordered in mind and already
married. Given a substantial sum of money, she went her own
way, apparently better off than she had been.

Dr. North, reflecting on this story, classified the case with
the same words used by Mitchell in reference to Mary Reynolds, "double consciousness." What causes this strange behavior? In his study of Mary Reynolds, Mitchell had hardly
attempted to answer this question. He did not then really
know the answer, and in this novel, *Characteristics*, confessed
so:

> Some people explain these strange facts by our having two
> hemispheres in the brain; but the power to write and to
> speak are the function only of the left side of the brain, and
> speech is lost but in part, and writing altogether, or not at
> all in other instances. I see no explanation. Whatever be the
> cause, it is such as may disappear and reappear in a minute.[8]

While Mitchell, in this particular story, was unable to give a
causal explanation of double consciousness, his picture—the
decided contrast between the two personalities—fits the explanation offered by present-day psychiatrists, that the second
personality represents a flight from the first.

SIBYL MAYWOOD

Mitchell's best and most extensive treatment of dual personality is in *Dr. North and His Friends*, a sequel to *Characteristics*.

[8] *Ibid.*, p. 151.

The book contains most of the principal characters of the earlier work, as well as some new characters, and it is planned on the same pattern, episodes concerning Dr. North and his friends as well as the conversations they have with one another. The dual personality is not merely, as in *Characteristics,* the subject of one single episode, but is one of the chief characters, Sibyl Maywood, an important member of the circle of Dr. North's friends. While the interest in this discursive book moves from one subject to another, it always returns to Sibyl. The story of her personality, told though it is with interruptions, dominates the entire book and provides the central interest. Mitchell pictured, often in considerable detail, her deterioration from a quite normal person to a physically anemic young lady afflicted with double consciousness, and he indicated the path of her development back to normal.

At the outset Sibyl had recently arrived from the New England village where her family had been settled for generations. She was slightly deformed. One shoulder was higher than the other and she walked with an obvious halt. But "above this crooked frame rose a head of the utmost beauty."[9] Her hands were graceful and her manner gracious. Particularly remarkable was her voice, which had such a pleasing quality, said Dr. North, that he found it difficult to concentrate on the sense of her words. "I sat reflecting," he continued, "upon the irony of fate which should have forever denied to this voice the privilege of saying to a man, 'Yes, I love you.' "[10] Sibyl was a poor girl, but Mitchell, ever conscious of family position, pointed out that her ancestors had once been rich and socially important. Financial disaster had struck the family generations earlier and, ever since, it had been in modest circumstances. Fresh from this background, Sibyl was quite unaccustomed to such brilliant people as she met in the circle of Dr. North's friends.

Among those in the circle who were to play an important part in her affairs, were Dr. North's wife, Alice; Mr. Vincent and his wife; St. Clair, the poet and sculptor; and Claybourne,

9 S. Weir Mitchell, *Dr. North and His Friends,* p. 42.
10 *Ibid.,* p. 43.

the scholar, who had brought Sibyl into this distinguished company. She was his cousin, come to live in his home and to work as his secretary. In spite of her limited background, she attracted at once the interest of all the circle.

Among those present when Sibyl made her first appearance in the novel was the attractive young bachelor, Victor St. Clair. He was a charming but capricious person, inclined to do as he pleased, yet willing on occasion to be ruled by the combined will of others in the group. He went his own way, for the most part, indulging his likes and dislikes. In his sculpturing he worked as he pleased, with little regard for money or the sentiments of others. When a wealthy business man whom he despised commissioned a bust, he did it—in his own way, bringing out all the mean and brutal qualities he saw, or thought he saw, in the man, sculptoring an indictment; and then, in great glee, he sent it to the man, insisting he wanted no pay for a work he so enjoyed doing. In his relations with the other members of the circle he was usually self-indulgent, though he sometimes showed some respect for their opinions and interests. When he felt like it, he stayed away for long periods and then suddenly appeared as a frequent visitor. His enthusiasms were intense, but often short-lived. He had broken the hearts of many women who had failed to understand him. Attracted by this or that feature in a girl, he would use her as a model, and otherwise devote his attentions to her; then, noticing some imperfection, his interest would suddenly cool, and he would turn elsewhere, leaving the girl to make her own explanations of what had happened.

When he first looked at Sibyl, St. Clair was immediately attracted by her beautiful face and watched it intently, with the interest of an artist in search of a subject. He was doing a vase in illustration of Keats's "Ode to a Grecian Urn," and decided she would be an appropriate model for one of the figures on that vase. His interest was impersonal, merely artistic. To St. Clair "all novel forms of beauty in women or in men caused . . . . uncomplicated, childlike admiration. . . . He was just now filled with admiration of the face and hands of Sibyl Maywood."[11]

After this initial meeting, St. Clair spent much time with Sibyl, read, sang and talked with her, and used her as a model. After completing the vase, he did a pedestal of rose-gray marble, carving in relief, on one side, the portrait of a Greek youth, on the other side, the portrait of Sibyl. When Mrs. Vincent asked why, he explained, "Oh, because her face has, like the girl's face on the vase, a history of joy which can never mature or be more than it is. And then, it is beautiful, and I wanted to do it."[12] Mrs. Vincent was dismayed at this lack of concern for the girl's feelings. How could he so coldly exploit the tragedy of this crippled girl? "It was a great liberty," she told him, "and you put it there because she, too, is never to realize maturity of joy. Incredibly brutal, I call it."[13]

Mitchell emphasized early that there was danger for Sibyl in this new relationship with St. Clair. She was far more susceptible than some of the women he had already left brokenhearted. She was extremely artless and simple, unschooled in the diplomacy of courtship. She would not know how to weigh his light words, nor how to sift admiration from affection. Furthermore, she was emotionally soft. A long time ago she had lost, within a year, father, mother and brother. Her emotional instability was revealed clearly one day when the discussion turned to Tennyson's *In Memoriam*. Out of her own deep grief she spoke impulsively:

> I do not feel in this verse the agony of loss, the death which is many deaths in one, the funeral of countless hopes, of sweet expectations, of—oh, of many things. . . .[14]

Suddenly, as the talk of death and grief continued, Sibyl broke into tears and hysterical laughter.

The girl's stability had been weakened, too, by her physical

11 *Ibid.*, pp. 186-187.
12 *Ibid.*, p. 184.
13 *Ibid.*, p. 185.
14 *Ibid.*, p. 134.

deformity about which she was extremely sensitive. One day when St. Clair displayed his vase, set on a broken-backed kitchen chair, Claybourne scoffed, "It is like putting a beautiful head on a distorted body. . . . The pedestal ruins the vase."[15] Sibyl overheard, and slipped away—to weep alone. Later she confessed to Dr. North, "I am a disabled wreck of a woman; and I must go on and on."[16]

All the ingredients of a tragedy for Sibyl seemed to be present: St. Clair's attractiveness and her susceptibility, his continued attentions, and her obvious response to his appeal. Mrs. Vincent was the first to speak bluntly of the danger, remarking to Dr. North, "I wish St. Clair would keep away from her. It is the old story."[17] North, also aware of the inevitable trend of events, agreed, "The girl will fall in love."[18]

As time went on their fears were confirmed. St. Clair continued to see Sibyl often, and once they came upon him reading poetry to her "with passionate emphasis."[19] Mrs. Vincent became more and more uneasy, and again spoke to Dr. North about Sibyl:

> Do you know that Victor St. Clair . . . . goes almost daily to visit her? He takes her flowers, he reads to her. . . . The only time I have seen him of late he raved about her beauty. . . . This girl is susceptible to passion; she is sensitive to all forms of beauty. . . . She was meant to love and to be loved. . . . How will it end? . . . In a little while St. Clair will drop her as he has done others. . . . Some one must talk to him.[20]

Mrs. Vincent's predictions were apparently coming true; St. Clair was beginning to find fault with Sibyl's beauty, and to lose interest. "The mouth is a trifle too large. It is too expressive," he said.[21] Urged by Dr. North and by Mrs. Vincent, he

15 *Ibid.*, p. 74.
16 *Ibid.*, p. 145.
17 *Ibid.*, p. 76.
18 *Ibid.*, p. 77.
19 *Ibid.*, p. 181.
20 *Ibid.*, p. 189.
21 *Ibid.*, p. 190.

went away, and wrote a note to Sibyl saying he had an errand in the South.

As a result, the young lady was suddenly faced with a very disturbing situation. The frequent visits by St. Clair, the admiration and the attentions were abruptly ended—and in their place was only a brief note of explanation, with no assurance or even indication that the relationship would continue where it had left off. Sibyl, artless and inexperienced, had not measured his attentions accurately. Without any sound evidence of his feelings, she had surrendered her own.

Mitchell presented no picture of her problems at this stage, but the inference can be drawn plainly enough. She had endured a shocking rebuff. What could she do about it? She was unable to face the harsh, unpleasant fact—and live it down, unable to admit to herself and to others that she had given her love where it was not wanted. In Mitchell's previous case studies—both literary and medical—this inability to face the realities of one's own life was often a first step to mental disorder. Sibyl was now driven toward the psychological mechanisms of evasion. She had to live with a cruel fact without admitting its existence.

When she next appeared in the story, several weeks after St. Clair had returned, she seemed tired, ill. "I came upon her in my drawing room yesterday," Mrs. Vincent reported, "looking at St. Clair's photograph. She put it down hastily and took up another."[22] Dr. North, to whom Mrs. Vincent reported this observation, realized its significance, but they feared they were already too late to help. Soon another incident occurred which confirmed their fears. One evening at a gathering of Dr. North and his friends, Sibyl again met St. Clair. She showed less warmth and sympathy toward him than formerly—until the subject of Keats's vase came up. Apparently, although Mitchell did not say so, this vase brought back the old associations, and Sibyl became unguarded in her reactions toward St. Clair. When he broke into a song which they had once

22 *Ibid.*, p. 200.

sung together she joined with him, becoming eager and impetuous like a child. "We must sing, now, 'The Holy Hour,'" she exclaimed. "Sing it; I want it now, at once."[23] She spoke with assurance, trust, and with an easy use of the imperative mood. When St. Clair, obedient, sang the song, she became strangely silent and then, before it was finished, disappeared into the house. When she came down again, she started walking slowly toward St. Clair. Dr. North called her name, but she did not hear. He called again and still again, but she failed to hear, and when he walked toward her she seemed not to notice him at all. By this time they were near St. Clair, and Dr. North took her arm. "Where am I?" she asked, obviously in a trance, and then in a low voice of ecstasy continued, "My love, I am coming, coming." Instantly she became rigid from head to foot and Dr. North caught her falling form. She had fainted.

The next morning, though she was weak, her mind was clear. However, she was "quite unable to recall this unpleasant little drama."[24] What had happened to Sibyl? Mitchell merely described the "little drama" and made no effort, at the time, to analyze it. But the inferences to be drawn are plain enough. Sibyl, before this episode, had suppressed her feelings toward St. Clair, and had acted in the proper manner toward a young man who was merely a casual friend. She had lived with her rebuff by ignoring its existence, at least in her outward behavior. But her feelings were too strong to be suppressed, particularly when they were encouraged by the presence of St. Clair and the old associations, the vase, the garden, and his singing again the songs they had sung together in happier days.

Mitchell's description of Sibyl's sleepwalking, it might be added, was certainly in keeping with fact as well as with present-day interpretations. "The acts which the somnambulist carries out in his dream-like state," declare Thorpe and Katz, "are ordinarily those which he desires to do in the wak-

23 *Ibid.*, p. 206.
24 *Ibid.*, p. 209.

ing state but which he fears or dreads."[25] The relevance to Sibyl is obvious.

The artist, troubled by Sibyl's all too significant behavior, went away for the next few months, distressed as he had never been before and blaming his own folly. With St. Clair away, she showed definite improvement in health and self-control; in fact, she seemed to improve almost too quickly and completely. References to St. Clair apparently caused her no uneasiness or embarrassment. She spoke of him as any of the others might have, "tranquilly," and "without trace of emotion."[26] Mrs. North, puzzled by the remarkable recovery, had a long talk with Sibyl, but came away reassured, as she reported to her husband: "She likes St. Clair, but I am sure she has not lost her heart. She discussed him quite coldly. . . . She does not love him, Owen, I am sure of that." Dr. North, however, was not so certain. How explain that sleepwalking scene in the garden? "In some way he disturbs her, but whether consciously to her or not I cannot say."[27]

Mrs. North then hit upon the explanation which reconciled the contradiction, which accounted for Sibyl's expressions of love for St. Clair as in the garden scene, and for her apparent indifference to him in her more normal behavior. "If Sibyl were two people," she said, "I could comprehend it." Dr. North felt immediately the truth of this observation. "I had seen enough of the double consciousness of some hysterias," he explained, "to feel no surprise at this flash of feminine insight."[28]

When after some months St. Clair returned, Sibyl seemed to meet the challenge well, and neither sought nor shunned him. But Dr. North, who observed her closely, felt cause for uneasiness. She became often too self-absorbed, or too silent. Though she seemed to be making no apparent reaction to the presence of St. Clair, Dr. North had his doubts, and began to suspect that the artist's "mere presence affected her without her being

25 Thorpe and Katz, *op. cit.,* p. 385.
26 S. Weir Mitchell, *Dr. North and His Friends,* p. 213.
27 *Ibid.,* p. 213.
28 *Ibid.,* p. 213.

consciously aware of it."[29] All doubt soon disappeared, for the presence of St. Clair eventually brought on another clear manifestation of Sibyl's alternate consciousness, as in the earlier garden scene. It happened one evening some weeks later when St. Clair, Sibyl, Dr. North and the others were present. Sibyl, as usual, went upstairs to bed at nine, for Dr. North had prescribed regular, early retirement. The artist, after that, went to the piano and sang, as he often did.

The next morning Sibyl was decidedly unwell. Called to her room, Dr. North noticed there was candle grease on her gown. He found, too, that there was candle grease on the stairs. Although she thought she had gone to sleep at once he understood just what had occurred: Sibyl had come half-way down the stairs—unobserved—and heard St. Clair as he sang to the others. She had done this, not deliberately and knowingly, but in an abnormal state, in a "condition of somnambulism, or double consciousness."[30] Although she had heard St. Clair sing, she had no conscious recollection of it. "I was driven to the conclusion," said Dr. North, "that this woman had ceased to love St. Clair. . . . but that in some state of unresisting dual consciousness she was the victim of an overmastering passion."[31] In brief, her conscious personality did not love him, but some part of her personality did.

At this point Mitchell took occasion to disparage the too easy diagnoses of doctors confronted by such cases as Sibyl's. He brought into the story a Dr. Randolph, who described Sibyl's trouble as a plain case of anemia. But, declared Dr. North, one has to ask what caused the anemia. Dr. Randolph, he added, betrayed "no evidence of intimate knowledge of her life."[32] Mitchell knew well enough from his own medical experience with nervous women that physical disabilities of all sorts could result from psychological causes, and certainly anemia could and frequently did.

29 *Ibid.*, p. 221.
30 *Ibid.*, p. 229.
31 *Ibid.*, pp. 232-233.
32 *Ibid.*, p. 231.

With the passing of summer, and with St. Clair away on his travels, Sibyl's condition again improved. But there remained, too, ominous signs of his continued influence. On the grounds of Claybourne's home where she stayed, stood St. Clair's vase illustrating Keats's poem, set there at her wish. In the chilly autumn weather she would sit near the vase to read or sew. Furthermore, on the window in her room she kept, covered and concealed, the pedestal which the artist had made for the vase. Sibyl herself realized, in some degree, that her behavior was strange; she knew that she did things and yet had no memory of having done them. She found her new pen-wiper blackened, for example, and yet could not remember using it. Actually she had been using it in the performance of the most revealing of her unconscious acts. St. Clair came to Dr. North with the evidence, four anonymous love letters. The artist had no idea who could have written them. Dr. North supplied some hints when he explained the nature of such anonymous letters. They are produced, he said, "by the craving for confession. . . . purely for the satisfaction of emptying a burdened mind."[33] The anonymous writer of the letters, he continued, must have spoken to herself as follows: "He will see it, he will read it, he will never know, he will imagine me beautiful, charming, and, alas! I am not!"[34]

The letters revealed well the deeply submerged feelings of Sibyl, her compulsion to love St. Clair and to express her love to him. In these letters, apparently, she could safely express herself. She could dream of St. Clair as her lover, alone with her, and she could picture herself as altogether beautiful, free of the physical defect that, she felt, made love in the real world impossible. Excerpts from the letters illustrate clearly the suppressed personality of Sibyl. From the first letter:

> If I—ah, do not dare to smile—if I love you, where is the harm? We shall not ever meet. You are a spirit to me, as much outside my world as if you were dead. . . . Be kind to me in thought. Imagine me poor, lonely, often in the society

[33] *Ibid.*, p. 286.
[34] *Ibid.*, p. 286.

of your best and noblest words. I can bear it no longer, and must speak to you directly, as I am now doing. What good will it do me? Ah! you a poet, and know not the joys of confession? Consider mine as though it were the revelation of a dream; and thus without shame I can say I love you. I do not ask you to write to me. In some other world we shall meet, and I may say, "It was I."[35]

From the second letter:

You adore beauty. I am beautiful; and you shall see me in spirit only. Thus shall I be the more beautiful, because imagination will lend her artful aid. All this I may with daring say, because we shall never meet. It remains the guilt-less vanity of a dream. I shall appear to your spirit with the radiant loveliness of immaterial conceptions.

Ah, the sweet foolishness of love! I lay on the grass yes-terday and surrendered myself to the easy prosperity of day-dreams. My sleep dreams are often sad. We were in a boat on a swift river. You had the helm. I lay facing you.[36]

From the third letter:

Sometimes I sit alone and cry because of having sent these letters. . . . I am sick with the anguish of a giant fear, the fear to lose that which I have not. . . . No, you will never see me. I should die of shame; and yet, I am fair to see, strong and beautiful.[37]

Thus in these letters Sibyl expressed her most deeply sub-merged wishes and fears, truths about herself which pride and self-esteem would never permit her to face directly and openly, beautiful dreams of escape from the unbearable realities of her loveless life.[38]

The fourth letter was not reproduced, for reasons easy to imagine. Mitchell, speaking through Dr. North, gave a suffi-cient hint. "No woman, unless in a passion of love, could have written a part of the last letter."[39] Mitchell, it seems, was too

35 *Ibid.*, p. 288.
36 *Ibid.*, pp. 289-290.
37 *Ibid.*, pp. 291-292.
38 These letters illustrate vividly the view, held by Freud, that dreams and the unconscious contain suppressed wishes.
39 *Ibid.*, p. 292.

honest to withhold the hint, yet too bound by the proprieties to give more.

Was it Sibyl who wrote the letters, asked Alice North after some hints from her husband. His reply was a clear statement of Sibyl's dual personality:

> Yes and no. You saw her in the garden in her trance state, a product of hysteria. She has periods when she does things of which later she has no remembrance. Thus she ordered the pedestal put in her own sitting-room, as the butler told me; and she herself assured me that she found it there and had been surprised. In her sound state she is able to control herself, and has, I think, overcome the impression made by St. Clair's thoughtless admiration of her head and face. In these times of alternate consciousness she obeys her emotional nature; she is even vain of her beauty—is, in fact, no longer our modest Sibyl. This is my conclusion. I may be wrong.[40]

Returning to St. Clair with the letters, Dr. North advised the artist not to answer them. St. Clair, who had no idea who wrote them, wondered why not. It will "encourage a folly," said North. When the young man persisted in his intention to answer the letters, Dr. North informed him they were written by Sibyl." She wrote. . . . in a state of alternate consciousness," he explained. "The real Sibyl does not know that she wrote these letters. It is an hysterical phenomenon, strange to you, not unfamiliar to me."[41]

St. Clair was extremely disturbed to learn it was Sibyl who had written the letters. "It's a damned lie!" he shouted at first, overwhelmed with emotion. The reader may be inclined to wonder here just what St. Clair's emotions were, but Mitchell withheld the information, quite deliberately keeping the reader in suspense. He liked to give his novels the traditionally happy ending. He wished to prepare for it well enough to make it logical when it came, but not so fully as to enable the reader to foresee it too plainly.

40 *Ibid.*, p. 293.
41 *Ibid.*, p. 302.

Some time after his interview with St. Clair, Dr. North's wife questioned him about Sibyl. Mitchell thus gave himself another opportunity to comment:

> Sibyl is very loving, very emotional; is a too easy prisoner of sentiment. . . . Moreover, she is what people call nervous. She is apt to lose control of herself, to cry readily, to be subject to ungoverned excesses of mirth or grief. She lives too near the danger-line of loss of power to discipline her emotions. It may sound absurd to say that such people are liable to moral anarchy. In other words, owing to temperament and ill health, she has been and may again be hysterical. . . . She fluctuates strangely as to her physical state. Always she is gravely anemic. . . . No one can anticipate the extent to which the sensitiveness of hysteria may go. Undoubtedly this poor child allowed herself to care too much for our thoughtless man of genius.[42]

Before concluding this conversation, Dr. North sounded a hopeful note: "I think also that if a man as affectionate as Victor ever came to have for Sibyl that which we call love both natures would prosper under its wholesome influence."[43]

St. Clair continued to meet Sibyl quite often, since they both moved within the same circle of friends. But she was obviously losing her health and Dr. North, convinced that St. Clair's presence was the cause, urged that Claybourne take Sibyl to Europe. Soon afterward the afflicted young lady sailed away with her guardian.

For the next few months the news from Italy concerning Sibyl continued good. As her health and strength improved, even her limp became less conspicuous. All this happiness seemed suddenly threatened when word came that St. Clair had joined her and the others. But when Dr. North and his wife followed by going to Italy, they found Sibyl in fine condition, quite erect in posture and with color in her cheeks. More important, her relationship to St. Clair had obviously improved. Her manner toward him was easy, assured and even

[42] *Ibid.*, pp. 369-370.
[43] *Ibid.*, p. 373.

somewhat commanding. "Our reckless Victor," observed North, "was being tamed."[44]

Mitchell did not inform the reader plainly that the couple was married or even engaged, but he left no doubt that everything was ending happily, that the girl who had fled into an alternate consciousness to escape a problem, could now, with that problem happily solved, return to her own wholesome personality.

[44] *Ibid.*, p. 496.

Chapter IX

DIPSOMANIA

Roger Grace

In Mitchell's novel *Circumstance* one of the characters suffers from dipsomania. Judged by the standards of present-day psychologists Mitchell's portrait is scientific. He attempted to understand the circumstances that shaped the man, and to portray him accurately, without reproach or disparagement. Roger Grace was a sick man who suffered from "a malaria of the mind, of the morals."[1]

At the outset of the story he was a bachelor of forty, a banker who had come from humble beginnings. Of late he had been taken with social ambitions, but was too sensitive to choose the nearest way, refusing to be helped in any manner that could seem the least bit compromising. Although his attorney belonged to the exclusive circle to which he aspired, Grace refused to ask his help, thinking the man might feel obliged to agree. The attorney's wife called upon him once for a contribution to a charity, and he responded handsomely, but even then refused her help. "I hope you won't bother about it," he told her. "I always get what I want. I wouldn't like you to think that I am buying my way. I should dislike anyone to say that."[2]

He not only gave generous amounts to worthy causes but he

[1] S. Weir Mitchell, *Circumstance,* p. 386.
[2] *Ibid.,* p. 92.

145

did so with the gracious manner of a sensitive person who understood and protected the feelings of those who received. When he insisted upon lending fifty dollars a month to Martin Blount, the needy and promising medical student, he overcame the young man's resistance by pointing out how much satisfaction he himself would get from the arrangement. "You have had, as I had, a hard life; let me feel that I am saving a good man from needless risks. And now good-bye; I'm very, very much obliged to you."[3]

Grace's activities in the earlier part of the novel constitute a record of generosity. He helped various people who were to play a part later in his career, particularly in the episodes associated with his dipsomania. In addition to Martin Blount there was Lionel Craig, the irresponsible spendthrift; there were the two Markham sisters, genteel ladies of reduced means; and there was Cyril Knellwood, the rector who subdued his strong, physical appetites and devoted himself, out of principle, to the service of others.

Roger Grace admired Knellwood, particularly for his "completeness of self-control." The reason was revealing, for Roger Grace's own self-control, admirable as it seemed, was far from complete. This was, at most, only hinted at in the earlier part of the novel. In an interview with his attorney's wife, Grace confessed, "When I am tired or troubled . . . . I go out to my flower-farm, and if that does not help me I am past remedy." "He was curiously near," added Mitchell, "to a desire to make the only confession of his guarded life."[4]

It was to Mr. Knellwood that he finally did make his confession, and then only under pressure of circumstances which were rapidly becoming unbearable. He was troubled by serious financial problems. His own financial position was not too badly threatened, but the position of the Republic Trust, with which he was closely associated, did seem precarious, and Grace was extremely anxious to prevent its downfall. He felt a social obligation to support so old and important an insti-

3 *Ibid.*, p. 103.
4 *Ibid.*, p. 91.

tution, and he was prepared to risk large sums of his own money in behalf of the Trust.

Under the stress of his difficulties Grace felt himself weaken. His collection of paintings by Van Dyk and others, which usually brought him much pleasure, failed now to interest him. His ability to sleep serenely, no matter what the trials of the day, deserted him. He felt himself slipping helplessly into the weakness he could not control, his old need for alcohol.

There was something new in his life this time, which made him dread his weakness more than ever, and that is why he turned to Knellwood. Roger Grace was considering matrimony. His affections for Clementina, the younger Markham sister, had grown, and he had reason to believe she might agree to marriage. Now, feeling the pull toward drink, he became acutely troubled; how could a man such as he involve so gentle a creature in his own sordid misery? His distress was feeding upon itself.

How had he ever developed his weakness? He told his story to Knellwood:

Before I was born my father and grandfather died drunkards. I never knew it until I was a man. I had no inclination that way. I never have had the usual form of this temptation. I can to this day take without risk, at dinner, my glass of wine. When I was about thirty I had a commercial disaster and lost heavily. This was in May. I was seized with a sudden desire to drink—oh, to put it brutally, to get drunk. From that day to this it comes again once in two or three years. Sometimes, as last spring, I can overcome it. This year it is on me like—oh, nothing I can liken it to will let you know its power. When it comes as it does this year I am gone. I yield. I give up.[5]

This confession indicates several of Mitchell's views. The hereditary factor, to which he attached great weight, is still today regarded as important and is generally considered in case histories. Of more interest, perhaps, is Mitchell's observation that the man's first great desire came after a commercial dis-

5 *Ibid.*, p. 310.

aster, and that he wished not merely to drink, but to get drunk. Present-day students recognize, as Mitchell did here, that alcoholism is an escape from harsh realities. Baldwin L. Keyes, for example, in a recent study, wrote as follows:

> The consumer of alcohol seeks the cortical depressant action of alcohol and finds its transient effects a great relief to him, since through them he is separated somewhat from the full realities of himself and his situation, his anxieties and his inhibitions. . . .[6]

A recent psychiatric work offered a similar explanation:

> The reason that the use of alcohol by human beings has persisted down through the centuries is because of the quality it has of rosily blurring the hard, unpleasant, and forbidding outlines of reality, and if taken in sufficient quantities, it has the power of effacing reality altogether. It is fantasy in a bottle. . . . Alcohol is always a narcotic. . . . complete shedding of all adult responsibilities may be observed so that the drunkard becomes as helpless as an infant. . . . From careful consideration of the vast amount of human material available for study, it becomes increasingly evident that alcohol in excessive amounts is the most commonly utilized technique to accomplish unconsciously an escape from mature responsibilities.[7]

Roger Grace was somewhat different from most alcoholics in that he usually remained completely sober; he indulged for short periods with long intervals between. It was only when he found himself overpowered by circumstance, as now by the oppressive financial and other difficulties, that he had to turn to drink. But when such times came, as he explained to Knellwood, he felt utterly helpless:

> I am impotent when it comes. I use all the brains I have to defend my good name. I go away to some remote little town. I calmly arrange to be cared for, not as Roger Grace; then I drink and drink. When I am through with it I go to

[6] Baldwin L. Keyes, "The Problem of Alcoholism," *Archives of Neurology and Psychiatry*, LIV (April, 1947), p. 513.

[7] Edward A. Strecker, Franklin G. Ebaugh, Jack R. Ewalt, *Practical Clinical Psychiatry* (Philadelphia, 1947), pp. 418-419.

some spring and cleanse myself of the consequences. I return at last, feeling physically well and clear in mind.[8]

This story of Grace is very similar to a case history described in a recent study by Ernst Simmel:

> The alcoholics called dipsomaniacs have drunken sprees only sporadically, sometimes periodically, with relatively long intervals of pseudo-normality. . . . they often remain away from their homes for weeks or months and, remaining drunk, engage in all kinds of activities until they wind up in the routine desolate state of helplessness in accordance with the established custom of alcoholics. . . . One of my patients. . . . used to travel through the country by train, always arriving sooner or later in the city in which his married sister lived.

Simmel then tried to explain what had caused this behavior. His explanation, representative of some modern psychiatric thinking, went far beyond anything Mitchell ever hinted at —and, it might be added, beyond what many present-day observers feel bound to accept:

> It was this sister, who during his childhood had substituted for his mother, to whom fell the task of sobering him up and caring for him. The addict thus acts out his pregenital masturbatory fantasies by returning in effect to his mother as her baby to be nursed and taken care of.[9]

While Mitchell never carried his search for causes to such obscure regions, he did go back into the man's youth in an effort to indicate the background causes of the disease. In his confession to Knellwood, Grace told of his lonesome youth and of his extreme sensitiveness:

> I need not say that I have been in constant terror of exposure. I am a more sensitive man than you would think it

[8] S. Weir Mitchell, *Circumstance*, p. 311.

[9] Ernst Simmel, "Alcoholism and Addiction" *The Psychoanalytic Quarterly*, XVII (1948), p. 18. For another description of an intermittent alcoholic like Grace, see Herman Wortis and Leonard R. Sillman, *Studies of Compulsive Drinkers* (New Haven, 1946). The person described "was a periodic drinker and, at one time, managed to abstain for ten years." p. 70.

possible for one like me to be. I have lived, I think, an upright life. I have tried to be all a man ought to be. In my
own church, in hospitals, and financial boards I am, I believe, useful and respected. Of late years I have learned how
to enjoy what my youth never knew, the social contact with
men and women whose happier chances have brought them
refinement and cultivated tastes. I made friends—you, the
Swanwicks, and others. My God! Knellwood, if this were
ever known I should simply give up and go away for years.[10]

With this knowledge of Grace's background and sensitive
nature it is easier to understand how burdened he was by the
pressures of a mounting financial crisis, and why, in the midst
of the crisis, he ran away, leaving behind all the vexing responsibilities. To Knellwood he left a note of explanation:

I go because I must. I go to the neglect of plain duty. No
one who has not been in the clutches of a temptation like
mine can imagine the almost mechanical certainty of its
action. It is like a machine. I have an awful joy in having
yielded. I look forward and can hardly wait. Burn this.[11]

Usually Grace was heard from after seven or eight days, but
this time nearly two weeks lapsed without a word. Meanwhile,
with the business situation growing ever more critical, his
leadership was sorely missed. But no one knew where to find
him. It was known only that a huge mail awaited him at Bedford whenever he might arrive there. When Knellwood observed that two years ago on one of his periodic absences Grace
had come to Bedford from Carlisle, the clue was sufficient.
Martin Blount, the young medical student, was sent to Carlisle,
where he found Grace in a dilapidated hotel, lost in a drunken
stupor. He took charge, watched "at the bedside of the friend
who had so unaccountably fallen."[12] When the night passed
and dawn came, Grace woke up and called for liquor. Refused, he fell back to sleep; but when he awoke again at seven,
though he recognized Blount, he continued to insist on a

10 S. Weir Mitchell, *Circumstance*, p. 311.
11 *Ibid.*, p. 319.
12 *Ibid.*, p. 377.

drink. When the young man refused, he pleaded, threatened and searched.

At nine o'clock, wrote Mitchell, whose report of the recovery was meticulous, Grace had become obedient and full of sad humiliation:

> The lines of enfeebling ravage, the heavy, swollen lids, the slackened look of lost energy told their wretched story; but the brain was recovering, the immense vitality of the man was seizing again the fallen reins of self-control. He uttered a sentence from time to time, brief, disjointed, and then was long speechless.[13]

Soon he asked for a cigar and, smoking it, observed, "It tastes good. You must not let me drink any more. By evening I shall not need it, not for a year. I must get away to Bedford at once."[14]

In characteristic fashion, Mitchell brought the story to a happy ending. Grace, recovered from his weakness, returned to the battles of business, carried through successfully and married Clementina. But in describing these later events, Mitchell offered one more important insight into the character of Roger Grace. The unscrupulous Lionel Craig, having learned his employer's secret, sent him an anonymous letter of blackmail. He would keep the secret, he promised, for three hundred dollars. Grace was generally a strong character, a man of confidence and decision, looked to by others for leadership in time of crisis. He knew, too, that this blackmail, if successful, would be only the beginning of continued demands for money. Furthermore, he learned that the blackmailer was the weakling, Craig, who almost certainly would shut up at the mere threat of arrest. But in this matter Grace was too sensitive to act with his usual force. He was "a strong man become the fool of fear."[15] He could not bear the thought of his secret weakness becoming known, for he imagined all his friends, espe-

13 *Ibid.*, p. 379.
14 *Ibid.*, p. 379.
15 *Ibid.*, p. 392.

cially Clementina, would be shocked. In unreasoning dread, he sent the money to the blackmailer.

This entire matter was well resolved before the end of the novel, and Craig was properly punished; but the episode did reveal more clearly than ever the kind of man Grace was. By emphasizing a central weakness in his character, it made more comprehensible his periodic falls from sobriety.

PETER LAMB

Peter Lamb, the dipsomaniac in *Westways,* was an entirely different sort of person from Roger Grace. He was a "scamp," a "sinner" who seemed to have no sense of right and wrong. Unlike Grace, who remained sober most of the time, Lamb was quite habitually drunk, as often as he could manage to get the liquor.

In the first scene in which he appears Lamb was ill, recovering from "an attack of delirium tremens and reassembling his scattered wits."[16] He had just been seeing bugs, snakes and various nonexistent creatures. On orders from the doctor, he was under guard of the not-too-bright Billy, who was to keep him in bed and away from further drink. Billy's job was no easy one, for while he was watching, "an unendurable craving for drink beset the man Lamb, who was the prey of slowly lessening delusions."[17] As his mind cleared, Lamb was better able to think of ways to outwit his guard. Mitchell knew how clever so desperate a man could become:

> Lamb fell to thought of how to get that whiskey. The ingenuity of the man who craves alcohol or morphia is sometimes surprising even to the most experienced doctor. The immorality of the means of attainment is never considered. If, as with Lamb, a lie or worse be needed, there is a certain satisfaction in having outwitted nurse and doctor.[18]

Soon Lamb's wits were sufficiently integrated for him to try

16 S. Weir Mitchell, *Westways,* p. 116.
17 *Ibid.,* p. 114.
18 *Ibid.,* p. 115.

them out on Dr. McGregor, who called upon him. Whiskey, he pleaded to the doctor, would strengthen him, would, in fact, save his life, for he was dying without it. But the doctor was not fooled. "That man," he thought, "is giving his whole mind to thinking how he can get whiskey. He will lie, cheat, steal, do anything to get it."[19]

Having failed with the doctor, Lamb tried his tricks on Mr. Rivers, the clergyman, who came in just as the doctor left. Adopting an air of repentance, he urged the clergyman to pray for him. When Rivers was on his knees, face in hand, Lamb broached his ingenious argument: he wanted to pray, but couldn't, he was "so harried inside." Just a little liquor, he urged, would enable him to pray. The clergyman proving adamant, Lamb tried one more person, Josiah, the barber, an escaped slave. When, at Lamb's request, Josiah came to shave him, he asked for whiskey, and when the barber refused, threatened to expose the ex-slave. The threat failed, and at a later date Lamb did take his revenge.

Mitchell not only presented this graphic picture of a dipso-maniac in the anguish of thirst, but he gave some indication of the cause of the man's illness. It was partly due to hereditary influence, for Lamb's father was "a sodden drunkard," although "not otherwise bad."[20] Later in the story Mitchell offered a somewhat more extensive discussion of the back-ground and personality of Peter Lamb. It was after Lamb had carried out his revenge against Josiah by reporting the fugitive slave's location, and so driving him out of town. When word got around that he had informed on Josiah, Lamb himself found the town too unfriendly. Blaming the minister for his predicament, he burned the parsonage to the ground. Commenting on the man's behavior, Mitchell explained that not only was his father a drunkard, but his mother had spoiled him:

He had been for several days enough under the influence of

19 *Ibid.*, p. 116.
20 *Ibid.*, p. 115.

whiskey to intensify what were for him normal or at least habitually indulged characteristics. For them he was only in part responsible. His mother had spoiled him. . . . What share in his evil qualities his father's drunkenness had, is in no man's power to say. His desire to revenge the slightest ill-treatment or the abuse his evil ways earned had the impelling force of brute instinct.[21]

When Lamb was accused of burning the parsonage, and feared arrest, he stole his mother's meager savings, about sixty dollars, and ran away. Would he begin a new and better life in new surroundings? Not likely, Mitchell implied. It was his view, expressed through Dr. McGregor, that Lamb was incurable, "a hopelessly ruined wild beast," and would "live to do much mischief."[22]

When Lamb reappeared in the story it was after he had done his last great mischief, the rape of a young girl. Captured and found guilty, he pleaded for mercy. When that failed and he faced execution, he cried out, "If I only could have a little whiskey."[23] His wish was granted and he walked to his death reeking with liquor.

Mitchell's description of the death scene indicated once more his understanding sympathy toward even the worst of men. When the bandage was put over Peter's eyes, he whispered a final word to Mr. Rivers, minister from his home town, "Tell my mother I was shot—not how—not why."[24] Dr. McGregor standing by was moved to observe: "Human wickedness is very incomplete."[25]

21 *Ibid.*, pp. 196-197.
22 *Ibid.*, pp. 116-117.
23 *Ibid.*, p. 424.
24 *Ibid.*, p. 426.
25 *Ibid.*, p. 427.

Chapter X

INSANITY

PHILETUS RICHMOND

MITCHELL'S MEDICAL practice was concerned mostly with nervous diseases, and included some insanity. In reply to an inquiry he explained that he treated "all forms of disease especially those of the nerves except such insane as need restraint."[1] He was frequently consulted on problems of insanity, and at one time made an investigation of asylums, including their medical and psychiatric procedures. In 1894 he delivered an epochal address before the Medico-Psychological Association, which represented the organized psychiatrists of that day. It was "a blistering verbal chastisement."[2] Mitchell singled out particularly the failure of these psychiatrists, with all their rich opportunities in the asylums, to do research into the problems of insanity, to probe causes and devise treatment.

In his fiction there are two fairly extensive studies of insanity, Philetus Richmond in *Far in the Forest* (1889), and Benedict Norman in *John Sherwood* (1911). Neither is the central character, but both play prominent parts. There is also,

[1] From an unpublished letter, dated December 21 (no year given), in the College of Physicians of Philadelphia.

[2] John C. Whitehorn, "A Century of Psychiatric Research in America," *One Hundred Years of American Psychiatry*, ed. by J. K. Hall, Gregory Zilboorg, and Henry A. Bunker, p. 167. Three other articles in this volume discussed this same memorable address which so sharply exposed the contemporary weaknesses in psychiatry.

in *Constance Trescot* (1905), a study of John Greyhurst, who came perilously near to insanity.

Philetus Richmond was, at the beginning of the story in which he appears, an apparently hale personality. By the end he had become a hopeless case in an insane asylum. Mitchell portrayed, in some measure, the causes and process of the transformation. At the opening of the story Philetus was sixty-five years old, but strong and vigorous, "an ample-shouldered giant" with "physical stateliness." Fifteen years earlier he had married an attractive girl of twenty, and despite their age difference, she had grown to love him. When shortly after the birth of their pretty daughter Philetus became hopelessly blind, his wife showed more devotion than ever. In spite of the blindness they were happy: "There was enough of mutual admiration to flavor the love which the child served to knit anew with ties which grew increasingly stronger year by year."[3]

Philetus, when we first meet him, had shortcomings which were to contribute to his downfall. "Like many men who marry much younger women," Mitchell explained, "he was more or less jealous, a peculiarity intensified by the suspiciousness from which the blind rarely escape altogether."[4] Furthermore, he was "incapable of taking a single glass of liquor without being morally poisoned. He knew and hated this single weakness, but could at times be led into self-indulgence."[5] Another factor playing an important part in his mental breakdown was his mystic philosophy derived from Swedenborg, his attempts to explain the simplest events of everyday life in terms of divine purpose and spiritual cause. Mystic thinking, Mitchell believed, could encourage insanity:

> The mystically minded are of all men the most apt to be illogical, are above others prone to be disturbed mentally by the permanent entertainment of a false belief which seems at

3 S. Weir Mitchell, *Far in the Forest* (New York, 1903), p. 62.
4 *Ibid.*, p. 62.
5 *Ibid.*, p. 63.

last to become a part of the structure of the mind and to affect all its decisions.[6]

Philetus' jealousy, weakness for alcohol, and mysticism were alone not enough to drive him insane. At least one other factor was needed, the appearance of a young man to stir the jealousy and aggravate the weaknesses already present. Such a man, ideally suited for the unhappy role he was to play in the blind man's life, was the young, attractive, educated German, John Riverius. Miriam Richmond, Philetus' young wife, liked him at once. "Now, my Phil ain't an ill-lookin' man, but he don't hold himself up like that Riverius."[7] While she was, in general, very favorably disposed to the young man, she remained altogether wifely in her feelings. Her love and interest remained with her husband, and she gave him no reasonable grounds for jealousy. In spite of John's superior learning, she considered Philetus the wiser man.

However, from the first her husband was jealous. "For all he was two weeks in my house," said Philetus, "I never kin call him rightly."[8] Mitchell saw here, it seems, the same psychological significance in forgetting that Freud was later to point out.[9] Even after being reminded of the name, Philetus refused to use it: "I don't like that there man much," he said. "He's too sot in his ways. He's the kind hangs about women. I never cum home he ain't a trapseyin' 'round, talkin' to Myry."[10] This charge was wholly unfounded.

While his antagonism arose mainly from jealousy, Philetus did have other grievances. Not only was John too superior and commanding in tone, but he habitually ridiculed Philetus for his mysticism. This was particularly irritating, for the blind man took great pride in the acuteness of his senses, in his

[6] *Ibid.*, pp. 187-188.

[7] *Ibid.*, p. 30.

[8] *Ibid.*, p. 46.

[9] Sigmund Freud has discussed at some length the causes of forgetting, and has pointed out, in particular, how we tend to forget what we dislike. See *A General Introduction to Psychoanalysis* (New York, 1943), p. 48.

[10] S. Weir Mitchell, *Far in the Forest*, p. 46.

"thinking eye" and in his mystical interpretation of what he perceived.

As a follower of Swedenborg, he was constantly finding symbols and lessons of God all about him. His own blindness, he explained, was caused by the devil:

> We're awful mean fighters, men air. The devil he's a lot fairer; he jus' runs in on you, and it's a squar' rough-and-tumble. I've had times with him,—times; 'twasn't hypocrisy done it. That ain't my failin'. That gits you in the teeth. Manuel Swedenborg says so. Anyways, some devil's got my eyes, cause maybe they wasn't the Lord's servers.[11]

When a jam was broken and the logs whirled destructively downstream, striking the shores and destroying the trees alongside, Philetus commented:

> It's like the damned broke loose. . . . It's like the devils on a spree. Them trees has souls. All things has bodies, but there is a spiritual body. Hear 'em yell. . . .
> Them logs is preachin' now. You just listen to them.[12]

Philetus was vulnerable to criticism not only because he so cherished his odd views, but because he was also a man of strange tenderness and delicacy of feeling. He stopped a hunter once from killing a doe, saying it was like killing in church on Sabbath, or like killing a woman. When his mystical ideas, which he felt deserving of respect or even awe, were bluntly ridiculed by the well-intentioned but thoughtless John Riverius, he became deeply angry. "He 'ain't no comprehension of any man's ways 'cept his own," he charged.[13] He was annoyed, too, by the logical effectiveness of the attack, which merely hurt his feelings without changing his views:

> He disliked greatly to have his mystical fancies lightly regarded. He liked as little the precision of thought with which, in his graver mood, Riverius met and overthrew his theories.[14]

11 *Ibid.*, p. 85.
12 *Ibid.*, p. 107.
13 *Ibid.*, p. 144.
14 *Ibid.*, p. 53.

Philetus' jealousy and antagonism became ever more aggravated. He was constantly imagining, at the smallest hint, that John was making private visits to his wife, especially after he had accepted a job from John, running a mill. "I'd give a lot fur to see that 'ere man's face," he would say to himself. "Then I'd know. Ther's things goin' on, goin' on—Oh, Lord, fur to see!"[15]

One day, when he declared his suspicions to his wife, she answered him with honest indignation: "For a right smart man, you can get yourself to believe more nonsense than the biggest ass in Rollins's camp."[16] Mitchell added his own comment:

> The wifely indictment was just and Philetus knew it for the time. Morbidness like his is apt enough to fall before the shaft of reason, sped from the bow of whole-minded vigor.[17]

Philetus retreated, quite aware of his own mental aberrations: "I don't say I ain't wrong, Myry. I'm kind of flurried in the head these last weeks."[18] Just what was causing these "flurries" Mitchell did not explain. Quite likely, however, he attributed much to the effect of alcohol. He mentioned it quite frequently in the story and always pictured Philetus at his worst under the influence of drink.[19]

Philetus' jealousy became a fixed idea, divorced from reality. There was a man, Ance Vickers, who did make improper advances to Miriam, but Philetus was as blind to these as he was alert to the imagined advances of John Riverius. In fact he made of Ance Vickers a close associate and companion in

15 *Ibid., p.* 86.
16 *Ibid.,* p. 120.
17 *Ibid.,* p. 121.
18 *Ibid.,* p. 121.
19 Mitchell's contemporaries, it might be added, considered alcohol a common cause of insanity. "In my own experience," wrote Hammond, an outstanding specialist in mental diseases, "it takes precedence of all other known causes, fully twenty percent of the cases that have come under my observation being due to alcoholic liquors used in excess." See William A. Hammond, *Treatise on Insanity* (New York, 1883), p. 660.

drink, and hired him as helper in the mill in spite of orders not to do so.

One day he was in the woods with Ance and the other men, drinking and feeling bitter about his fancied grievances. The men, seeing an opportunity for sport, began to play upon these grievances. They talked about the orders he had to take from his employer, until he cried out in defiance, "Ther' ain't no man kin boss Philetus Richmond."[20] Then they taunted him where it hurt most, with reference to his wife's fondness for John, until the old man shouted with "savage pain." When at this moment John appeared on the scene, Philetus was tenderly susceptible to any new injury—and his employer quickly supplied one. In front of all the men he fired Philetus for disobeying the order concerning Ance. "All right," was all that Philetus answered; but his mind took a new turn after that.

He drank more, spoke of John as "a hard man" who made "no 'lowance for folks,"[21] and when he was alone, spoke aloud more violent thoughts. Some "stringent passionate need forced from his lips the troubling results of thoughts too keenly felt for silent guard." He was overheard muttering about the vengeance of God:

> 'He has said to me in the night season, Burn; he has said to me in the daylight, Slay; the woman that deceiveth shall surely die; the man that beguileth shall perish; fire shall follow him, fire shall devour his substance.' It's gettin' clearer. Thar's this here tree as he smote with lightnin', or he might have minded to rot it with worms, or vex it with galls, or put it in my head to ruin it with an axe. Ain't it him all the same as does it?[22]

His mystic thoughts enabled him to persuade himself that he personally was to become an instrument of the Lord to work vengeance upon the deceiver, John Riverius. Not only did he speak such thoughts himself, but he heard voices, "imperative counsellors," Mitchell called them. "For days they were gone

20 S. Weir Mitchell, *Far in the Forest*, p. 149.
21 *Ibid.*, p. 161.
22 *Ibid.*, pp. 176-177.

or faintly heard, and again, as now, they screamed in his ears wild and eager counsels."[23] Eventually he burned the new mill put up by John. When questioned he admitted nothing, "Him as done it might have been a firebrand in the hands of the Lord."[24] Asked point blank if he had burned the mill, he replied, "No; I didn't do it." Alone, speaking to himself, he justified this lie: "When the hand of God air on a man . . . . that thar man he does as he's bid. 'Tain't him, but the Lord. I said it wasn't me, and it wasn't."[25]

The burning solved no problems. He continued to imagine that there was something improper between John and his wife. This fixed idea was becoming ever more dangerous:

> . . . . the malevolent effects of a fixed idea were becoming more and more serious. . . . In the domain of morbid psychology the terrible effects of these absolute and false ideas are well understood, and they are among the many causes which lead to inexplicable crimes.[26]

Even Philetus himself, at times, mistrusted his mental condition. He saw visions, he said, which made him do things he wasn't bid to do. "Sometimes," he added, "I think I ain't 'countable."[27] To quiet his mind he turned more frequently to drink, for, as he explained, "It makes me comfortable, drink does. It puts away them visions."[28]

For the most part Philetus continued to take his visions seriously. Their effect was to incite ever more sharply his hostility toward John Riverius. "I hate him," he exclaimed. "Twice I seed him come to my house at night, and when I got up he was gone."[29] Nothing could prevail against this fixed

23 *Ibid.*, p. 178.
24 *Ibid.*, p. 186.
25 *Ibid.*, p. 186.
26 *Ibid.*, pp. 187-188. See William A. Hammond's *Treatise on Insanity.* This book, published in 1883, about six years before Mitchell's novel, was one of the outstanding works on insanity of that time. Hammond's discussion of the effects of a fixed idea (p. 273) is similar to Mitchell's.
27 S. Weir Mitchell, *Far in the Forest*, p. 189.
28 *Ibid.*, p. 190.
29 *Ibid.*, p. 191.

idea, except temporarily. When the kindly, sympathetic Mrs. Preston, to whom he confessed his thoughts, told him how wrong he was, he disagreed. However, her words did have some influence, as Mitchell explained:

> The strong protest of a healthy, positive person had had for a time a useful value in the way of control which it temporarily exerts over persons in the state of mind which beset Philetus. The influence did not last very long. . . .[30]

One day an incident occurred which brought matters to a climax. John, planning a new business venture, decided to offer Philetus the job of looking after it. Knowing that Philetus disliked him, and still not suspecting why, he decided to broach the matter to Miriam first so that she might present the idea to her husband. No sooner did he finish his brief business with her than Miriam had another caller, Ance Vickers, who had been trying for some time to make improper advances. When Miriam grabbed a rifle to order him out, there was a scuffle, and she was accidentally killed. Ance ran away, leaving the dead woman on the floor.

Before he discovered the death of his wife, Philetus learned that John was visiting her alone. He hurried home in a fury of suspicion:

> His unbridled imaginations were away with him on a path of vague fears. The wolves of anger, jealousy, insane suspicion, pursued his blind yet rapid steps.[31]

When he arrived home and found his wife dead, he decided at once who did it. His belief was confirmed when his little daughter remarked that John had just been there. "He's the man," Philetus explained. "I knowed somethin' was a-comin'."[32] He hurried away, informing everyone that John had been visiting his wife at night and now had murdered her; he "wandered from group to group, relating his hallucinations as realities."[33]

30 *Ibid.*, p. 192.
31 *Ibid.*, p. 234.
32 *Ibid.*, p. 235.
33 *Ibid.*, p. 245.

At the end of the novel the dying Ance confessed before all concerned that he had killed Miriam, without intending to. "I done it, Phil. 'Twasn't him. . . . O Lord, forgive me. You jus' curse me, Phil, and let me die."[34]

To which Philetus replied, "You didn't go to hurt her. I ain't no harder nor Christ, Ance." And he took the hand of the dying man. Those were the last words spoken by Philetus. Mitchell did not let us know just what were the blind man's detailed reactions, but he seemed to imply that Philetus was retreating from reality into his own thoughts, for even while Ance lay dying, Philetus seemed to forget about him. He "leaned against a tree, self-absorbed and motionless."[35]

Philetus was not cured by Ance's dramatic revelation of his error. In describing the status of the chief characters fifteen months later, Mitchell made a final reference to the blind man: "Poor old Philetus Richmond is cared for in an asylum —a hopeless case."[36]

The picture of Philetus, enlightening though it may be, remained incomplete. Mitchell described him at various moments in his developing insanity, but never very fully. He failed to give his readers the intimate revelations and details that might have enabled them to perceive the world as Philetus did and live his life with him for awhile.

MR. HAPWORTH

In *John Sherwood* (1910) Mitchell again presented an insane character, Mr. Hapworth, victim of paranoia. He had escaped from an asylum before the opening of the story, and had been living for many months alone in the woods. In the first part of the novel Mitchell tried to portray this strange man, to reveal how he talked, acted and felt toward his few neighbors in the secluded woodland settlement. As the story proceeded, Mitchell made a more ambitious effort. He con-

34 *Ibid.*, p. 297.
35 *Ibid.*, p. 298.
36 *Ibid.*, p. 302.

fronted this character with the same sort of situation which
had called forth his original paranoiac behavior. The author
brought to this settlement the wife that Hapworth had fancied was faithless and the man he had accused as her accom-
plice, and thus was able to present to the reader the spectacle
of a paranoiac completely dominated by his delusions.

Hapworth first appeared in the story when the friendly John
Sherwood called upon him in his isolated retreat. His speech
was that of an educated man, his features were refined, he was
clean-shaven and neatly dressed. Yet he seemed odd. He lacked
some of the thoughtful courtesies customary in a man of his
appearance and speech, and he seemed suspicious, guarded,
and antagonistic to the friendly overtures of his visitor.

As the story unfolded Mitchell revealed, bit by bit, mainly
through the words of people who knew him, something of the
past history of Hapworth, whose real name was Benedict Norman. Two years before the opening events of the story he had
been an active clergyman with a parish. But he had become
unreasonably jealous of his wife, whom he had recently married, and had threatened to kill her, and finally did fire at her.
He fled, was captured, and put in an asylum. There he insisted he had killed his wife and that the police were after
him. When his wife was brought before him to refute his delusion, he cried out that she was dead and fell into a faint.
The delusion remained, and a few days later he escaped from
the asylum, and eventually found his way to the forest.

He brought his delusions with him. John Sherwood found
him "uncomfortably beyond the boundaries of mere eccen-
tricity."[37] One day he came across Hapworth praying aloud,
"plainly in the grip of some overwhelming anguish."[38] Another time he noticed the man laugh at a witticism, then
change abruptly to a grave expression. Sometimes Hapworth,
absorbed in a discussion, would lose his customary look of
melancholy and his habit of glancing about as though in
dread. At other times, he would suddenly introduce a jarring

[37] S. Weir Mitchell, *John Sherwood,* p. 134.
[38] *Ibid.,* p. 122.

note into a conversation. Talking once with Sherwood about the sound of the ocean, he explained he didn't like it, for it was "too like the cry of a soul in distress."[39] Sometimes he would abruptly introduce the subject of death. "I do not fear it and indeed I should welcome it. I am of opinion that self-destruction ought to be made legally possible, considered by a Court and authorized."[40]

Even in the wild forest Hapworth was finding no peace, no escape from the psychological twist that had sent him into isolation. It seemed to Sherwood that the insane man was considering suicide:

> I had watched him of late with increasing belief that when at night he stood with me on the rock, talking visibly but not audibly, he was facing the temptation to end a life of, to me, mysteriously complete unhappiness.[41]

Asked point blank by Sherwood if he were planning suicide, he said he had thought of it once, but had now given it up. "I have reached a decision of late which relieves me of the responsibility of ending my life. What it is, I beg you will not ask me."[42]

Just what the decision was, Mitchell did not then divulge. Soon, however, a revealing incident occurred. While in a boat Hapworth fell overboard, was rescued, and put to bed. Suddenly he became wildly frightened: he wanted to run away from the detectives he fancied were outside his tent looking for him. Assured they were not there, he said he must have been dreaming. Upon being questioned, he could remember nothing of his fall overboard or his rescue, and had nothing to say of the entire incident except that the men who rescued him did him an evil turn.

The view of Hapworth as seen through Sherwood's eyes has its limitations, for Sherwood had neither the skill nor the opportunity to observe him closely. We learn what Hapworth

39 *Ibid.*, p. 133.
40 *Ibid.*, pp. 136-137.
41 *Ibid.*, p. 137.
42 *Ibid.*, p. 138.

said and did, but we do not get the informed medical interpretation that Mitchell was prepared to give. Since the story
was being told in the first person by Sherwood, Mitchell could
not, as he sometimes did, speak up as the all-seeing novelist.
In this circumstance he resorted to his favorite device: he introduced a doctor who would be able to comment on the disordered personality. Sherwood, troubled over what to do with
Hapworth, sent for Dr. Heath to observe the man and give his
professional advice. By a deft stroke of economy Mitchell had
Dr. Heath perform an additional role in the story: the doctor
was the very man whom Hapworth had known in the past,
and accused as the lover of his wife. Thus with the doctor's
visit to Sherwood the novel moves forward at a bound.

Dr. Heath, in giving his analysis of Hapworth, was particularly well informed. Not only had he known the man in the
past, but he observed him now in this forest retreat and received from Sherwood a competent report on his recent behavior. He was able to perceive Hapworth's contradictory attitudes and his retirement from reality:

> It is a too familiar story, belief without cause in his wife's
> being unfaithful, threat to kill her, a shot that misses, de-
> lusion at last that he had killed her. He is committed to an
> asylum, with still the firm belief of being a murderer. . . .
> He tells everyone what he did and yet fears arrest. It is of
> course like the contradictions of a dream. The fear of ar-
> rest drives him into escaping . . . . now he has, or may have,
> remorse and thinks he will surrender himself to the law.
> Then he hesitates, is in and then out of his dream, so to
> speak.[43]

Dr. Heath went on to describe how he had met Mrs. Norman
in the past, in a purely professional way, when her father was
ill, and how he had corresponded with her concerning her
father's illness. He had not seen nor heard from her since. The
sick man, he concluded, was a paranoiac, and too dangerous
to be loose outside an asylum. Dr. Heath was not yet aware

[43] *Ibid.*, p. 194.

that he himself was the object of Hapworth's—Norman's—baseless jealousy.

As one might expect, subsequent events confirmed his diagnosis. One day Hapworth, speaking with Sherwood, cried out that he did right to kill his wife, that the guilty man was Heath, and Heath too must die. "There are ways, things, voices you cannot hear, by day and by night telling me what to do."[44]

After warning the doctor of Hapworth's intentions, Sherwood asked, "Can you explain his delusion in any way, its origin, I mean?"[45] Dr. Heath replied that the delusion may have begun when he himself had corresponded with Hapworth's wife concerning her ill father. However it originated, he continued, it certainly was dangerous:

A man like Norman may seem to the every day layman rational and to-morrow he stops some stranger and says, "You called me a bastard," and shoots him. These men are as dangerous as a stick of dynamite in the hands of a boy. . . . You can be sure of nothing in regard to Norman except that he is just now as deadly as a cobra. . . . He has now or may develop at any moment a wild homicidal tendency. . . . I have handled too many human explosives to feel easy just now.[46]

A bit later in the story, Dr. Heath pointed out how brief such flare-ups could be:

The active mood of murderous fury is usually brief. He may then resume a condition of apparent competence for the everyday things of life.[47]

The climax came when Hapworth's wife, having learned of his whereabouts, visited him. When he saw her he chased her with an axe, screaming, "I'll make sure this time."[48] However, one of the men nearby was able to wrench the axe from him

44 *Ibid.*, p. 210.
45 *Ibid.*, p. 211.
46 *Ibid.*, pp. 211-214.
47 *Ibid.*, p. 237.
48 *Ibid.*, p. 232.

and prevent the murder. Hapworth ran away and later was found dead, victim of an accidental fall from a cliff.

Mitchell's delineation of Hapworth represents authentically a well-known type of insanity, paranoia. Not only did Dr. Heath make that classification in the story, but Mitchell himself did, too, in one of his letters to Mrs. Mason, written while he was still at work upon *John Sherwood:*

> I am at present up to my ears in work on my last novel . . . . it has in it a great deal of personal observation, thought, and a typical characterization of the paranoiac such as none but a physician could, I am sure, have drawn, and yet these people in mild and unsuspected form affect the lives of many.[49]

The description of the jealous paranoiac that one finds in present-day studies fits very well the portrait drawn by Mitchell. Hapworth, for example, behaved in characteristic fashion when he seized upon the innocent professional correspondence between his wife and the doctor, and regarded it as proof of infidelity. As modern students report, it is precisely such little incidents that provide, in the mind of the jealous paranoiac, evidence of his wife's interest in another man:

> If his wife shops for a new outfit, she has met another man; if she returns an hour late, she must have stopped to visit with her paramour; or, if she calls someone on the telephone, she must be calling her "boy friend."[50]

Hapworth's threat against Dr. Heath was also typical of a paranoiac's behavior:

> Many an innocent acquaintance or total stranger has been threatened and even attacked by a jealous husband, wife, or lover.[51]

Hapworth's conduct, aside from the delusion, was quite nor-

[49] A copy of the unpublished letter, dated August 26, 1910, is in the possession of Mrs. S. W. Macdonough.
[50] Louis P. Thorpe and Barney Katz, *op. cit.,* p. 683.
[51] *Ibid.,* p. 683.

mal. His guardedness toward strangers, his suspicious looks behind, his lonely prayers of anguish were associated with his delusion, particularly his fear of being pursued by detectives. Until one noticed these oddities Hapworth seemed normal. In this respect, too, Mitchell's study conforms to the descriptions of present-day psychiatrists:

> A diagnosis of paranoia is based on the presence of a systematized delusion in an individual whose contact with reality is preserved and who manifests no other marked symptoms of personality disorder. . . . Except for the presence of the delusion, the patient's behavior is considered to be "normal."[52]

As Mitchell characterized him, Hapworth was not amenable to logical argument where his delusion was concerned. When Sherwood confronted Hapworth bluntly, attacking his delusions straight-forwardly, he could make no headway at all. On one occasion, for example, Hapworth insisted that he had killed his wife, and would not hear any argument or proof to the contrary. His delusion system was stronger than any logic, impregnable to argument. In this respect, too, Hapworth's behavior was characteristic of the paranoiac as pictured by modern psychiatrists. They recommend, in treating paranoiacs, "the avoidance of argument and direct frontal attack."[53]

What were the causes of Hapworth's paranoia? Mitchell indicated, through Dr. Heath, how independent these causes were of Hapworth's control.

> I often wonder, John, how far men like Norman are responsible. Is he no more so than the axe with which he strikes? Is he hopelessly hurled into murder by the riot of a group of nerve cells? Was he ever in a state to win by effort the battle against advancing insanity?[54]

In the light of the context and of Mitchell's general point of view[55] it is quite clear he felt that Hapworth was the victim,

[52] *Ibid.*, p. 687.
[53] See *ibid.*, p. 688.
[54] S. Weir Mitchell, *John Sherwood*, p. 236.
[55] See Chapter V.

to a large degree, of forces outside his control. Mitchell indicated quite clearly some of the circumstances which combined to push the man toward insanity. At the very outset of
his marriage he had feelings of insecurity, which made him
particularly susceptible to jealousy. His very name, *Benedict*
Norman, had been against him, a name, as Mitchell wrote, so
odious to Americans it was practically never given to a new-
born boy. The unfortunate man had himself tried to escape
it by adopting another. Hapworth's physique, too, contributed
to his feelings of insecurity, for he was "a feeble little man,"[56]
and married to an exceptionally attractive young woman.

Hapworth had even stronger reasons for insecurity in his
marriage: his wife did not really love him. "I suspected," John
Sherwood declared after becoming well acquainted with her,
"that Helen Norman had made a marriage in which the
passions had no share. I could read between the lines that
duty, not love, made her enduringly face death and resolutely
search for the man whom she knew to be so dangerous."[57] Certainly, during the last year of the marriage, after his jealousies
were manifest, she lived in misery, as she herself declared:

> When my father was long ill in Italy, Mr. Norman was
> kind beyond the common and I came to care for him. You
> would understand why, if you had known him in his better
> days. We were married before my father's death and, re-
> turning to Baltimore, within a month this dreadful thing
> came on, oh, even before we came back. I did not under-
> stand at first. Then I knew. I lived a year amid wild
> jealousies and threats of my life, oh, more than threats![58]

Mitchell did not state plainly that all these facts made Hapworth feel insecure and therefore played a part in the development of the paranoia. It must be admitted, too, that if
Mitchell did have a clear understanding of the entire pattern
he did not make the most of it. He did not indicate as clearly
as he might the relationship of each fact to the development of

56 *Ibid.,* p. 213.
57 *Ibid.,* p. 279.
58 *Ibid.,* pp. 255-256.

Hapworth's disease, nor did he present in any detail Hapworth's own reactions to the various circumstances which worked against his sanity. But the facts which Mitchell presented, however inadequately utilized, are in harmony with the present-day belief that some cases of paranoia result from "feelings of inadequacy and inferiority."[59]

JOHN GREYHURST

John Greyhurst was never a well-balanced personality, even at the outset of the novel. He was thin-skinned and impulsive. He stamped roughly over the feelings of others, but expected his own to be treated with delicacy. He could not get along with his wife, and divorced her. In his service as a Southern officer in the Civil War he had quarreled with the other officers and injured his usefulness. His record as a lawyer in private life was no better. As his fellow lawyer Averil pointed out, he was both impulsive and dangerous.

But Mitchell, ever aware of the good in the worst of men, presented favorable comments too. "I do not think him a rascal," said Averil.[60] "He is not a bad fellow," observed another acquaintance, "and is enough of a gentleman to be sorry after his damned vanity has made him say something disagreeable."[61] In the course of the story Greyhurst murdered, suffered remorse, had hallucinations, felt himself at the brink of insanity, and at last committed suicide. Mitchell described not only the causes of these changes, but many of the accompanying thoughts and feelings of the man who endured them.

An important cause of Greyhurst's difficulties was his wild temper, which was aggravated by his immediate environment:

In the ordered life of a more complex society Greyhurst's readiness to take offense would have caused amusement and been checked in any excessive manifestation. In the wilder West, and in St. Ann, where he had lived since the war, the

59 Thorpe and Katz, *op. cit.,* p. 685.
60 S. Weir Mitchell, *Constance Trescot,* p. 160.
61 *Ibid.,* p. 168.

individualities of men were less conventionally governed. He was felt to be a dangerous man, and as resentments were here apt to result seriously, he was either avoided or treated cautiously by his old comrades in arms.[62]

Greyhurst was a lawyer when the story opened, a representative of the Southerners in their dispute with their absentee landlord. The legal contest in which he opposed Trescot was of the utmost importance to him, for he was in debt and needed to win, although the weight of legal evidence was against his clients. He knew his own weakness and was determined to keep a tight rein on his temper during the trial. At first he behaved himself well enough, speaking quietly and examining witnesses with extreme courtesy. But as the opposition scored important points, his temper wore thin, and he began irritating the witnesses he cross-examined. As the trial progressed, he lost control of himself completely, called Trescot a liar and otherwise insulted him.

On the evening before the verdict the impulsive lawyer, alone in his library, had time to reflect on his conduct. Like all Mitchell's characters who suffered moral degeneration, Greyhurst failed to look honestly upon his actions and took refuge in rationalizing. Instead of recognizing that he was himself his own worst enemy, he blamed Trescot for all his failures at court:

> . . . . he recurred, as was habitual with him, to some human instrument as responsible; and now it was, above all, the Yankee lawyer whose triumph would cost him so dear, and who had insulted him, and, although Greyhurst did not confess it, had preserved that serenity of temper which exasperates those for whom a slight is an outrage, and a hasty word an insult. . . . He was no master of himself, and now an evil mood possessed the hour. He drank more than was his habit, and at last went to bed. . . .[63]

The next day the jury, as he feared, decided the case against him. In the crowd after the trial he saw Trescot come toward

62 *Ibid.*, p. 168.
63 *Ibid.*, p. 217.

him, and reach with his lame hand for something in his pocket. Greyhurst, acting on a mad impulse, drew his gun and killed the man who had just defeated him in the courtroom. A moment later he was horror-stricken at what he had done. Trescot never carried a gun. Alone, and confronted by the act he had committed, he tried to see it favorably, still rationalizing:

> He tried to think that according to his Western code, he was justified. He had been told that Trescot never carried arms. He had not believed it at the time, and now fell back on this remembrance. Most men went armed, and certainly Trescot had seemed to him about to draw a pistol; and the man had said he was responsible, which in St. Ann meant that he was prepared to expect attack.[64]

But this specious view would not stay, and he was confronted more and more clearly with the tremendous fact that he had killed an innocent man. The reality became too hard to face, and he "drank glass after glass of whiskey, until he had drugged himself into a state where he ceased to reason."[65] Although he was legally exonerated, he could never completely succeed in his efforts at self-justification. A dreadful feeling of guilt persisted:

> He never willingly walked over the ground where he had seen Trescot fall. . . . He still excused his act as justified by what Trescot had said, and by the self-belief encouraged in his trial by those who swore they thought Trescot was about to draw. . . . He was measurably successful, but never could deal as readily with his remembrance of the agonized face of Constance Trescot.[66]

Greyhurst was troubled, too, in his sleep. Mitchell described his difficulties with the informed knowledge of a neurologist who had studied the subject:

> There is, however, a little space of time when the specters of thought or memory possess the scene. In the brief interval

64 *Ibid.*, pp. 222-223.
65 *Ibid.*, p. 223.
66 *Ibid.*, p. 248.

between the waking state and sleep, when the will is becoming dormant, and imagination plays us sad tricks, he saw her as she stood before him pronouncing the sentence which he never could forget.[67]

His sensitiveness to criticism, and his feelings of guilt made him an easy prey, as has been described in an earlier chapter,[68] to the implacable campaign of revenge waged by Constance. Mitchell presented, at times, some illuminating insights into the struggle that went on in Greyhurst's mind as he tried to fight off the reminders of his crime which Constance so unremittingly placed before him, and as he tried to bend those facts he couldn't forget into a more favorable pattern:

> As he walked homeward in the darkness he took refuge in that which had somewhat helped him at an earlier period. During his trial men swore to their belief that the younger man was in act to draw his pistol. This, as he thought of it in cold blood, justified his own action as defensive. He clung to this view of the matter; set it before his mind as true, and, with sophistry which was scarcely self-convincing, so manipulated the facts that at last mere repetition of the mental states did assist him to escape from the self-reproach which fell upon him when Averill had struck him with the verdict of a man whom all men honored. The telegram and Mrs. Trescot's letter had forced him again to think it all over. He realized how small had been his victory over the recording power of memory.[69]

But all his efforts proved futile:

> A new and overwhelming realization of what he had done to this woman swept over him in a storm of self-reproach and pity. . . . How would this end? There must be a limit to the ability of this woman to torture him, and to his own capacity to suffer. . . .[70]

Once only, he tried an appeal to her mercy, "My God! have you no pity? Cannot you see how I suffer?" Her reply ended

67 *Ibid.*, p. 248.
68 See pp. 110 ff. of the present work.
69 S. Weir Mitchell, *Constance Trescot*, pp. 261-262.
70 *Ibid.*, p. 275.

all hope of an adjustment by such means: "I have for you such pity as you had for him and me!"[71]

Because his sufferings had so weakened him, one sharp additional blow, the sudden sight of Trescot's picture, disordered his senses:

> The test of endurance had been beyond his powers, and had produced on his nervous system an effect such as could never have been anticipated.

He began to see hallucinations of the man he had killed. Mitchell's description here has the meticulous detail of the informed neurologist:

> . . . . he looked up and saw, as if some ten feet away and a little to the left, the face of the man he had killed. For a moment he was simply astonished. It was larger than life and smiling, and not like the photograph. He rubbed his eyes, closed and opened them, and moved about. The phantom kept its place; and at last he observed that if he looked down he lost it. He was, as I have said, intelligent, and recognized in this vision the effect of long strain and sudden shock. . . . He awakened the next day still seeing the face, at times dimly, at others clearly. Its persistency troubled him. Was it a symptom of some impending mental disaster? Had his head been clear of late—his memory unimpaired? When the mind of the sensitive becomes critical concerning the health of its own processes, there is peril in the way. He found himself caught in machinery not readily arrested by the will which set it in motion. He had always been in vigorous health and had rarely had occasion to consult a physician. He had, however, lacked power to dismiss unpleasant thoughts, and now the terror of decay of reason haunted him unceasingly.[72]

In this plight he called on Dr. Eskridge, and thus Mitchell had an opportunity once more to speak his views as a doctor on the troubled personality of Greyhurst:

> He [Eskridge] was reflecting upon what had made Greyhurst what he was, when the man . . . . entered the room.

[71] *Ibid.*, p. 284.
[72] *Ibid.*, pp. 303-304.

As they had met of late, on the street or elsewhere, he had casually noticed the slight loss of soldierly carriage, and the absence of a certain defiant challenge in his expression. Now, as they sat down, he cast on Greyhurst a quick look of observant attention, and saw that the large frame had lost flesh . . . . he knew him to be free from grave organic maladies.[73]

Greyhurst had come to the doctor as a patient with a nervous disorder, troubled by his hallucination, and anxious about his sanity:

I have of late been troubled—not all the time, I ought to say—by an occasional sensation of quite causeless fear—well, something like the terror a timid child has when alone in the dark.[74]

Under the gentle prodding of the doctor he continued:

I have also been annoyed by seeing a face in the air, a little to the left. It is lost when I look down. It appears as if made of gossamer, and I see things through it. Does it or the other trouble represent any probability of mental failure?[75]

Before answering his question the doctor elicited further information. The patient had lost his appetite, had at times an inexplicable fear, and couldn't get rid of the vision which was nearly always present. He had always been troubled with an impulsive temperament which was made even worse by the pampering and indulgence he had received as a child.

After his examination the doctor ended the interview with an assurance: the phantom would fade away unless the cause that occasioned it were repeated. Mitchell had many times commented on the salutary effect of confession, and here he provided an example. Greyhurst, walking home, felt a "great sense of relief" and found "that he had lost the smiling face of George Trescot."[76]

But the relief was only short-lived, and made all the more

[73] *Ibid.*, p. 318.
[74] *Ibid.*, pp. 318-319.
[75] *Ibid.*, p. 319.
[76] *Ibid.*, p. 323.

painful the last blow inflicted by Constance, breaking the marriage Greyhurst had long ago set his heart on. Constance communicated with the young lady Greyhurst was devoted to, and persuaded her that he was an evil man. It was then he saw the phantom again; unable to bear more, he rushed to the home of Constance and, standing before her, put a bullet to his head.

Chapter XI

MITCHELL AS A NOVELIST

As THE foregoing survey has attempted to show, Mitchell's accomplishments as a psychiatric novelist were considerable. He portrayed a number of characters suffering from various types of mental illness, and each from a strictly realistic viewpoint. Only in his first story, "The Case of George Dedlo," was there any alien mysticism at all, anything outside the framework of Mitchell's own knowledge and observation; and in that story the impossible climax, the limbless Dedlo walking on spiritual legs, was intended merely as a satire on spiritualism. The story in general was based upon the factual observations of a neurologist whose opportunities to study the nerve injuries of amputees had been unprecedented. It was essentially a fictional version of some of the material which Mitchell later published in his important contribution *Injuries of Nerves and Their Consequences*.

In all his many studies of mentally ill people Mitchell was equally realistic and informed. Dr. Wendell was the study of a man whose character underwent a slow and gradual process of deterioration. The author traced his downfall step by step, showing how each prepared the way for the next, and how his entire course of action was the inevitable result of his temperament and the circumstances in which he was placed. His career illustrates vividly some of the principles involved in the development of conditioned responses, principles which

Mitchell learned and utilized in his treatment of nervous disorders. Richard Darnell was a similar study. He followed the
same general pattern of deterioration as Dr. Wendell and illustrates the same principles. His childhood days, too, were
described, because of their importance in the growth of those
habits which later destroyed him.

Octopia Darnell was an outstanding illustration of hysterical
illness. She was chronically weak, pale and thin, an invalid
confined to her couch. There was no physical reason why she
should not get up, meet her responsibilities in the world, and
regain the health that can come only from activity. Mitchell
not only described her illness as of hysterical origin, but he
exposed precisely the psychological mechanism involved and
the way it helped her to get what she wanted. He revealed,
too, how easily she could get well when the proper stimulus
was applied. His portrait has the authenticity that could come
only from his large experience with just such women, and it
has, too, the insights which were dependent upon his special
medical knowledge. Octopia illustrates some of the observations he made in his *Lectures on Diseases of the Nervous System*. Constance Trescot was another study in hysterical illness.
Mitchell described in detail the emotional shocks that made
her ill and the weaknesses in her temperament and training
that made her succumb to blows a different personality might
have been able to withstand. Ann Penhallow was as soft and
generous as Constance was hard and unrelenting; yet Ann,
too, became hysterically ill and resorted to the same disagreeable behavior patterns as Octopia and Constance. Mitchell
revealed the psychological cause that could make even so admirable a character put on the semblance of physical disability, and become really ill in the process.

Mr. J. C. was a study in dual personality. He had been
leading a quiet life as a refined Oriental scholar married to a
genteel lady when he suddenly escaped his circumstances by
becoming an uneducated clerk married to an uneducated
woman. In his new personality he could remember nothing
of his original one; he showed no recognition when confronted

by his first wife, nor had he ever heard of the man when his own original personality was described. When he reverted to his first personality he could remember nothing of his second. His career paralleled closely, in its psychological characteristics, the career of Mary Reynolds, an actual person, the subject of a medical paper which Mitchell had written earlier. Sibyl Maywood was a more elaborate study in dual personality. Sibyl, a very sensitive young girl, suffered a shock when the young man she was in love with suddenly lost interest in her. She was able to suppress this unpleasant fact from her conscious personality, but her deepest feelings broke through into a second personality. Walking in her sleep she spoke her love aloud, but upon waking into her normal state could remember nothing. She wrote anonymous emotional letters to the man she loved, but had no recollection of them in her normal state. In these studies of dual personality Mitchell illustrated clearly the interpretation held by present-day psychiatrists, that the second personality represents a flight from the first.

Roger Grace was an example of dipsomania in an otherwise admirable person, a successful banker of exceptional kindness and generosity. Once every year or two, when the strains of life would become particularly difficult, he would be seized with an uncontrollable desire for drink. He would escape to some obscure town, lose himself altogether for a week in a drunken stupor, and return refreshed and better able to face his problems. Peter Lamb, also afflicted with dipsomania, was a completely different sort of person. He was drunk as often as he could obtain liquor, and otherwise a cruel and dangerous criminal. In his presentation of this man, as well as of Roger Grace, Mitchell indicated some of the causes in temperament and background which helped develop the disease.

Philetus Richmond, a blind man married to a much younger woman, lost his contact with reality and eventually had to be confined as insane. His feelings of anxiety and insecurity were intensified by the presence of a younger and better-educated man. He had hallucinations of the man visiting his wife at night, and he heard voices commanding him to take revenge. Benedict Norman was a feeble, little man suffering from paranoia. He had tried unsuccessfully to kill his wife, but refused to be persuaded that he had failed. He believed, on no evidence whatever, that she had been unfaithful, and tried to kill the man he imagined as her lover. The impulsive John Greyhurst, in a fit of temper, had murdered an innocent man. Although he was legally exonerated on the plea of self-defense, he was constantly reminded of the real facts by the dead man's widow, who had witnessed the crime. He began to have hallucinations of the dead man's smiling face, ever before him several feet to his left. It stayed with him when he stood still and also when he walked, always at the same distance. He began to question his own sanity, and indeed seemed perilously near to losing it when, goaded beyond tolerance, he appeared before the widow and shot himself in the temple. In this study of the first phases of insanity, as well as in the other two studies, Mitchell stressed the role of feelings of anxiety as background causes of insanity, as do psychiatrists today. The three portraits together represent authentically three different stages in the growth of insanity. In John Greyhurst we see a man take the first definite steps, in Philetus Richmond we see a man complete the process, in Benedict Norman we see a man as he acts and thinks after he has become insane.

Mitchell described all his mentally ill characters from his viewpoint as a scientist. He tried to show the causes in heredity, background or circumstance which produced the disorders he pictured. Even the worst of his characters were presented not as complete villains, but as ill people, made so largely by forces outside their control. He communicated this viewpoint not only through the action of the story and through the comments of the various doctors who appeared as characters, but through the very language of his narrative, which was replete with scientific metaphors and analogies.

Mitchell's psychiatric fiction becomes all the more impressive when one appreciates how much original work he had to do in the field of science before he had the necessary background. Before he could portray such characters as Octopia he had to do his own original work in psychiatry; and before he could do that he had to develop his scientific viewpoint toward people and his ability to apply that viewpoint to problems of human personality. In our own age it may be difficult to grasp how much of an effort he had to make; for today novelists may take for granted much of what he had to formulate for himself. One needs only to remember Mitchell's famous address before the psychiatrists of his time to appreciate how rare were his own habits of research into the problems of nervous disorder and personality illness. He could rightfully scold his audience for their failures in research. With all their rich opportunities as guardians of the insane in hospitals and elsewhere, they had added almost nothing to knowledge of the mentally ill. Most of them carried on no experiments or investigations, and published no papers. Worse than that, they seemed to lack the fundamental viewpoints and methods necessary to such research.[1] The human personality was one of the last areas to come within the sphere of science; in the late nineteenth century, psychology was hardly a science, and there were but few men trying to make it one. Even the great William James, after vigorously attacking the problem, found other fields more inviting. Most doctors were still quite helpless before the problems of mental illness. Mitchell was one of the few who made an effective beginning. His productive research in physiology and in neurology had taught him an approach which he found equally productive in his study of human personality disorders.

In his fictional studies of nervous disorders he stood alone. He was the first novelist in American literature to present such clinically accurate portraits of mentally ill characters. No one else had ever done anything like it, except Oliver Wendell

---

[1] Speaking of Holmes, who died in 1894, Oberndorf observed: "The most advanced psychiatrists of his day were concerned almost exclusively with the abolition of forcible restraint and punishment of the insane and the introduction of more humane attitudes and methods in custodial asylums." *Op. cit.*, p. 5.

Holmes. But even Holmes's work lacks much of the merit of Mitchell's. His three novels, in the first place, lack the range of subject one finds in Mitchell. There are but three important studies: Elsie Venner, who has been classified as an example of schizophrenia; Myrtle Hazard, an example of hysteria; and Maurice Kirkwood, an example of gynophobia (morbid fear of women). These studies, furthermore, lack the objective, factual detail of Mitchell's presentations. Clarence P. Oberndorf, who has edited Holmes' psychiatric novels, calls *The Guardian Angel,* which contains the study of hysteria, "psychiatrically by far the most significant of Holmes's three novels." Yet Myrtle Hazard, the central character, seems shadowy and unreal beside Mitchell's studies in hysteria, particularly Octopia Darnell. Mitchell's portrayal seems based, as indeed it was, on extensive, first-hand knowledge. He pictured Octopia in conflict with normal people, and confronted her with dramatic situations which exposed her character. Myrtle Hazard was allowed to live in a world of her own from which even the reader is shut away. She is herself less interesting than some of the author's comments about her.

This difference between Myrtle and Octopia typifies a larger difference between their two authors. Mitchell was more of a literary realist, particularly in his presentation of mental illness, than was Holmes. There were no mystical fancies woven into Mitchell's portraits, whereas Holmes, in the tradition of Hawthorne, employed unreal and impossible allegory to present his ideas. He attributed to Elsie Venner reptilian characteristics and explained them by the fact that her mother, during pregnancy, was bitten by a snake. There is nothing like that in Mitchell.

Holmes himself was quite aware of the fancifulness of his conception. He received a number of questions concerning this reptilian influence on Elsie Venner, and in the second preface written in 1883, explained his attitude:

> In the first place, it is not based on any well-ascertained physiological fact. There are old fables about patients who

have barked like dogs or crowed like cocks, after being bitten or wounded by those animals. There is nothing impossible in the idea that Romulus and Remus may have imbibed wolfish traits of character from the wet nurse the legend assigned them, but the legend is not sound history, and the supposition is nothing more than a speculative fancy. Still, there is a limbo of curious evidence bearing on the subject of pre-natal influences sufficient to form the starting-point of an imaginative composition.[2]

In the original preface to the work, it might be added here, he made a confession which indicates how much his literary method differed from Mitchell's. The latter's fictional presentations of ill people were based on his actual knowledge, and illustrated what he had observed in his practice and experience. Holmes deliberately indulged in romance, and drew Elsie Venner from his imagination, as he himself freely admitted:

> In calling this narrative a "romance," the Author wishes to make sure of being indulged in the common privileges of the poetic license. Through all the disguise of fiction a grave scientific doctrine may be detected lying beneath some of the delineations of character. He has used this doctrine as a part of the machinery of his story without pledging his absolute belief in it to the extent to which it is asserted or implied. It was adopted as a convenient medium of truth rather than as an accepted scientific conclusion. . . . The Author must be permitted, however, to say here, in his personal character, and as responsible to the students of the human mind and body, that since this story has been in progress he has received the most startling confirmation of the possibility of the existence of a character like that which he had drawn as a purely imaginary conception in Elsie Venner.[3]

Holmes had accomplishments of his own as a psychiatric novelist, and they are amply recognized by Clarence P. Oberndorf in his recent study. Like Mitchell, Holmes emphasized how much men were, in their actions, thoughts and personali-

2 Oliver W. Holmes, *Elsie Venner* (New York, 1891), p. ix.
3 *Ibid.*, pp. vii-viii.

ties, the product of causes they could not control. He not only shared some of Mitchell's pioneer views, but developed other insights which his contemporary never revealed. In his study of Myrtle Hazard he described with unusual appreciation the effect of infant experience on adult life. Early in the story he set down, in some detail, Myrtle's impressions of the world as she lay in her cradle in the far away tropics of India where she was born:

> So her earliest impressions,—it would not be exact to call them recollections,—besides the smiles of her father and mother, were of dusky faces, of loose white raiment, of waving fans, of breezes perfumed with the sweet exhalations of sandal-wood, of gorgeous flowers and glowing fruit, of shady verandas, of gliding palanquins, and all the languid luxury of the South.[4]

He described, too, her impressions when, still an infant, she returned home to America:

> During the long voyage, the strange mystery of the ocean was wrought into her consciousness so deeply, that it seemed to have become a part of her being. The waves rocked her, as if the sea had been her mother; and, looking over the vessel's side from the arms that held her with tender care, she used to watch the play of the waters, until the rhythm of their movement became a part of her, almost as much as her own pulse and breath.[5]

Holmes's unique observations are often obscured, so enwrapped are they in their awkward, banal stories. They appear more clearly in the comments of the author than in the actions of the characters. Holmes's novels make tedious reading much of the time.[6] Not only do the characters seem un-

---

[4] Oliver W. Holmes, *The Guardian Angel* (New York, 1892), p. 26.
[5] *Ibid.*, p. 26.
[6] Mitchell, apparently, never wrote at any length about the novels of Holmes. He did, however, on a number of occasions record his opinions of his other contemporary psychological novelist, Henry James: "I do not read Henry James, not because I do not see a certain greatness in his powers, but because this immense analysis seems to me unnatural and because I expect a novel to interest me. If it does not, I have nothing to

real, but the stories are poorly constructed, and slowed up with lengthy digressions. Some of Mitchell's novels, such as *When All the Woods Are Green,* are also extraordinarily dull, and one wonders how anyone ever enjoyed them. But his better novels maintain the reader's interest quite well. Certainly he was a more skillful storyteller than Holmes.

Mitchell, however, did have his shortcomings as a novelist. In the first place, he was limited by his own literary theories. He did not make the fullest use of his psychiatric experience and understanding. He was bound by a severe sense of decorum, sharing with some of his contemporaries the attitude toward fiction expressed by Howells when he wrote that he wanted his novels to be fit reading for young ladies. In his medical writings, however, Mitchell seemed to be candid enough when the situation called for it—far more candid and outspoken than he ever became in his fiction. When he faced the general public he dropped the freedom of a doctor and assumed what he considered the obligations of a gentleman. He explained his point of view in his book *Doctor and Patient:*

> It would be easy, and in some sense valuable, could a man of large experience and intelligent sympathies write a book for women, in which he would treat plainly of the normal circle of their physiological lives; but this would be a method of dealing with the whole matter which would be open to criticism, and for me, at least, a task difficult to the verge of the impossible. . . . The man who desires to write in a popular way of nervous women . . . . must acknowledge, like the Anglo-Saxon novelist, certain reputable limitations. The best readers are, however, in a measure cooperative authors, and may be left to interpolate the unsaid.[7]

He expressed himself again on the subject in a talk before the students of Radcliffe College:

---

say to such books. I liked his earlier style novels, and think that there is something precieuse in his later style." From an unpublished letter to Mrs. Mason, dated September 10, 1908. A copy of the letter is in the possession of Mrs. Macdonough.

7 S. Weir Mitchell, *Doctor and Patient,* pp. 11-12.

It is impossible to speak frankly as to certain matters. I never could, and never will, lecture medically to women. And so I must talk as best I can, and you must read unspoken wisdom between the lines.[8]

Mitchell felt bound to be reticent not only on the subject of sex, but on other aspects of human life. The details of sickness and the behavior of patients, which he knew so well, he felt were inappropriate in a novel. He disapproved of that school of realistic writers who painted meticulously and in detail the more sordid aspects of life. Much of the great knowledge he accumulated as a doctor had no place, he felt, in literature:

Since, however, the growth of realism in literary art, the temptation to delineate exactly the absolute facts of disease has led authors to dwell too freely on the details of sickness. . . . Mr. Trollope's "Gamma" is an instance in point, where every one will feel that the spectacle of the heroine going seasick to death, owing to the administration of tartar emetic, is as disgusting and inartistic a method as fiction presents. Why not have made it croton oil? More and worse of this hideous realism is to be found in About's books, such, for instance, as "Germaine". . . . As to the recent realistic atrocities of Zola, and even of Tolstoi, a more rare sinner, if we exclude his disgusting drama of peasant life, I prefer to say little.[9]

In numerous places Mitchell expressed his disgust with the French realistic novel, perhaps never more effectively than in *Circumstance* when he had Mrs. Hunter, as wicked a female as graces his fiction, express her taste in reading by turning to a French novel.[10]

[8] S. Weir Mitchell, *Address to the Students of Radcliffe College* (Cambridge, 1896) , p. 10.

[9] S. Weir Mitchell, *Doctor and Patient,* pp. 72-73. See p. 144 and p. 148 for further examples of Mitchell's reticence. He would not discuss the cyclical restrictions imposed upon women after puberty.

[10] Although Mitchell disparaged the French realists for their "hideous realism," he also disparaged unrealistic descriptions. He felt that sordid details should be omitted from fiction, but he wanted accuracy in whatever was presented. "The difficulty of the modern novelist in giving symptoms and preserving the entire decorum of his pages has amused me a

Mitchell's fiction certainly was much affected by his self-imposed restraints. In his own day his literary friends, sharing his views and aware of all the unpleasant details he might have crammed into his stories, approved his practice. Owen Wister, for example, singled out this restraint for praise in his address to the College of Physicians of Philadelphia at the special meeting upon the death of Mitchell:

> It is preposterous to suppose that any Balzac or Flaubert or de Maupassant knew more of evil and sorrow and pain than Dr. Mitchell. Four years of mutilated soldiers and fifty of hysteria, neurosis, insanity, and drug mania, unrolled for him a hideous panorama of the flesh, the mind, and the soul. But when in one of his books he makes a doctor say: "Who dares draw illness as it is? Not I," he gives the clue to his fiction. He omits nothing needful, it is the superfluous that he discards. . . . Consider what we should have had if Balzac or Flaubert or Zola had known what Dr. Mitchell knew about women![11]

Mitchell was restrained not only because of his literary theories, but also because of his professional ethics, as he indicated in the words of Dr. North:

> Concerning most of life's strangest experiences my lips are professionally sealed. Sometimes they may be told when

little. Depend upon it, he had best fight shy of these chronic illnesses; they make queer reading to a doctor who knows what sick people are; and above all does this advice apply to death-beds. As a rule, folks get very horrible at such times, and are a long while in dying, with few of their wits about them at the last. But in novels people die marvelously possessed of their faculties; or, if they are shot, always jump into the air exactly as men never do in fact." See *ibid.*, pp. 73-74.

In his correspondence Mitchell sometimes expressed in colorful language his dislike of the French novelists: "As for the novel you speak of, I read it, half of it, with disgust and a glad sense that it is only among the French that we find genius devoting itself crudely to such matters as this book deals with. No Englishman of genius has as yet done this. I put the book into the fire and found that it did not even burn so satisfactorily as to contribute the comfort of decent warmth." A copy of the unpublished letter, dated October 3, 1908, and addressed to Mrs. Mason, is in the possession of Mrs. S. W. Macdonough.

11 Owen Wister, "S. Weir Mitchell: Man of Letters," *S. Weir Mitchell, Memorial Addresses and Resolutions* (Philadelphia, 1914), pp. 154-155.

years have gone by and death has removed all concerned.[12]

Perhaps the greatest single cause of Mitchell's restraint was his Philadelphia background. As a gentleman of the city's cultured class, he was particularly restrained in his approach to the offensive subject of sex. His personal conduct had always been puritanical. As a boy in college he had shunned the local prostitutes; as a medical student in Paris, although he had sufficient funds, he had kept aloof from the wild life of the city, consuming his energies in study and his money on books and medical equipment. From his earliest childhood, particularly as a result of his mother's training, he had been brought up in an atmosphere of puritanism. He had been required to attend Sunday school and church frequently, to shun card-playing and, on Sundays, all games whatsoever.[13]

Throughout his life his behavior toward women was reserved. His personal associations were limited to ladies of his own social level who shared his cultural interests and moral standards. It is true, however, that he did become quite fond of some of these feminine friends, particularly Sarah Butler Wister, whom he considered the most interesting woman he ever met. How his wife reacted to such relationships there appears to be no record, but evidently he himself felt she should be sympathetic. When married women grow wise, he wrote, "they will want their husbands to have women friends."[14] One may speculate concerning the sublimation involved in these friendships, but there was never a hint of scandal nor the least indiscretion. In his novels Mitchell observed the same proprieties that he did in his personal life. In fact even his lady friends, who shared his general attitude, felt he was too restrained in his treatment of love scenes.

In addition to these limitations resulting from his sense of propriety, he was handicapped in another way. Some of his most important characters were evidently based on persons he

---

12 S. Weir Mitchell, *Dr. North and his Friends*, p. 362.

13 See Earnest, *op. cit.*, p. 9.

14 S. Weir Mitchell, *When All the Woods Are Green*, p. 208.

knew professionally, but not with any great personal intimacy. In presenting such people, he described the symptoms of the disordered personality, and to some extent the immediate and background causes—only enough to give the reader some definite understanding. But he could not introduce many of the personal, intimate details which bring a character vividly to life.

To the present-day reader the most interesting characters in some of Mitchell's novels are those suffering from mental illness. As a result, he finds an unhappy disproportion in the construction of such novels. While the main story is about quite normal people, the main attraction is in the abnormal minor characters. In *Roland Blake,* for instance, the central characters are Blake and Olivia. What reader could doubt, early in the narrative, that they would end up in one another's arms? The suspense Mitchell tried to build up is a mockery, and serves only to interfere with the story of Octopia, who commands every scene in which she appears. In *John Sherwood,* too, the man who dominates the story is not the chief character, John Sherwood, who tells it in the first person and who is part of nearly every scene, but rather Mr. Hapworth, the paranoiac. Mitchell had more of importance to say of this man than of any other character in the novel. Nevertheless our understanding of him is inadequate, unsatisfying. There is more space devoted to the way the others feel about him than to the far more intriguing picture of the way he feels about them, and about himself. As a result the reader is given the commonplace reactions of ordinary people rather than the exceptional reactions of the disordered personality.

What is true of Hapworth is true of Mitchell's disordered personalities in general. We do not see the world through their distorted eyes. We do not relive with them their agonies, their sensations, their plans. We get all too seldom the detailed re-creation of a disturbed personality such as Dostoyevsky accomplished in *Crime and Punishment,* or Shakespeare in *Macbeth* and *King Lear*—especially through those soliloquies which by their intensity speak many pages in a few lines.[15] Nor do we get the sort of detail given by Clifford Beers, who wrote the story of a man afflicted with delusions quite similar to Hapworth's. This man, too, thought he had committed a crime, thought the police were after him, unduly suspected people, and had tendencies dangerous to others and himself. Clifford Beers drew a memorable picture of the man's mind in all its detail, presented his feelings, thoughts, sensations, hopes. The reader relives the experience of a manic-depressive, knows how it feels to be so disordered. Yet Beers showed no more understanding of the principles governing abnormal character than Mitchell did. There was, however, one crucial difference: Mitchell was writing of people he had known as patients; Beers was writing of himself, of his own past agonies during the time when he had been a manic-depressive.

Mitchell, in fact, seldom used his own personality as a source of literary material. The idea of searching into his own deepest thoughts and feelings and portraying them in his novels, however disguised, was quite foreign to him. When he finished his first draft of *John Sherwood*, for example, he noted in his diary, August 19, 1910: "It is too autobiographical and must have a complete revision."[16] The discerning Mrs. Mason called attention to this reticence in one of her many letters to him:

> I have always noted that you put very little of yourself in your work, though much of your own observation, or *objective* experience. That is modern and scientific, but to my mind the divine spark lies in the personal life. . . . You are a bit afraid of emotional writing, and rightly enough, as things go. This is *not* a criticism. One may be too cold, as Mr. Howells is. He writes symphonies in gray, as I have said elsewhere. You are far more sympathetic.[17]

15 Mitchell, of course, had none of the techniques for depicting the stream of consciousness, such as Joyce, Proust and their successors developed. He had little need for such techniques since he seldom tried to give detailed pictures of the inner life.

16 The diary, unpublished, is in the possession of Mrs. Macdonough.

17 Mrs. Mason to S. W. Mitchell, December 26. 1899. A copy of the unpublished letter is in the possession of Mrs. S. W. Macdonough.

About two weeks later she wrote again on the subject:

> You do put a great deal of personal experience and observation in your novels. The sentiment is sane and healthy, which certainly is not a fault, but you do not deal in soul tragedies that are apt to be outlets for strong personal feeling, or suffering.[18]

Mitchell was troubled by such criticism, but he could hardly disagree completely. Certainly he was aware of his own reticence, and occasionally referred to it. His diary of March 7, 1907, contains the entry: "No man can reveal his whole life. No man dare. The wisest are the most silent."[19]

In his personal life, too, Mitchell was extraordinarily reticent, even with his wife after long years of happy marriage. When their twenty-two year old daughter died, Mitchell could not speak freely of himself to her. "Ah, dear lady, if I could only tell you all of my life as honor forbids, you would know what you are and have been to me and my later life."[20] The death of his daughter did result in a clear expression of his personal grief, the poem *Ode on a Lycian Tomb*. Because it was so personal, however, he decided at first not to publish it in a magazine, but later changed his mind.

In his novels Mitchell represented himself primarily through the various doctors. They were not portrayed with any intimacy at all, but were employed for the light they could cast upon the mental illness of characters more important than themselves. By this practice Mitchell not only kept his own inner life out of his fiction, but the inner lives of his abnormal characters as well. He presented them from the point of view of the doctor, too often giving the reader an analysis of a case rather than the creation of a personality.

It seems that Mitchell never fully appreciated his own unique qualifications. The disordered personalities which he almost alone among the American novelists of his time could

[18] Mrs. Mason to S. W. Mitchell, January 6, 1900. A copy of the unpublished letter is in the possession of Mrs. Macdonough.
[19] Quoted in Earnest, *op. cit.*, p. 236.
[20] *Ibid.*, p. 237.

create he drew merely as minor characters, giving the chief roles to less interesting people. It is true, he probably didn't know these mentally ill persons intimately enough to make them the central characters—but apparently he never tried to know them that well. He never deliberately set out, it seems, to utilize his position as doctor to pry loose information he could use in his fiction. Not for him was Zola's note-taking technique, the deliberate study of men and women for the purposes of fiction. In his contacts with his patients Mitchell was, first, last and always, a doctor, and whatever he might learn for his stories was incidental. His medical career, as he often stated in reply to questions, was his chief pride and interest.[21] The mentally ill characters who got into his novels seemed apart from the main design. He evidently was quite surprised himself, in reviewing his work, to find that somehow so many of them had made their way into it.

So unobtrusive, in general, were Mitchell's mentally disordered characters that most contemporary discussions of his work failed to appreciate his accomplishments in portraying them. The magazines rarely even mentioned his fictional studies of mental disease. No journal reviewed Mitchell's novels more consistently than the *Nation;* since its reviews were quite characteristic of the contemporary failure to recognize what Mitchell had accomplished, and since he himself commented more frequently on the *Nation's* criticism than on any others, a brief survey of its reviews may be revealing.

Its criticism of Mitchell's first novel was certainly unappreciative. *In War Time*, the *Nation* said, was not wholly successful. While that verdict might not seem too harsh, the reasons in support of it reveal a lack of sympathy with Mitchell's entire purpose. The *Nation* admitted that the book had "a well considered theme, and characters in themselves of much more than ordinary promise." Why then did it "fail of great suc-

<hr>

[21] Mitchell declared to B. R. Tucker, for example, that literary pursuits were "unimportant when compared with medicine, and that he was much more interested in his profession than in anything else." Beverley R. Tucker, *op. cit.*, pp. 58-59.

cess"? The final catastrophe was "too shocking." As for the protagonist, Dr. Wendell, whose deterioration Mitchell had described so meticulously, he was altogether unsuitable as a chief character. One has no business writing a novel about such a man:

> It never can be wise to neglect the old rule, discovered long before the evolution of the modern novel, that the principal figure must, so to speak, command the reader. It will not do to make him either a villain or a coward. Be the end never so tragic, the feeling excited must be only terror or pity. If the pity passes into contempt of the man, it is all over with admiration.[22]

In its review of Mitchell's next novel, *Roland Blake*, the *Nation* was even harsher. The review missed altogether the informed portrait of Octopia Darnell, who was not even mentioned. Indeed, the entire novel was dismissed in a most disdainful manner:

> Mr. Mitchell's stories are readable; the memories of the war are very actual and living with him; but his conceptions are too hasty and too carelessly worked out to deserve more than a careless reading.[23]

[22] "Recent Novels," *Nation*, XL (March 26, 1885), p. 265. *In War Time* did receive an appreciative review in *Lippincott's Magazine:* " 'In War Time' is an eminently sane and delicate interpretation of the lives of a group of people, each of whom is made admirably real by a succession of minute and carefully studied touches." See "Recent American Novels," *Lippincott's Magazine*, XXXV (February, 1885), p. 216.

[23] "Recent Novels," *Nation*, XLIV (January 6, 1887), p. 18. It was probably in reply to this review that Mitchell published in the *Critic* a caustic letter on reviewers: "The most carefully written book," he said there, "is often dismissed with as little care as the most slovenly novel." See S. W. Mitchell, "A Novelist's Thoughts on Critics," *Critic*, VII (April 23, 1887), p. 202. The *Critic* itself had reviewed *Roland Blake* favorably, though it made no particular comment on Octopia: "It is, indeed, a noteworthy tale, fine in its subtle study of character and changes in character, its nice individualizing of each personality, and its clever conversations. . . . Each character stands clearly by itself, though perhaps the ladies are a little more prominent than the hero; and the keen analysis of motive and action is as marked a characteristic of this as of Dr. Mitchell's other books." See "Recent Fiction," *Critic*, VI (December 15, 1886), p. 317. More discerning than any of the reviewers was Mitchell's friend Mrs.

Mitchell's careful presentation of the insane Philetus Richmond in *Far in the Forest* also failed to evoke appreciation from the *Nation*. The review mentioned him as a "blind giant," and that was all. However, it did say that the characters in the novel were "solid and vigorous" and that the final tragedy was "the natural result" of all that went before, "an inevitable catastrophe."[24]

The *Nation's* reviews of *Characteristics* and its sequel, *Dr. North and His Friends,* were equally unconcerned with Mitchell's ventures into abnormal psychology. The chapter on dual personality in *Characteristics* and the extensive treatment of Sibyl Maywood in *Dr. North and His Friends* were not mentioned. After describing some of the very definite weaknesses of *Characteristics,* the *Nation* called it, truly enough, "not very exciting," but added that the conversation was "sane and even in tone."[25] As for *Dr. North and His Friends,* the *Nation* dismissed that book with elaborate sarcasm:

> Almost everybody who believes himself to be intelligent may be heard, at one time or another, expressing a regret that the age of conversation is past. An attempt to read the conversations between 'Dr. North and his Friends' is likely to stifle such regrets; indeed, to convert them into an ardent prayer that the art may not be revived, at least in our time.[26]

Mason. In a letter to Mitchell she showed her appreciation of Octopia: "She is too real not to have been drawn from life. You deal with very subtle shades of motive and feeling and give a singularly delicate analysis of many forms of unconscious self-deception. It is quite possible that the multitude, intent upon striking events, may overlook many of your finest points." A copy of the unpublished letter, dated December 27, 1886, is in the possession of Mrs. S. W. Macdonough.

24 "Recent Novels," *Nation,* XLVIII (January 27, 1889), p. 530. Other reviews likewise ignored Philetus. However, The *Critic,* although making no mention of Philetus, did observe that *Far in the Forest* contained "some clever analysis of character." See "Recent Fiction," the *Critic,* XI (June 8, 1889), p. 283.

25 "More Novels," *Nation,* LV (December 8, 1892), p. 437.

26 "Recent Novels," *Nation,* LXXII (February 28, 1901), p. 182. While some other reviews treated the book more kindly, they likewise failed to appreciate Mitchell's scientific knowledge in the portrait of Sibyl Maywood. The *Critic,* for example, did little more than mention Sibyl, though

In 1900 Mitchell published in book form a collection of short works, including the "Case of George Dedlo." The title story, "The Autobiography of a Quack," the *Nation* dismissed as "only an unpleasant expression of a transient craze for realism." As for Mitchell's story of an amputee, describing in such accurate detail his reactions to his missing limbs, the *Nation* considered it of "no more general interest than has a surgeon's report of a famous case, which he describes accurately without sentiment or sympathy." But isn't even such a report worthwhile, deserving of praise? Evidently not to the *Nation*. "If these be doctor's diversions," the review concluded, "a doctor's life is indeed a distressing one."[27]

The *Nation*'s review of *Circumstance*, although fair in its judgments, made no mention of the dipsomaniac Grace.[28] The review of *Constance Trescot*, however, did show some appreciation of the fact that Mitchell had drawn upon his medical experience, a fact rather difficult to overlook since Constance is the chief character and dominates the novel:

> Constance Trescot is not a monster, but just a perfectly selfish woman, which is, perhaps, about the same thing. After her husband's death she becomes a monomaniac, but is none the less responsible for her actions. Dr. Mitchell has had ample opportunity to observe many women similarly constituted, and his delineation of Constance is as clear and assured as if she had been the subject of notes.[29]

---

it did refer to *Dr. North and His Friends* as "a book such as only a wise and learned man could write, for it garners the wit and wisdom of a lifetime." "Fiction," the *Critic*, XXXVIII (January 1901), p. 86.

27 "More Novels," *Nation*, LXXI (August 23, 1900), p. 157.

28 See "More Fiction," *Nation*, LXXIV (March 20, 1902), The *Dial* did praise Mitchell's portrait of Mrs. Hunter; but it, too, failed even to mention Mr. Grace, the banker who suffered from dipsomania. See William Morton Payne, "Recent American Fiction," *Dial*, XXXII (February 1, 1902), p. 88.

29 "More Fiction," *Nation*, LXXX (June 1, 1905), p. 441. The *New York Times* also noticed the psychological treatment of Constance: "Constance Trescot, first as the loving wife, later as the avenger of her husband's murder, is an excellent exhibition of Dr. Mitchell's ability at strong delineation of character. It is a tale wherein the psychological element, however, does not overcloud the romantic interest." See "Summer Reading," *New York Times* (June 17, 1905), p. 391.

The *Nation*'s review of *John Sherwood* was less complimentary. Not only did it contain no hint that Mitchell's treatment of Hapworth was an informed study of a paranoiac but even the praise in the review was inane: "We suppose Dr. Mitchell's popularity as a writer is due to his optimism. His interpretation of human character is always cheerful and wholesome." When the reviewer went on to find definite fault, he wrote a sentence which really stirred the ire of Mitchell: "But the chief fault of this writer is not a matter of correctness: it is a certain thickness of speech amounting almost to an impediment."[30]

In a letter to Mrs. Mason, Mitchell referred to this criticism, declaring (not too convincingly) that the story was told in the first person by John Sherwood, and that the style represented the character and not the author. Furthermore, Mitchell went on to say, the reviews in the *Nation* habitually missed the general design of a novel:

> The capacity to feel the tone and the general trend of a novel is one which I have missed always in the *Nation*'s reviews.
> I should like to thank the writer of the review in the *Dial* for just what the other review misses.[31]

While the review in the *Dial*, which Mitchell so praised, also failed to comment on Hapworth, it did show more understanding of the chief character, John Sherwood, who recovered his health and a wholesome outlook by escaping from the strains of business into a life close to nature.[32]

30 "Current Fiction," the *Nation*, XCIII (August 10, 1911), p. 122.

31 A copy of the unpublished letter dated August 11, 1911, is in the possession of Mrs. S. W. Macdonough.

32 William Morton Payne, "Recent Fiction," *Dial*, LI (July 16, 1911), p. 48. The *New York Times* review, it should be noted, did point out that *John Sherwood* contained some of its author's medical knowledge: "There is rather more of the physician's knowledge than the novelist's art in Dr. S. Weir Mitchell's story . . . . which amounts to a little sermon on physical and spiritual well being plus several interesting pathological studies." See "Dr. Mitchell's Little Sermon," *New York Times* (August 6, 1911), p. 483.

After its long sequence of not too favorable accounts, the *Nation,* in writing of Mitchell's last novel, *Westways* (1913), offered a compliment, perhaps a dubious one in the light of the past reviews: "This story is quite up to the standard of Dr. Mitchell's earlier work."[33] There was some praise for the battle scenes, but none for the informed treatment of the hysterically ill Ann Penhallow, nor for any of the other characters reflecting the medical knowledge Mitchell drew upon. But in this respect, the *Nation's* review was no different from the reviews in other magazines. In their comments on this book, as on his novels in general, the literary writers of his day showed no real appreciation of the unique qualities which Mitchell, as a result of his medical background, was able to bring to his novels.[34]

This lack of appreciation should not be surprising. One of the causes has already been mentioned, the relatively minor roles which Mitchell assigned to his mentally ill characters. But perhaps more important, the critics of the period had little awareness of psychiatry; its use in novels simply did not attract their attention.[35] There was not yet the fusion of psy-

---

[33] "Current Fiction," *Nation* LXLVII (October 3, 1913), p. 384.

[34] In his address upon Mitchell's death Owen Wister did pay brief tribute to Mitchell's fictional studies in mental illness: "His novels abound with studies of decay. *Hugh Wynne* and *Circumstance* offer us senile change; *Roland Blake,* hysteria; *Far in the Forest,* the insanity of persecution; *In War Time* and *Constance Trescot,* the progressive moral rotting of their chief characters—nor does this finish the list," Wister, *op. cit.,* pp. 154-155.

[35] The critics failed also to see the psychiatric merits of the novels of Holmes. The *Nation* in an editorial on American novels commented as follows on the fiction of Holmes: "We acknowledge that 'Elsie Venner' and 'The Guardian Angel' are interesting books. . . . But the artist is hampered by his scientific theories and by his lack of fervent emotional sympathy. His characters do not go; they do not drag him along; they do not drag us. We seem to see that they disappoint their creator. . . ." See "The Great American Novel," *Nation,* VI (January 9, 1868), p. 28. Even the distinguished James R. Lowell, whom Mitchell considered a great critic, in a long review of *Elsie Venner,* hardly touched on its psychological aspects: "The story is really a romance, and the character of the heroine has in it an element of mystery; yet the materials are gath-

chology and literature which has become a trend in our own day, which has given us the stream-of-consciousness technique, the application of determinism to character, the portraits of disordered personalities, and the probings into childhood and infant experience to explain the adult personality.

While it is easy to point out the contemporary failure to appreciate Mitchell's unique achievements, it is quite a problem to bring home those achievements to the present-day reader. If only Mitchell had written one novel that could clearly represent him at his best, one rich in his virtues and free of his worst shortcomings, towering over the others! He didn't. However, three or four of his novels do stand out above the others. In some respects *In War Time* was his best work. Dr. Wendell is certainly one of his outstanding characters, derived from his personal knowledge of doctors and from his scientific conception of personality. The woman Dr. Wendell loved, Mrs. Westerley, was also one of his most memorable creations, a wholesome personality with a generous sense of humor and a delicate sense of honor.

While Octopia Darnell is perhaps Mitchell's best character creation, drawn largely from his special knowledge of hysterically sick women, the novel in which she appears is weak. The protagonist, Roland Blake, is hardly more than a traditional hero of romance, and the woman he loves is, at best, an inferior Mrs. Westerley. The plot, too, is weak, full of too obviously contrived coincidence.

About a dozen years after *Roland Blake* Mitchell wrote the novel which contemporary opinion in general rated as his best, the historical novel of the American revolution, *Hugh Wynne* (1897). "It is interesting from first to last," wrote the *Critic*. "It is easily the author's best work in fiction."[36] The

---

ered from every-day New England life, and that weird borderland between science and speculation where psychology and physiology exercise mixed jurisprudence. . . ." There is no other discussion of the psychological content of the novel. See "Review and Literary Notices," *Atlantic Monthly*, VII (April, 1861), p. 511.

36 "Literature," *Critic*, XXVIII (October 16, 1897), p. 215.

Dial considered it "the most important novel of the American Revolution thus far written."[37] Mitchell's literary friends, too, were enthusiastic in their praise of the book. Thomas Aldrich went so far as to say that there were two great American novels, *The Scarlet Letter* and *Hugh Wynne*.[38]

The popularity of *Hugh Wynne* was well earned. The book marked an advance in the art of the historical novel in America. While it has some of the characteristics of the romantic novel, it also has some of the same realism that distinguishes Mitchell at his best. Although he was able to write the first draft of this long novel in six weeks, he had devoted seven years of research gathering his material. In writing it he did not resort to his imagination as an easy substitute for solid knowledge, but drew his historical characters with the same meticulous effort at accuracy which he used in his portraits of the mentally ill.[39]

There is much merit in *Hugh Wynne*. There are some interesting characters, particularly Hugh's father and Hugh's aunt; there are some effective, satiric pictures of the stern Quaker brotherhood; there are stirring appeals to love of country and of liberty. But the love story which dominates the book is weak. There is Hugh Wynne, the gallant hero; Arthur Wynne,

[37] William Morton Payne, "Recent Fiction," *Dial*, XXIII (November 16, 1897), p. 286.

[38] Burr, *op. cit.*, p. 237. George Meredith, however, dissented from the chorus of praise. "Pardon me," he wrote to Mitchell, "for regretting the days of Roland Blake." *Ibid.*, p. 215.

[39] For Mitchell's own description of his methods as a historical novelist see *Dr. North and His Friends*, pp. 264-265. How seriously Mitchell took his duty to speak the truth in his historical novels, and in his novels generally, may be gleaned from his correspondence concerning his fictional *The Youth of Washington* (1904). In a letter to S. Pomeroy he defended the unfavorable picture he had presented of Washington's mother; his facts came from Washington's own letters, he said. When the Century Company wished him to delete the offending passages, he wrote a strong protest to the publisher's representative, his friend R. W. Gilder: "I did not write this book for children—not for any false consideration would I make myself lie about G. W. . . . As to change from the true to the false by omission—ah never—Nevertheless accept my honest thanks." Both these unpublished letters were written on June 10, 1903 and are in the Library of the University of Pennsylvania.

the obnoxious villain; and Darthea Peniston, the lovely young lady. She is generally intelligent, but remarkably slow to understand that Hugh is really a much better young man than the villain, who was also courting her. Early in the story, the reader can plainly foresee the ending, and can hardly take seriously the suspense Mitchell tried to inject into this old triangle.

In spite of all the praise and popularity it enjoyed, *Hugh Wynne* has steadily declined in appeal. Mitchell's skill and inventiveness in imparting to a historical subject the glamor and suspense of fiction seem less striking today than half a century ago. As a novel, the work has less merit than some of Mitchell's others. It has no character as outstanding as Mrs. Westerley, Dr. Wendell, Mrs. Hunter, or Octopia Darnell. And, except to a minor degree in the study of the senility of Hugh's father, there is no portrait based on medical knowledge. No other novel of Mitchell's has had so great an opportunity to keep the favor of the reading public. If it has given way to more recent books it must always be accorded a place in the development of the American historical novel.

When one asks what is Mitchell's best, he remembers, too, the novel *Circumstance*. It has Roger Grace, the dipsomaniac; it has the two genteel sisters stricken with poverty—a delightful though minor pair—and it has, as its chief character, the unscrupulous Mrs. Hunter, one of Mitchell's most notable portraits, a woman of extraordinary wile. Mitchell himself considered *Circumstance* one of his outstanding works. In a letter to Mrs. Mason written toward the end of his career when all but the last of his novels was published, he classed it with *Constance Trescot*:

> You ask me what I think you would like in my work. . . . Of my novels, I think you would take for choice of approval, as works of fictive art, two novels, *Constance Trescot* and *Circumstance*.[40]

[40] A copy of the unpublished letter, dated August 4, 1911, is in the possession of Mrs. S. W. Macdonough.

In discussing Mitchell's best, one must say a word, too, about *Constance Trescot,* for, as has been mentioned, it was Mitchell's own first choice. Certainly it is his most tightly organized novel. Everything in the first half prepares for Constance's revenge, which occupies the last half. However, since Constance dominates the novel completely, her weaknesses as a character, discussed earlier, are outstanding flaws in the novel. There are serious shortcomings, too, in the plot. The preparatory action is all too elaborate. The important part of the story does not really begin until Constance sets out in pursuit of revenge against Greyhurst, but by that time the novel is nearly half-written. While the first half remains always on the subject, it is too prolonged, too filled with details of background. Furthermore, the machinery of the story seems unduly cumbersome. The descriptions of the law-suit and of the court procedure are prolix and overburdening.

While there is no single novel of Mitchell's which combines all his best, the general body of his work is too good to be forgotten. Not only does it contain much discerning character study, but it represented a new trend. In his scientific approach to personality, in his informed portraits of the mentally ill, Mitchell utilized for fiction—however inadequately at times— knowledge of human behavior which psychologists and doctors, including himself, were discovering. At present, the histories of American literature give Mitchell but scant attention. Only A. H. Quinn, in his *American Fiction* (1936) , has discussed his work at any length, but succeeding histories have not yet followed this precedent. Mitchell's novels should be evaluated anew,[41] for his accomplishments deserve to be recalled more widely and wrought into the tradition of American culture.

[41] Ernest Earnest in his recent biography of Mitchell expresses the same view, declaring that Mitchell "deserves to be restored to the canon of American literature." *S. Weir Mitchell,* p. 235. Both A. H. Quinn and Ernest Earnest, it may be of interest to note, are Philadelphians.

BIBLIOGRAPHY

BOOKS

Beers, Clifford. *A Mind That Found Itself*. New York, 1942.

Berg, Charles. *Deep Analysis*. London, 1946.

Brill, A. A. (ed.). *The Basic Writings of Sigmund Freud*. New York, 1938.

Burr, Anna Robeson. *Weir Mitchell*. New York, 1929.

Burt, Struthers. *Philadelphia, Holy Experiment*. New York, 1945.

Coignard, John. *The Spectacle of a Man*. New York, 1937.

Castiglione, Arturo. *A History of Medicine*. New York, 1947.

Dercum, F. X. (ed.). *Nervous Diseases*. Philadelphia, 1895.

Earnest, Ernest. *S. Weir Mitchell: Novelist and Physician*. Philadelphia, 1950.

Fay, Jay W. *American Psychology Before William James*. New Brunswick, 1939.

Freud, Sigmund. *A General Introduction to Psychoanalysis*. New York, 1943.

——. *Collected Papers*, Vol. III. London, 1925.

Goodman, Nathan G. *Benjamin Rush*. Philadelphia, 1934.

Guthrie, E. R. *The Psychology of Learning*. New York, 1935.

Hall, J. K., Zilboorg, Gregory and Bunker, Henry A. (eds.). *One Hundred Years of American Psychiatry*. New York, 1944.

Hammond, William A. *Treatise on Insanity*. New York, 1883.

Hartwell, Samuel W. *Practical Psychiatry and Mental Hygiene*. New York, 1947.

Hawthorne, Nathaniel. *The Scarlet Letter*. New York, 1946.

Holmes, Oliver W. *A Mortal Antipathy*. New York, 1886.

——. *Elsie Venner*. New York, 1891.

——. *The Guardian Angel*. New York, 1892.

Ingersoll, A. J. *In Health*. Boston, 1877.

Oberndorf, Clarence P. *The Psychiatric Novels of Oliver Wendell Holmes*. New York, 1946.

Quinn, Arthur H. *American Fiction*. New York, 1936.

Mitchell, J. K. *Five Essays*. Philadelphia, 1859.

Mitchell, S. Weir. *The Autobiography of a Quack and Other Stories*. New York, 1903.

——. *Characteristics*. New York, 1903.

——. *Circumstance*. New York, 1903.

——. *Clinical Lessons on Nervous Diseases*. Philadelphia, 1897.

——. *Constance Trescot*. New York, 1905.

——. *Doctor and Patient*. Philadelphia, 1889.

——. *Dr. North and His Friends*. New York, 1905.

——. *Far in the Forest*. New York, 1903.

——. *Fat and Blood*. Philadelphia, 1877.

——. *Hugh Wynne*. New York, 1898.

——. *Injuries of Nerves and Their Consequences*. Philadelphia, 1872.

——. *In War Time*. New York, 1903.

——. *John Sherwood*. New York, 1914.

——. *Lectures on Diseases of the Nervous System, Especially in Women*. Philadelphia, 1881.

——. *Lectures on Diseases of the Nervous System, Especially in Women*, 2nd ed. Philadelphia, 1885.

——.*The Guillotine Club and Other Stories*. New York, 1910.

——. *Roland Blake*. New York, 1903.

——. *The Red City*. New York, 1907.

——. *When All the Woods Are Green*. New York, 1903.

——. *Westways*. New York, 1914.

Mitchell, S. Weir, Morehouse, George R. and Keen, William W. *Gunshot Wounds and Other Injuries of Nerves*. Philadelphia, 1864.

Rees, J. R. (ed.). *Modern Practice in Psychological Medicine*. New York, 1949.

Rush, Benjamin. *The Autobiography of Benjamin Rush*. Princeton, 1949.

——. *Medical Inquiries and Observations Upon the Diseases of the Mind*. 3rd ed. Philadelphia, 1827.

Sherman, Mandel. *Basic Problems of Behavior*. New York, 1941.

Strecker, Edward A., Ebaugh, Franklin G., and Ewalt, Jack R. *Practical Clinical Psychiatry*. Philadelphia, 1947.

Thomas, Atha and Haddan, Chester C. *Amputation Prosthesis*. Philadelphia, 1945.

Thorpe, Louis P. and Katz, Barney. *The Psychology of Abnormal Behavior*. New York, 1948.

Tucker, Beverley R. *S. Weir Mitchell*. Boston, 1914.

Wertham, Frederic. *Dark Legend*. New York, 1941.

Wortis, Herman, and Sillman, Leonard R. *Studies of Compulsive Drinkers*. New Haven, 1946.

PAMPHLETS

Mitchell, J. K. *Lectures on Some of the Means of Elevating the Working Classes*. Philadelphia, 1834.

Mitchell, S. Weir. *Address to the Students of Radcliffe College.* Cambridge, 1896.

——. *Commemorative Address at the Centennial Anniversary of the Institution of the College of Physicians of Philadelphia, January 3, 1887.* Philadelphia, 1887.

——. *Hints to Nurses.* A printed leaflet, among the Mitchell papers in the College of Physicians of Philadelphia.

——. *Mary Reynolds: A Case of Double Consciousness.* Philadelphia, 1889.

——. *The Annual Oration Before the Medical and Chirurgical Faculty of Maryland.* Baltimore, 1877.

ARTICLES

"Current Fiction," *Nation,* XCIII (August 10, 1911).

"Current Fiction," *Nation,* LXLVII (October 3, 1913).

"Dr. Mitchell's Little Sermon," *New York Times* (August 6, 1911).

"Fiction," *Critic,* XXXVIII (January, 1901).

Hinsdale, Guy, "Recollections of S. Weir Mitchell," *The General Magazine and Historical Chronicle,* L (Summer, 1948).

Howells, William Dean, "Recollections of an Atlantic Editorship," *Atlantic Monthly,* C (November, 1907).

Keyes, Baldwin L. "The Problem of Alcoholism," *Archives of Neurology and Psychiatry,* LIV (April, 1947).

"Literature," *Critic,* XXVIII (October 16, 1897).

Lowell, James R. "Reviews and Literary Notices," *Atlantic Monthly,* VII (April, 1861).

Mitchell, S. Weir, "A Novelist's Thoughts on Critics," *Critic,* VII (April 23, 1887).

——. "Experimental Contributions to the Toxicology of Rattlesnake Venom," *New York Medical Journal,* VI (January, 1868).

——. "Nervousness in the Male," *The Medical News,* XXXV (December, 1877).

——. "On Some of the Disorders of Sleep," *Virginia Medical Monthly,* II (1876).

——. "On the Modern Methods of Studying Poisons," *Atlantic Monthly,* XXII (September, 1868).

——. "Paralysis from Peripheral Irritation," *New York Medical Journal,* II (March, 1866).

——. "Phantom Limbs," *Lippincott's Magazine,* VIII (December, 1871).

——. "The Poison of the Rattlesnake," *Atlantic Monthly,* XXI (April, 1868).

——. "Researches Upon the Venom of the Rattlesnake," *Smithsonian Contributions to Knowledge,* XII (1860).

——. "Spinal Arthropathies," *American Journal of the Medical Sciences,* LXIX (April, 1875).

——. "The Treatment by Rest, Seclusion, etc., in Relation to Psychotherapy," *The Journal of the American Medical Association,* L (June, 1908).

Mitchell, S. Weir, "The True and False Palsies of Hysteria," *Medical News and Abstracts,* XXXVIII (February, 1880).

——. "Was He Dead?" *Atlantic Monthly,* XXV (January, 1870).

"More Fiction," *Nation,* LXXIV (March 20, 1902).

"More Fiction," *Nation,* LXXX (June 1, 1905).

"More Novels," *Nation,* LV (December 8, 1892).

"More Novels," *Nation,* LXXI (August 23, 1900).

Payne, William Morton. "Recent Fiction," *Dial,* XXIII (November 16, 1897).

——. "Recent American Fiction," *Dial,* XXXII (February 1, 1902).

——. "Recent Fiction," *Dial,* LI (July 16, 1911).

"Recent American Novels," *Lippincott's Magazine,* XXXV (February, 1885).

"Recent Fiction," *Critic,* VI (December 15, 1886).

"Recent Fiction," *Critic,* XI (June 8, 1889).

"Recent Novels," *Nation,* XL (March 26, 1885).

"Recent Novels," *Nation,* XLIV (January 6, 1887).

"Recent Novels," *Nation,* XLVIII (January 27, 1889).

"Recent Novels," *Nation,* LXXII (February 28, 1901).

Richardson, Lyon N. "S. Weir Mitchell at Work," *American Literature,* II (March, 1939).

Simmel, Ernst. "Alcoholism and Addiction," *The Psychoanalytic Quarterly,* XVII (1948).

"Summer Reading," *New York Times* (June 17, 1905).

"The Great American Novel," *Nation,* VI (January 9, 1868).

Welch, William H. "S. Weir Mitchell: Physician and Man of Science," *S. Weir Mitchell, M.D., LL.D., F.R.S., Memorial Addresses and Resolutions,* Philadelphia, 1914.

Wister, Owen. "S. Weir Mitchell: Man of Letters," *S. Weir Mitchell, M.D., LL.D., F.R.S., Memorial Addresses and Resolutions,* Philadelphia, 1914.

UNPUBLISHED MATERIAL

Gilder, R. W. A letter to The Century Company. Historical Society of Pennsylvania. October 5, 1904.

Mason, A. G. Letter to S. W. Mitchell. December 27, 1886. Copies of
    of this and of the following letters by Mrs. Mason are in the
    possession of Mrs. S. W. Macdonough.
——. Letter to S. W. Mitchell. December 26, 1899.
——. Letter to S. W. Mitchell. January 6, 1900.
Mitchell, J. K. A letter to General George P. Morris. Historical
    Society of Pennsylvania. November 28, 1840.
——. A letter to John Tomlin. Historical Society of Pennsylvania.
    July 25, 1843.
——. "Vindication of Rush." A paper in the College of Physicians
    of Philadelphia. The manuscript, sixteen handwritten pages, is
    undated.
Mitchell S. W. Address to Liberal Art Students. The manuscript,
    undated, is in the possession of Mrs. S. W. Macdonough.
——. Diary in the possession of Mrs. S. W. Macdonough. April 2,
    1906.
——. Diary: April 19, 1910.
——. Letter to ——. May 28, 1863. Historical Society of Pennsyl-
    vania.
——. Letter to Mrs. A. G. Mason. September 24, 1885. Copies of this
    and of the following letters to Mrs. Mason are in the possession
    of Mrs. S. W. Macdonough.
——. Letter to R. W. Gilder. Library of the University of Pennsyl-
    vania. June 10, 1903.
——. Letter to S. Pomeroy. Library of the University of Pennsyl-
    vania. June 10, 1903.
——. Letter to Mrs. Mason. April 26, 1905.
——. Letter to Mrs. Mason. September 10, 1908.
——. Letter to Mrs. Mason. October 3, 1908.
——. Letter to Mrs. Mason. August 6, 1910.
——. Letter to Mrs. Mason. August 4, 1911.
——. Letter to Mrs. Mason. August 11, 1911.
——. Letter to Mrs. Mason. July 19, 1912.
——. Letter to Mrs. Mason. November 22, 1912.
——. Letter to Mrs. Mason. March 30, 1913.
——. Letter to Mrs. Mason. Undated.
——. Letter to Taylor in the College of Physicians of Philadelphia
    (undated).
——. Letter to Thayer. September 28, 1910. Mrs. S. W. Macdonough.
Letter to ——. December 21 (no year given). Library of the College
    of Physicians of Philadelphia.
Reynolds, Mary. Manuscript. Library of the College of Physicians of
    Philadelphia.